National Security and Refugee Protection

International Refugee Law Series

VOLUME 27

The titles published in this series are listed at *brill.com/irls*

National Security and Refugee Protection

Critical Comparative Analysis of the Cases of the European Union, the United States and South Africa

By

Laura Planas Gifra

BRILL | NIJHOFF

ISSN 2213-3836
ISBN 978-90-04-70451-0
ISBN 978-90-04-70452-7 (PDF)
DOI https://doi.org/10.1163/9789004704527

Library of Congress Control Number: 2026914312

Brill Nijhoff and Koninklijke Brill BV are part of De Gruyter Brill.
www.degruyterbrill.com

Questions about General Product Safety Regulation: productsafety@degruyterbrill.com

Contents

PART 2
Case Studies

Tables

Introduction

The framing of migration as a security threat has become a defining feature of contemporary global politics. While the securitization of human mobility is not unique to the 21st century, the attacks of September 11, 2001, marked a pivotal moment in intensifying and institutionalizing security-oriented approaches to migration governance. In the aftermath of 9/11, counter-terrorism reshaped how states perceive and manage cross-border movement, introducing preventive, risk-based, and exceptional logics that were progressively extended to asylum and refugee protection. Since then, migration, and refugee flows in particular, have increasingly been governed through the lens of security, leading to restrictive laws, heightened border controls, and the externalization of borders and of protection responsibilities.

Terrorism thus functioned as a powerful catalyst for a new and more robust wave of securitization, particularly in Western states. In recent decades, terrorism has become one of the most politically and socially destabilizing global phenomena. Its impacts have extended worldwide, prompting states from different regions to adopt increasingly restrictive security measures. Simultaneously, the outbreak of violent conflicts – particularly the Syrian civil war – has driven massive refugee flows, many of which reached the borders of the European Union. These two developments converged in the public imagination and political discourse: refugees and asylum seekers were not only seen as a strain on national welfare systems and cultural cohesion but were also increasingly portrayed as potential security threats. The events of September 11, 2001, subsequent terrorist attacks, and the 2015–2016 refugee crisis together reinforced the idea that irregular migration and refugee flows constitute a risk to national security. Right-wing and xenophobic parties in Europe seized on this moment to construct a narrative of "invasion", blaming refugees for social unrest, economic instability, and even for the terrorist violence itself, often based on ethnicity or religion. These conditions fostered a fertile ground for securitization and growing xenophobia across destination countries.

It is important to note that this book does not treat terrorism as the sole or even dominant driver of contemporary refugee securitization. Terrorism is examined in Chapter 1 because of its foundational role in triggering a more intense and institutionalized security turn in migration governance, particularly in the early 21st century. Over time, however, these security rationalities have been reinforced and rearticulated through other discourses, such as irregularity, criminality, economic burden, and cultural threat, often mobilized by populist and far-right actors. Refugee securitization today therefore

 | HTTPS://DOI.ORG/10.1163/9789004704527-002

operates through a plurality of overlapping frames, many of which persist independently of any concrete terrorist threat.

It is in this context that this manuscript arose. The present book examines the securitization of refugees as a deliberate state practice aimed at moving migration from the domain of ordinary politics to that of national emergency. It critically analyses how migration – and particularly refugee flows – have been framed as existential threats justifying exceptional measures. The present analysis lies under the assumption that the securitization of migration, including of refugees, is an actual practice of states to bring migratory issues to the security domain with the justification that the society and the state need to protect themselves from these external security threats. This manuscript is the evolution of a doctoral thesis defended in 2022. The text has been updated and reframed in the context to study specifically the securitization of refugees.

Furthermore, to provide a comparative and nuanced understanding, this study focuses on three case studies: the European Union, the United States, and South Africa. These cases were selected for their contrasting historical, political, and socio-economic contexts, as well as their varied exposure to terrorism and migration flows. The European Union and the United States have both been prominent targets of terrorist organizations and have developed extensive legal and policy frameworks connecting migration control to security concerns. South Africa, although less affected by transnational terrorism, provides an important comparative example from the Global South, demonstrating how securitization practices have expanded beyond traditional Western contexts and beyond the terrorist threat. Analysing these three cases allows for an exploration of both similarities and differences in how states rationalize and operationalize the securitization of migration.

This analysis does not deny that large-scale refugee movements may generate genuine security challenges in certain contexts, particularly for fragile states; rather, it distinguishes such indirect or structural concerns from the securitization of refugees as threats in themselves, a distinction emphasized by Milner (2009). As Loescher further argues, refugee movements can raise security concerns primarily when they interact with fragile political contexts or inadequate governance, rather than because refugees constitute inherent security threats (Loescher, 1992; 2001). And empirical research on conflict spillover also emphasizes that while refugee flows may coincide with instability, causality is mediated by host-state capacity and political choices, not refugee presence alone (Salehyan and Gleditsch, 2006). Therefore, refugees are perceived as security problems not because of their actions, but because they challenge the territorial and political assumptions of the state system itself (Haddad, 2008). While refugee movements can give rise to genuine, often indirect security concerns, such as pressure on state capacity or regional stability, this does not in itself justify the securitization of refugees as security threats.

At the practical level, it is extremely important to be aware of securitization processes – in whatever area they take place – and to understand how they happen. When extraordinary measures are applied to the general population, but also to especially vulnerable groups –such as that of refugees – these can make their lives even more difficult than they already are. Extraordinary measures should be proportionate and held only so long as the security threat persists. But once the particular threat is over, these measures should come to an end. Is this the case for the securitization of refugees? Is it justified to treat them through the lens of national? If so, are these measures proportional and temporarily limited? Do all countries apply them in the same way and in the same contexts? Who is the actor responsible for pushing these measures? These are some of the questions this book seeks to answer.

If societies base their national identities on race, ethnicity, or religion, and rancour those who are different, we will build less inclusive societies in the future and conflicts will undoubtedly be more likely to arise. Higher border controls, restrictions of the rights of asylum seekers, rising administrative burdens for these collective, or the externalization of migration, create societies based on the securitization of those who are different. Threats are often seen everywhere. And countries are built with national security at the forefront of its interests, instead of prioritizing individual rights. And when the protection of the individual – and not the state – is the goal of national and international security strategies, liberal democratic values are at stake.

This book falls within the fields of Public International Law, Security Studies, and Critical Migration Studies, drawing on interdisciplinary perspectives to explore the relationship between migration, security, and state sovereignty. It engages particularly with critical security theories, including the Copenhagen School's concept of securitization, and critical legal approaches to migration governance.

The analysis follows a qualitative, comparative methodology based on legal and political analysis. Primary sources include international legal instruments, domestic legislation, policy documents, and judicial decisions. Secondary sources encompass academic literature in the fields of migration studies, security studies, and international law. The case studies are examined through the theoretical lens of securitization, focusing on discursive framing, legal measures, and policy shifts. Attention is given to how political elites and public discourse contribute to the construction of migration as a security threat, and how this framing translates into restrictive legal and administrative practices affecting refugees.

This book makes several key contributions to the academic literature on migration, security, and refugee studies. First, it offers a comparative, critical analysis of the securitization of migration, with a specific focus on the treatment of refugees, a group traditionally seen as deserving of international protection but increasingly framed as a security threat. Through an in-depth examination of three distinct cases – the European Union, the United States, and South Africa – the book identifies the diverse legal, political, and discursive mechanisms through which refugee securitization is constructed and operationalized. The comparative approach not only enhances the analytical depth of the study, but also helps explain why refugees are securitized, how this process unfolds in different contexts, and what outcomes it produces. In doing so, the book demonstrates that securitization is not confined to the Global North or to states with significant terrorist threats but has become a global and adaptable practice shaped by a range of political, economic, and social dynamics.

Second, the book contributes to critical security studies by applying the theory of securitization – traditionally developed in the context of military and political threats – to the domain of refugee law and migration governance. While much of the existing scholarship has explored the securitization of migration in Western liberal democracies, this study extends the field by incorporating a Southern perspective through the case of South Africa. This broadens the analytical scope and challenges assumptions that securitization is exclusively a reaction to terrorism. Instead, the study shows that securitization can also emerge from concerns about economic competition, social stability, and national identity.

Third, from a legal perspective, the book offers a critical examination of how international refugee law, particularly the principle of non-refoulement and the rights enshrined in the 1951 Refugee Convention, is being undermined by securitization practices. It highlights the growing tension between states' security interests and their international legal obligations, contributing to broader debates about the erosion of refugee protection norms and the rise of exceptionalism in migration law.

Fourth, this work dialogues with and builds upon critical migration scholarship by scholars such as Didier Bigo, William Walters, and Nicholas De Genova, who have theorized the relationship between migration control and security governance. By focusing specifically on refugees and connecting securitization practices to broader trends of human rights regression, the book emphasizes the need to re-centre human security in academic and policy debates.

Finally, the book also provides a pragmatic contribution by offering a framework for understanding the mechanisms, discourses, and legal instruments through which securitization is operationalized. This framework can serve as a reference for future research into national and regional migration policies, helping scholars and practitioners critically assess when and how migration is transformed into a security issue, and with what consequences.

In sum, this book aims to enrich interdisciplinary discussions by situating the study of refugees at the heart of contemporary security and migration debates. It calls for a revaluation of current practices and for a reaffirmation of the humanitarian principles that should guide the governance of forced migration in an increasingly securitized world.

This book has been divided in two parts. The first part studies the processes in relation to the securitization of migration. It first contextualizes the situation of migrants today; migratory flows, the massive arrival of asylum seekers in the European Union – which will be useful to later understand the context in which securitization measures in the EU have been applied – and it also explains the conflicting debates on the definitions of the concepts of 'refugee' and 'terrorism', as these will be often used in this thesis. After this initial contextualization, it goes over the concept of securitization, and it explains the ways in which these measures are applied in practice by different states around the world. This is a way to put different nations as an example besides the three main cases of study of the thesis. The idea of this second part is to prove that the securitization of migration is a practice that is widely applied in different regions of the world. Migrants have been placed as a national security problem and they have been many times blamed for the social and economic deficiencies of the country, which has aggravated their situation, rights, and integration into host societies.

The second and last part is the one making specific reference to three cases: that of the European Union, the United States, and South Africa. Here we will see the laws which have been used in these countries to advance in the securitization processes, linking immigration to security threats from which the country needs to be protected. As it will be seen, the global war on terror has been used many times as a justification to advance in measures to control migration, but counter-terrorism measures are not the only argument to contend immigration flows. There are other political, social, and economic arguments presented by governments – and supported by the media – linking migration with national security. These will be all explored in these chapters. To close with the presented research, a last section in relation to the conclusions will set forth the main findings of the thesis and offer a few ideas on the prospects which may be awaiting in this field in the coming future.

References

Haddad, E. (2008) *The Refugee in International Society: Between Sovereigns*. Cambridge: Cambridge University Press.

Loescher, G. (1992) *Refugee Movements and International Security*. London: International Institute for Strategic Studies.

Loescher, G. (2001) *The UNHCR and World Politics: A Perilous Path*. Oxford: Oxford University Press.

Milner, J. (2009) *Refugees, the State and the Politics of Asylum in Africa*. Basingstoke: Palgrave Macmillan.

Salehyan, I. and Gleditsch, K. S. (2006) 'Refugees and the spread of civil war', *International Organization*, Vol. 60(2), pp. 335–366.

PART 1

Linking Migration and Security

CHAPTER 1

The Complexities of the Definitions of Refugee and Terrorism

This chapter analyses the different conceptualizations of *refugee* and *terrorism*. Not only will this be useful to comprehend the basic terms that will be used over the next pages, but it is also essential to understand current debates on whether the meaning of these terms adequately reflects society as it stands today. As it will be described in the following lines, the definition of refugee has long been framed in international law, but it is still being discussed today.[1] On the other side, the definition of terrorism has extensively been analysed by academia, but there is no international agreed definition yet.

Therefore, this chapter will start reflecting on the discussion about the term "refugee", and in the second half of the chapter, the shift will be towards the concept of "terrorism". Regarding the first, even though the concept has been defined internationally and within different instruments, most definitions agree on the basic elements that distinguish refugees from other types of migrants, and most scholars take the definition of the 1951 Refugee Convention to be predominant. Nonetheless, there is an ongoing debate on how this definition forgets, for instance, climate refugees – those who are fleeing their countries because of climate devastation – who are currently growing rapidly in numbers worldwide.

On the other hand, and while there has been some intention to define the term terrorism at the international level, there has not been sufficient agreement to adopt a formal and well-established definition. The main consequence of this lack of agreement is that it has remained mostly defined domes-

1 A wide range of scholars have acknowledged that the definition of refugee has become outdated and that it should include victims of economic and political instability and natural disasters. The discussion will continue in section 2.3. For further readings see: Lentini (1985), *The Definition of Refugee in International Law: Proposals for the Future*, Boston College Third World Law Journal, Vol. 5 Issue 2; Chamberlain (1983), *The Mass Migration of Refugees and International Law*, 7 Fletcher Forum 93, pp.103–104; Fragoman (1970), *The Refugee: A Problem of Definition*, 3 Case Western Reserve Journal of International Law 45, 58; Plender (1977), *Admission of Refugees: Draft Convention on Territorial Asylum*, San Diego Law Review 45, pp. 54–55; Woods (1981), *The Term 'Refugee' in International and Municipal Law: An Inadequate Definition in Light of the Cuban Boatlift*, 5 ASILS International Law Journal, 39; Gunning, I., (1989), *Expanding the International Legal Definition of Refugee: A Multicultural View*, Fordham International Law Journal, Vol. 13, Issue 3.

 | HTTPS://DOI.ORG/10.1163/9789004704527-003

tically. In turn, this has meant that the way in which it has been shaped has been politicized, mostly depending on the circumstances and interests of the national government. Therefore, this chapter will seek to revise these two definitions and the controversies surrounding them.

1 Definition of Refugee and Determination of Their Status

Firstly, this chapter will go over the legal concept and rights expressed in international instruments relating to refugees, and the section will close with the debate on the problematic related to the meaning of refugee in the 21st century.

The current framework regarding the international protection of refugees dates back to the end of World War II. After the war, international conventions were revised and one of the most important outcomes was the creation of the UN Convention relating to the status of Refugees 1951 (from now on, the Refugee Convention or 1951 Convention). It entered into force on 22 April 1954. As a post–World War II instrument, the Convention was originally restricted only to those persons fleeing from events that had occurred before 1951 and only within Europe (UNHCR, 2010). The 1967 Protocol Relating to the Status of Refugees removed the geographic as well as temporal limitations of the Convention; thus, with its approval, these restrictions were removed to offer universal coverage. The Convention has been ratified by 146 States (UN, 2019), with the latest incorporation of South Sudan in December 2018. The United Nations High Commissioner for Refugees (UNHCR) is the UN agency dedicated to protecting refugees and making sure their rights are being safeguarded; hence, States are expected to act in collaboration with the agency to ensure that the rights of refugees are respected and protected.

As for its content, the Convention gives a definition of refugee, describes the rights of the displaced and determines the legal obligations of States to protect them, being one of the most remarkable principles that of *non-refoulement*. The definition is found in Article 1(A)(2) of the Convention, and it is described as any person who:

> Owing to well-founded fear of being persecuted for reasons of race, religion, nationality, membership of a particular social group or political opinion, is outside the country of his nationality and is unable or, owing to such fear, is unwilling to avail himself of the protection of that country; or who, not having a nationality and being outside the country of his former habitual residence as a result of such events, is unable or, owing to such fear, is unwilling to return to it.

This definition is the cornerstone of international refugee law and is generally seen as the minimum standard definition for the status of a person as a refugee.[2] The concept must be distinguished from other types of migrants. While a refugee is basically a person who flees his or her country because of persecution, war or violence, an asylum seeker is that who flees his or her country to seek sanctuary in another, and this sanctuary has not yet been processed. In the country of destination, they apply for asylum through individualized national procedures and must demonstrate that the fear of persecution in the country of origin is well-founded. Gaining asylum means that they are formally recognized as refugees, and thus their legal protection is also formally recognized, obliging states to give them material assistance (UNHCR, 2006). The rights of asylum seekers are also protected in the Universal Declaration of Human Rights, which states in its Article 14 that "everyone has the right to seek and to enjoy in other countries asylum from persecution". Hence, asylum seekers can find protection both under human rights law and refugee law.

Furthermore, asylum seekers are the ones to prove the existence of the a "well-founded fear" showing that there is a reasonable possibility that they will suffer prosecution if they were returned to their native countries, and this can be either an objective or subjective standard.[3] As to the grounds of this persecution, there has been some debate in the United States as to whether neutrality can count as political opinion for the purposes of obtaining refugee status. In this sense, this country has pronounced different decisions such as *Matter of Acosta*[4] – in which the Court decided there was no basis for persecution – and *Bolaños-Hernandez v. I.N.S.*[5] – in which persecution was considered to be proven for a former military member who refused to join the guerrillas because he wanted to remain neutral.

Refugees are also different from internally displaced people (IDP). The latter, as the name itself explains, are those who have been forced to flee but remain within the internal borders of their country. They might move to different regions at the national level, to internal camps or settlements, or even

2 There is a wide array of academic literature on the concept of refugee and the elements forming this definition. As an example see: Shacknove, A. (1985), *Who Is a Refugee?*, The University of Chicago Press Journals, Vol. 95, Num. 2, pp. 274–284; Weis, P. (1960), *The Concept of Refugee in International Law*, Journal du Droit International, Vol. 87, pp. 929–1001; Storey, H. (2016), *The Meaning of "Protection" within the Refugee Definition*, Refugee Survey Quarterly, Vol. 35, Issue 3, pp. 1–34; Worster, W. (2012), *The Evolving Definition of the Refugee In Contemporary International Law*, Berkeley Journal of International Law, Vol. 3, Issue 1, pp.94–160.

3 See *Matter of Mogharrabi*, United States, 19 I&N December 439 (BIA 1987).

4 *Matter of Acosta*, 19 I&N Dec. 211 (BIA 1985).

5 *Bolanos-Hernandez v. I.N.S.*, 767 F.2d 1277, 1284–5 (Ninth Circuit 1985).

to fields and forests, but unlike refugees, IDPs are not protected by international law, and as a consequence they cannot obtain many of the rights and assistance that refugees can access because of their status. This protection is not given to IDPs because they are legally under the protection of their own country. In 2017, more than 40 million were internally displaced people around the world (IDMC, 2017). In 2023, there was a new record, with 75.9 million. Two-thirds of these are a result of the conflicts in Sudan, the Democratic Republic of the Congo, and Palestine (IDMC, 2024).

Another and last distinction, but which is still useful to determine, is that of stateless persons. According to Article 1(1) of the 1954 Convention relating to the Status of Stateless Persons, this is the person "who is not considered as a national by any State under the operation of its law"; thus, to indicate when a person falls within this definition, one must see how a particular State applies its nationality law in the particular case. The most common problem for this collective is to get access to education, healthcare, employment, and freedom of movement.

Globally, UNHCR calculates that there are at least 10 million stateless people (UNHCR, 2024), although there is no exact data on how many stateless people exist worldwide, as data is based on that provided by the government and NGOs. Rohingyas make up the world's largest stateless population with over 3.5 million people (Rahman, 2024).

1.1 The Rights of Refugees

There are certain rights which are automatically acquired by refugees, some that she acquires when she has made her asylum application, and others that are guaranteed once the refugee status has been granted or after a certain period of residence (UNHCR, 2017). There are, amongst the most important, the protections afforded by Articles 31 and 33 of the 1951 Convention against the punishment for unlawful entry and for non-refoulement. In addition to these and regardless of their status, they also enjoy the right to religious practice and education (Article 4), to the acquisition of property (Article 13), to access to courts and legal assistance (Article 16), to education (Article 22), and to identity papers (Article 27). Once their asylum application has been submitted, these rights increase to include that of self-employment (Article 18), and to choose the residence and to freedom of movement within the territory of the host State (Article 26). Only when the refugee is staying lawfully in the country with the status of refugee or when she has fulfilled a determined period of residence (which varies depending on the country), she can enjoy the right of association (Article 15), to engage in wage-earning employment

(Article 17), to practice a liberal profession (Article 19), to housing (Article 21), to access the social security system (Articles 23 and 24) and to obtain travel documentation (Article 28).

Overall, there are two main strands of international law to offer protection to refugees. On the one hand, there is international refugee law, and on the other, international human rights law. Regional instruments to take into consideration are the European Convention on Human Rights, the European Union Charter of Fundamental Rights, the African Convention on Human and Peoples' Rights, the African Convention on Refugees, and the American Convention on Human Rights. Other international instruments containing rights for refugees are the following:

One of the most important principles at the core of international refugee law is the principle of non-refoulement. It prohibits States from returning refugees to the countries where they may be subject to persecution, as provided by Article 33 of the 1951 Convention. This principle is now part of customary international law and as such, it is binding on all States, whether or not they are parties to the 1951 Convention (UNHCR, 2006). Furthermore, the principle of non-refoulement prohibits not only sending refugees back to the countries where they would be subject to persecution, but it also prohibits the mass expulsion of refugees. We can find a codification of this specific notion of the principle in Article 12(5) of the African Charter on Human and Peoples' Rights. Therefore, if a State is in breach of this principle – or any other in customary international law – the State in question will be responsible for the internationally wrongful act under Article 1 of the 2001 ILC Articles on Responsibility of States for Internationally Wrongful Acts. However, we must not forget that there is an exception found in the 1951 Convention which permits States parties to deny asylum to those refugees who have committed particularly serious crimes or those who are guilty of acts contrary to the principles of the UN.

An important case in European Union law is that of *Soering v. United Kingdom.*[6] Held in 1989 at the European Court of Human Rights. It set the foundations for protection from removal under the European Convention, since the Court ruled that if the individual was removed to a third state, there would be a breach of the European Convention, as the person in question would be put at a situation where he or she would face a real risk of being tortured or receive inhuman or degrading treatment.[7] This case was a breakpoint for the Euro-

6 *Soering v. the United Kingdom,* nº 14038/88 July 7, 1989.

7 Article 3 of the European Convention on Human Rights states that "No one shall be subjected to torture or to inhuman or degrading treatment or punishment".

TABLE 1.1 Refugees' rights

International instrument	Articles	Main rights acquired
Universal Declaration of Human Rights	14	Right to seek and enjoy asylum
International Covenant on Civil and Political Rights	2, 7, 9, and 12	Non-discrimination; prohibition against torture or inhuman or degrading treatment; right to liberty and security and prohibition of arbitrary arrest and detention; right to freedom of movement and residence
International Covenant on Economic, Social and Cultural Rights	2	All rights of the Convention are enjoyed without discrimination
Convention on the Elimination of All Forms of Racial Discrimination	1 and 5	Non-discrimination; prohibition of discrimination for various rights such as security of the person, freedom of movement and residence, right to leave any country and to return one's country, right to nationality, etc.
Convention on the Elimination of All Forms of Discrimination Against Women	1	Non-discrimination
Convention for the Protection of All Persons from Enforced Disappearance	2, 13, and 16	"Enforced disappearance" is considered to be an arrest, detention, abduction or other forms of deprivation of liberty (…); non-discrimination; non-refoulement
Convention Against Torture and Other Cruel, Inhuman or Degrading Treatment or Punishment	3	Principle of non-refoulement
Convention on the Rights of the Child	10, 22, and 28	Family reunification; ensuring protection of refugee children; right to education

pean Convention as an instrument of protection of non-European citizens since not only did it forbid the treatments described in Article 3, but it also prohibited sending persons who could be put under threat of the treatments described in this Article if they were sent to third states which would likely extradite them. After the decision, Article 3 was applied to foreigners of the European Union in the cases of extradition and expulsion. Some of these cases are of particular interest because the Court took into consideration the status of asylum seeker of potential victims of Article 3 (Morgades, 2010).[8]

We need to keep in mind that refugee law was established to protect individuals who were dissidents from oppressive political systems. After World War II, states wanted to design a framework to deal with mass movements of people, but it was never a framework designed to deal with the current refugee flows. Furthermore, States have shown to be unable to cope with the ongoing refugee crisis and their national asylum systems have been overwhelmed by these large numbers of newcomers. As a result, many countries have many times denied responsibility for refugees, and understandings on the notion of responsibility have also differed between richer and poorer States. Mechanisms to shift away responsibility on refugees have multiplied and developed countries have tried to refrain refugee flows from entering their borders both in the high seas outside their national waters or by settling agreements with other countries so that responsibility for asylum seekers is placed somewhere else.

This is the case of the readmission agreements with African countries, which have become a way to facilitate repatriation of rejected asylum seekers (MEDAM, 2017). And it is also the case of the 2016 agreement between the EU and Turkey by which irregular migrants arriving in Greece from Turkey would be returned to the later, thus alleviating the pressure of refugee flows on European countries. In exchange, the EU promised economic benefits so that Turkey could establish an integration programme for the Syrian refugees it hosts, as well as easiness in getting EU visas for Turkish nationals (Triandafylliou, 2017).

As Hathaway (2007) recognizes, governments of developed States have erroneously challenged the protection given by the 1951 Convention, suggesting that "it sets only protection obligations of 'last resort'". He explains that States have set out a practice by which they think they can send refugees away to third States, which will accept refugees without sending them back to their

8 See *Ahmed v. Austria*, nº 25964/94, December 17, 1996; Recueil 1996-VI, *Hilal v. the United Kingdom*, nº 45276/99, March 6, 2001; ECHR 2001-II, *10 N. v. Finland*, nº 38885/02, July 26 2005, ECHR.

home countries. What they should do instead is to make sure these third States are truthfully engaged to the obligations of the Refugee Convention and be certain that they comply with the principle of non-refoulement.

Another current established practice is that refugees that arrive without permit are considered "illegal" by many governments, despite the fact that the determination of refugee as established by the Convention says otherwise. In this sense, it is important to note that Article 31(1) of the 1951 Convention declares that States should treat refugees as non-transgressors when they enter their territorial borders. Since there has never been any type of visa that lets a refugee travel to one's territory to make an asylum claim, using it would still be too risky for the individual. Hence, those arriving to the territory of another country seeking for sanctuary should not be considered as illegal, as it would be "completely inappropriate to stigmatize refugees arriving without visas as law breakers when a treaty we have freely signed provides exactly the contrary" (Hathaway, 2007).

In *R v. Appulonappa and B010 v. Canada*, the Canadian Supreme Court noted that Article 31 of the 1951 Convention meant that Canadian national law had to recognize that groups of people could try to enter a State illegally looking for refuge, and that the national government (in this case, the Canadian government) could not impose sanctions on refugees only to help others get into their State in an illegal manner. Hence, even domestic courts have used and continue using international law to shape human rights law and refugee law at the domestic level.

Nevertheless, even though the 1951 Convention recognizes the rights of refugees, it does not specify the process by which to concede asylum as such (Goodwin-Gill, 2014). While the principle of non-refoulement is not discussed, the terms to establish whether the terms 'persecution', or 'degrading' treatment are not defined, leaving wide discretion to caseworkers and national courts to decide whether there is a justified cause to get the status of refugee when an individual has applied for asylum in a particular country. There can be in certain situations problems of interpretation and balanced reasoning when discussing their cases (Pirjola, 2008).

Furthermore, many believe – erroneously – that refugees come to stay, which incentivizes this feeling of unwelcomeness to one's country. However, refugee status is not permanent and it stands so long as the prosecution in their countries of origin persists. Refugee law only protects individuals from the risk that they would have if they stayed in their countries and it seeks for safety in international borders as long as the threat they are escaping from persists. Therefore, gaining the status of refugee does not entitle to a right of permanent migration. On the contrary, what most refugees look for is a safe place while they cannot return home, and their ultimate goal is to go back to their lands. Voluntary repatriation reflects this idea, and although the right to return is only formally found in Article 5(1) of the 1969 OAU Convention, it is still a universal right.

1.2 Principal Critiques on the Concept of Refugee

There are different critiques to the concept of refugee. Contestation over refugeehood has been addressed, to start with, at a normative level through critiques of the moral foundations of refugee law. Gerver argues that the refugee regime rests on ethically arbitrary distinctions between different forms of harm and displacement, privileging persecution over other serious threats such as poverty, environmental degradation, or generalized violence (Gerver, 2018). From this perspective, refugee protection does not reflect a coherent moral theory of obligation, but rather a historically contingent compromise shaped by state interests and political feasibility. Gerver's critique exposes how exclusion is built into the refugee definition itself, rendering refugeehood a contested and selective status even before issues of implementation or securitization arise.

One of the most common criticisms is in relation to the 1951 Convention. This was made after the end of World War II, taking into consideration the migration movements that were there at the time, with the experience of the Nazi-war prosecutions and the European displacements (Millbank, 2000). Hence, this instrument was not thought to be used for the existing refugee flows of the 21st century.

Consequently, as time passed by, the Convention became outdated. Most recent refugee movements have started because of civil or ethnic wars, but also because of natural disasters. Every time more often, we are seeing people fleeing from their countries as a result of not being able to survive in the existing environmental conditions, affected by events such as tsunamis or hurricanes, to the lack of water because of dryness. Some even argue that those victims of economic unrest should also be considered as a category of refugees (Lentini, 1985). And while the Convention does not cover these groups of people, it seems unlikely that governments adapt and expanse the standing criteria. Altogether, it seems that it has become an archaic convention that cannot cope with the refugee movements we are facing nowadays.

Nevertheless, it must be noted that other scholars have also argued that rather than rendering the 1951 Convention obsolete, the problem lies on the fact that states have adapted its application to contemporary concerns by narrowing recognition through procedural and evidentiary standards, thereby contesting refugeehood without formally revising the definition (Hamlin, 2014). In fact, in her recent work, Rebecca Hamlin extends this analysis beyond asylum adjudication to examine how categories such as "refugee", "migrant", or "illegal immigrant" are politically constructed and mobilized across different governance contexts. She argues that these labels are not neutral descriptors but powerful tools that shape how states and societies respond to people on the move. Rather than reflecting objective differences between displaced populations, legal and political labels determine access to rights, protection, and moral legitimacy. Refugeehood thus emerges not simply from the circumstances of flight, but from political decisions about which forms of mobility are deemed deserving of protection and which are treated as illegitimate (Hamlin, 2021).

In addition, recent scholarship has also emphasized that refugeehood is not merely defined in law but actively produced and contested through state practice. Hamlin's work demonstrates how asylum adjudication functions as a political and administrative process in which states interpret, narrow, and reshape the refugee definition without formally amending international legal instruments. Refugee status thus emerges through discretionary decision-making, credibility assessments, and institutional priorities, revealing how exclusion often operates within, rather than outside, the existing legal framework. She conceptualizes refugee status not as a neutral legal category but as a politically produced status, shaped by institutional practices, credibility assessments, and shifting state priorities rather than by law alone (Hamlin, 2014).

In fact, the same categorization of "refugee" or "migrant" has been contested. As Crawley and Skleparis (2018) contend, the refugee–migrant distinction is not a neutral analytical tool but a politically charged boundary that obscures complex mobility trajectories while legitimizing exclusion. From this perspective, efforts to address marginalization should move beyond categorical prioritization and instead engage explicitly with the politics of bounding. That is, the processes through which categories are constructed, the functions they serve, and the consequences they produce. Denaturalizing these categories exposes how they operate as mechanisms of division and discrimination rather than as objective descriptors of human mobility.

What can be inferred from the categorization and treatment of refugees, as T. Alexander Aleinikoff explains, is that the state system has a vision of refugees as "problems" that must be "solved". And the "solutions" that states have found are based on focusing attention on countries of origin, supporting repatriation and human rights monitoring. But as Aleinikoff argues, the real risk lies in the fact that most of these countries are more committed to human rights protection in theory than in practice. And in turn, refugees are kept away from destination countries with no real protection to their rights (Aleinikoff, 1995/2003).

It is also key to stand out the understanding and application of the principle of non-refoulement used by the European Union. With the approval of Directive 2013/32/EU, the EU designed a serial of 'safe third countries' to stop and deal with the arrival of refugee flows, and it has become a way to reject asylum applications by certain nationals arguing that they already come from countries that are thought to be safe enough. Therefore, their applications are automatically rejected based on insufficient grounds and they are sent back to this 'safe third countries' from which they come from.[9] Thus, the problem does not only rely on the Convention itself, but the interpretation given by some actors to this instrument also arises questions and challenges the use of the international framework as it remains today.

Furthermore, as it has been stated in the previous lines, one of the criticisms by the standing literature is the fact that there are different groups separated from the definition of refugee (such as internally displaced peoples and asylum seekers) who are not granted the same rights as refugees. Thence, even though the first would maybe qualify as refugees if they had crossed international borders, only because they stayed within their country, they are not granted the same protection as refugees.

9 In this sense, it must be highlighted that the EU also closed an agreement with Turkey in March 2016 with the intention that the latter kept those migrants trying to enter the EU within its territory. Those migrants that came into the EU after the agreement were sent back to Turkey with their asylum applications declared inadmissible, shifting the responsibility to assess the applications to Turkish authorities in exchange of a monetary compensation and easiness between EU and Turkish visas. This European and Turkish agreement is different from others because of the use of the 'safe-third-country' concept (Alpes et al., 2017). Whether Turkish can offer the sufficient and necessary protection to refugees is highly disputed, and so is categorizing it as a safe third country. This debate is based on several grounds. Firstly, Turkey is one of the countries in the world that apply a geographical limitation to the 1951 Refugee Convention, restricting its protection only to nationals of the member state countries of the Council of Europe (Alpes et al, 2017). Furthermore, in 2014 the Turkish government passed the Law on Foreigners and International Protection which created a special organism to process asylum applications. This law also created a new status for non-European refugees, providing them with a lawful stay in the country and calling them "conditional refugees", but in practice, most of the times migrants in Turkey do not have access to education and employment at all (Alpes et al, 2017). There is even a 2017 report by Amnesty International that examined the situation of refugees in Turkey and which acknowledged that the risk of refoulement is in fact very likely to happen in this country (Amnesty International, 2017).

Recent academic work has further expanded on these critiques, offering interdisciplinary perspectives on refugeehood that challenge the traditional frameworks established by the 1951 Convention. The field of refugee studies has evolved significantly over the past few decades, moving beyond a purely legalistic or humanitarian framework to incorporate critical, anthropological, and political analyses. A landmark figure in this shift is Liisa H. Malkki, whose influential article "Refugees and Exile: From 'Refugee Studies' to the National Order of Things" (1995) critiques the tendency to depoliticize and dehistoricize refugees, treating them merely as humanitarian victims. Malkki emphasizes that refugees are often portrayed as "speechless emissaries" in need of rescue, rather than as political actors shaped by complex historical and national contexts. Her work has been fundamental in rethinking how displacement is framed and in challenging the assumptions embedded within international responses to refugee movements.

Building on these critical approaches, Alexander Betts has contributed to a broader understanding of the refugee regime as a product of international political dynamics. In works such as *Protection by Persuasion* (2009) and *Refuge: Transforming a Broken Refugee System* (2017, co-authored with Paul Collier), Betts highlights the governance failures of the current refugee system and argues for more innovative, development-focused solutions. Betts critiques the rigid North–South divides in refugee protection and advocates for greater agency for refugee-hosting states and displaced persons themselves. His research underscores the political contingencies that shape access to protection and redefines refugees not only as passive beneficiaries of aid but also as active economic and social agents.

Matthew J. Gibney further deepens the ethical and political dimensions of refugee studies. In *The Ethics and Politics of Asylum* (2004), Gibney explores how liberal democratic states reconcile the tension between their sovereign rights to control borders and their moral obligations to protect those fleeing persecution. He critically examines concepts such as membership, citizenship, and exclusion, arguing that the treatment of refugees raises fundamental questions about the nature of the political community. Gibney's work is crucial in framing refugee protection within broader discussions about human rights, state sovereignty, and political justice.

A growing body of literature also addresses emerging challenges not anticipated by the 1951 Refugee Convention, most notably climate-induced displacement. Jane McAdam is a leading scholar in this area, with her influential book *Climate Change, Forced Migration, and International Law* (2012) providing a comprehensive legal analysis of protection gaps faced by people displaced by environmental factors. McAdam argues that while these individuals are not recognized as refugees under current international law, their protection needs are urgent and require the development of new legal frameworks. Her work bridges refugee law, human rights, and environmental law, pressing for a more responsive international legal system.

Together, these contributions shift refugeehood from a purely legal category to a political and contested condition, thereby opening analytical space to examine how security logics subsequently intervene in protection regimes. These scholars illustrate that refugee studies have expanded far beyond the traditional parameters of refugee law. It now encompasses a multidisciplinary engagement with historical, political, ethical, and environmental dimensions of displacement. Theoretical approaches in the field increasingly challenge state-centric models of protection and call for greater recognition of the agency, rights, and dignity of displaced persons. Incorporating these perspectives enriches the study of refugeehood, showing that the experience of displacement cannot be fully captured by legal definitions alone. Instead, a critical and interdisciplinary approach is essential for understanding the structural forces that produce displacement, the evolving nature of mobility in the 21st century, and the pressing need to rethink international protection frameworks in an era of global crises.

In addition to legal and humanitarian approaches, recent critical scholarship has highlighted how refugee protection and counter-terrorism measures intersect with broader practices of governing mobility and security. Scholars such as Didier Bigo, William Walters, and Nicholas De Genova have drawn attention to the ways in which states increasingly frame refugees, asylum, and security as interconnected fields of management and control. This scholarship underscores that refugees are not only protected subjects but also often constructed as security threats, and that migration control mechanisms can replicate forms of exclusion, surveillance, and marginalization.

Didier Bigo's theory of the "security continuum" is particularly influential. In his work on the "ban-opticon", Bigo (2002; 2011) argues that practices such as refugee camps, externalized borders, visa controls, and terrorism databases are part of a single apparatus aimed at managing perceived risks. Migration and terrorism are thus entangled through a shared security logic, wherein mobile populations are simultaneously feared and controlled. Bigo's work invites a reconsideration of how humanitarian protection can, paradoxically, reinforce security practices that limit mobility and political agency.

Similarly, William Walters has critically analysed how migration governance operates through what he calls "bordering practices". In *The Politics of Insecurity* (2004) and later works, Walters shows how security is produced not only at territorial borders but through complex administrative and bureaucratic regimes that regulate asylum seekers and refugees within and beyond state territories. His concept of the "humanitarian border" points to the ambivalent role of humanitarianism itself in legitimating practices of exclusion, containment, and selective mobility.

Nicholas De Genova further develops this critical approach by focusing on the production of "illegality" and "deportability". In his seminal work *Working the Boundaries* (2005) and later articles, De Genova argues that immigration law and enforcement do not simply regulate movement; they actively create categories of people as illegal or criminalized. This process of illegalization ties into how refugees and migrants are constructed as potential threats, facilitating broader securitization agendas under the guise of migration control.

Finally, Giorgio Agamben's notion of the "state of exception" offers a theoretical lens to understand how extraordinary legal measures, such as those targeting refugees or suspected terrorists, become normalized. In *Homo Sacer* (1995) and *State of Exception* (2005), Agamben shows how certain individuals are stripped of legal protections and reduced to "bare life", subjected to sovereign power without the rights of citizenship. Refugee camps, immigration detention centres, and counter-terrorism frameworks can thus be seen as contemporary spaces of exception where fundamental rights are suspended.

Importantly, these dynamics of exception do not operate solely through spectacular or overtly coercive measures, but are also reproduced through routine administrative practices that quietly delimit access to protection. Building on this literature, qualitative scholarship has shown how refugee status is actively contested through credibility assessments embedded in asylum procedures. Jubany's analysis of asylum decision-making reveals how refugeehood is filtered through what she terms a "culture of disbelief", in which applicants are routinely met with suspicion and required to perform coherent, detailed, and emotionally appropriate narratives to be deemed credible (Jubany, 2017). These evidentiary expectations are shaped by gendered, racialised, and cultural assumptions that privilege certain forms of suffering while disqualifying others. As a result, exclusion from refugee protection often occurs not because claimants fall outside the legal definition, but because they fail to conform to institutionalized notions of credibility and deservingness.

Taken together, these perspectives illustrate that contestation over refugeehood unfolds across multiple sites, from exceptional legal spaces to everyday bureaucratic encounters, where power is exercised through both suspension and interpretation of the law. While the definition established by the 1951 Convention remains the reference point for this chapter, it is therefore essential to remain attentive to the broader political, institutional, and discursive dynamics through which refugee protection is shaped, constrained, and selectively granted in practice.

2 Definition of Terrorism

The analytical link between refugees and terrorism in this book does not rest on any empirical claim that refugees are more likely to engage in terrorist violence. Rather, it lies in the role terrorism has played as a powerful organizing frame for contemporary security governance. Since 9/11, counter-terrorism has reconfigured legal standards, evidentiary thresholds, and risk-based decision-making across multiple policy domains, including asylum and refugee protection. In this sense, terrorism marked a critical intensification of security-oriented approaches to mobility, introducing preventive, risk-based, and exceptional logics that were subsequently extended to the governance of refugees.

Importantly, the focus of this book is not limited to the refugee-terrorism nexus. Terrorism is examined here as a paradigmatic security category whose legal and political treatment has profoundly shaped broader approaches to borders, migration, and protection. While early post-9/11 securitization of refugees was closely tied to counter-terrorism concerns in Western states, these security logics have since diffused and diversified.

In the past decade, the securitization of refugees has increasingly been articulated through discourses of irregularity, criminality, economic burden, cultural threat, and xenophobia, further increasing after the so-called "refugee crisis". These dynamics demonstrate that although terrorism acted as a catalyst for a more intense and institutionalized securitization of refugees, contemporary security framings now operate well beyond the terrorist register.

The significance of including terrorism in this chapter lies in understanding how it has functioned as a gateway into wider security frameworks. Refugees have often been associated with terrorism in political rhetoric and legislation, but securitization now extends far beyond this frame. The objective of the book is to analyse how the refugee, despite being a legally protected figure, has been progressively reframed as a threat in diverse geopolitical contexts and through varied forms of security discourse. Terrorism, therefore, is only one – albeit important – dimension of this broader transformation.

The word 'terrorism' originated in 1793 during the French Revolution in France (COE, 2017). It was used to define the *Regime de la Terreur* or *le Government de la Terreur* (the Reign or Government of Terror) by the Jacobins, who with these words wanted to describe their own methods to fight the French

Revolution against the authorities of the State, who were repressing the population and making thousands of executions without fair trial (Matusitz, 2012). This period ended with the fall of Maximilien Robespierre, a top seed of this movement, in July 1974. Robespierre described the importance of terror in one of his speeches (Halsall, 1997):

> If virtue be the spring of a popular government in times of peace, the spring of that government during a revolution is virtue combined with terror: virtue, without which terror is destructive; terror, without which virtue is impotent. Terror is only justice prompt, severe and inflexible; it is then an emanation of virtue; it is less a distinct principle than a natural consequence of the general principle of democracy, applied to the most pressing wants of the country.

But today the word "terrorism" and its word families are extensively heard from politicians, mass media and citizens around the world, many times using it to refer to war conflicts, oppression moves in dictatorships, crimes committed by State leaders, and other sorts of disputes. There has been so much confusion with these terms to the point that it is now hard to distinguish between what really is terrorism and what is not. The lack of agreement on the exact use of this wording can lead to erroneous or inaccurate descriptions of events, and the fact that the United Nations has not been capable of adopting a convention on terrorism is proof of these ambiguous environments surrounding the definition and limits of terrorism. The UN had the willingness to create an international instrument in this field, but its member States seemed to be unable to reach an agreement on how to define the word terrorism. The UN General Assembly, however, tends to use the following definition:[10]

> Criminal acts intended or calculated to provoke a state of terror in the general public, a group of persons or particular persons for political purposes are in any circumstance unjustifiable, whatever the considerations of a political, philosophical, ideological, racial, ethnic, religious or any other nature that may be invoked to justify them.

This definition given by the UN focuses mostly on the intention of the attack, which would be to provoke terror in the population, rather than on the means

10 1994 United Nations Declaration on Measures to Eliminate International Terrorism annex to UN General Assembly resolution 49/60, "Measures to Eliminate International Terrorism", of December 9, 1994.

used to conduct it. This notion differs from that of the Security Council given eight years later, which is much more specific on the different intentions that can be pursued when committing such a crime. There can be, for instance, not only an objective of provoking terror, but also to "intimidate a population" or "compel a government", among others. And it does not only describe the intention of the attack, but also the means used (such as that of taking hostages) or the causes it seeks to inflame (such as causing death or serious injuries).

Soon after the September 11 attacks, the United Nations Security Council passed Resolution 1373, which required all States to take legislative action against terrorism, but it failed to provide a definition for terrorism (Hardy and Williams, 2011). Later on, the Security Council tried to give a definition in Resolution 1566,[11] although this is non-binding and lacks authority in international law (Schmid, 2012):

> Criminal acts, including against civilians, committed with the intent to cause death or serious bodily injury, or taking of hostages, with the purpose to provoke a state of terror in the general public or in a group of persons or particular persons, intimidate a population or compel a government or an international organization to do or to abstain from doing any act, which constitute offences within the scope of and as defined in the international conventions and protocols relating to terrorism.

Europe has also developed an instrument in this field: the European Convention on the Suppression of Terrorism of 1977. According to this, terrorist acts are all serious offences involving an attack against the life, physical integrity or liberty of internationally protected persons, as well as offences involving kidnapping or the taking of hostages (Symeonidou-Kastanidou, 2004). Hence, this definition is based on the subject over which there has been an attack as well as the type of offence, but it does not consider the motive nor the damage to determine whether an attack can be classified as terrorist or not (Llobet, 2008).

Studies have found that there are more than 200 definitions of terrorism. In this sense, Schmid and Easson compiled up to 260 in The Routledge Handbook of Terrorism Research.[12] Schmid, in this sense, has also worked to reach a

---

11 Security Council Resolution 1566 (2004) on Threats to international peace and security caused by terrorist acts, S/RES/1566 (2004).

12 Schmid, A. P. (2011), The Routledge Handbook of Terrorism Research, London and New York: Routledge.

consensus based on the opinion of academics and other professionals whom he interviewed. They described what they thought terrorism was, and he put together the elements that were mostly agreed on (Schmid, 2011). According to his compilations, terrorism is a "form or tactic of fear-generating coercive political violence" and it is also a practice of "calculated, demonstrative, direct violent action without legal or moral restraints". Its targets are mainly civilians and non-combatants, and its purpose is to cause propagandistic and psychological effects (Schmid, 2012).

It is important at this stage to acknowledge the relevance of the academic study of terrorism, which has been shaped by several key thinkers whose contributions offer essential insights into its nature, causes, and evolution. Bruce Hoffman in *Inside Terrorism* (2017) emphasizes that terrorism is the deliberate creation and exploitation of fear through violence for political, religious, or ideological purposes. Hoffman's work remains foundational for understanding terrorism as a dynamic, adaptive phenomenon, as he highlights the importance of publicity and evolving tactics, offering a historical trajectory from nationalist movements to contemporary transnational networks.

A strategic understanding of terrorist behaviour is provided by Martha Crenshaw, who argues that terrorism is often a rational choice made by groups when other strategies appear ineffective. In her seminal work "The Causes of Terrorism" (1981), Crenshaw emphasizes organizational decision-making and political context over simplistic moral narratives. Complementing this, David Rapoport's "Four Waves of Modern Terrorism" theory (2001) historicizes terrorism into successive ideological waves: anarchist (the anti-colonial, new left, and religious) with distinct motivations and characteristics. Together, Crenshaw and Rapoport have been instrumental in situating terrorism within broader strategic and historical frameworks.

The motivations underlying terrorist acts have been further explored by Louise Richardson and Jessica Stern. Richardson, in *What Terrorists Want* (2006), identifies revenge, renown, and reaction as the core drivers of terrorist actions, arguing that emotional and strategic motivations intertwine. Stern, through works like *Terror in the Name of God* (2003), focuses on the psychological dimensions, analysing personal trauma and radicalization pathways among individuals who join terrorist organizations. Their research underscores the need to understand terrorism not only as political violence but also as a deeply personal and emotional phenomenon.

Engaging with these scholars' insights enriches the understanding of terrorism beyond narrow legal definitions. They reveal terrorism as a multidimensional phenomenon requiring historical, psychological, and political analysis.

Thus, a comprehensive study of terrorism must incorporate both the structural factors facilitating it and the subjective experiences of its perpetrators, acknowledging that terrorism evolves across time and adapts to new social and political realities.

What seems to be clear among all definitions is that this terror is intentionally used through violence to create fear at non-combatant targets (Matusitz, 2012); hence, it is usually held on civilians and other defenceless persons who have no direct responsibility on the conflict itself. The intent is not to harm the people who have been victims of the attack, but to generate big and prompt propaganda. The echo of the attack is the ultimate goal, and creating impact is what differentiates terrorist violence from other crimes. This is because the damages it causes reach far beyond the immediate victims, but it can extend to governments, the military, and the rest of the population, even though they are not directly involved.

Furthermore, the perpetrators can range from small groups to big transnational networks whose aim is predominantly political (Schmid, 2012) although there can be other – separate or coexistent – religious and ideological reasons. Moreover, the acts usually come in a serial character, creating a climate of fear and expectation on whether other threats or violence can happen again. This is the way they establish fear within a society, which may lead to a manipulation of the political process of a country – or group of countries.

Another key difference for the delimitation of terrorism is whether this can be considered the equivalent of war crimes during peacetime. It needs to be clarified first that terrorism can occur both during armed conflict and during peacetime. The main difference is that when committed during wartime – whether these are international or national armed conflicts – the applicable law will be that of the 1949 Geneva Conventions and their 1977 Additional Protocols. Some domestic and international judicial bodies have started applying the laws of war to peacetime acts of terrorism (Scharf, 2001), setting a precedent. This is the case of *Juan Carlos Abella v. Argentina*[13] held at the Inter-American Commission on Human Rights in 1997. This case is about an attack that took place 1989 by 42 civilians during peacetime in Argentina. After hours of fighting, the civilians asked for surrender, but Argentine troops continued fighting until most of the people died or were heavily wounded. The Court ruled that this confrontation qualified as an armed conflict because it was a planned, coordinated, and executed armed attack against a military

13 Juan Carlos Abella v. Argentina, Case 11.137, Inter-Am. C.H.R., Report No. 55/97, OEA/Ser. L./V./I.95, doc. 7 rev. 271 (1997).

objective. This case sets a precedent that lowers the requirements to consider an attack as part of an armed conflict, which might lead future terrorist situations to qualify for application of humanitarian laws (and so, the laws of war). At the same time, this conclusion might lead to consider that terrorists act lawfully if analysed under the laws of war (Scharf, 2001).

The problem of not having a comprehensive definition of the term terrorism in international law may lead to conflicts with the principle of legality, enshrined in Article 15 of the International Covenant on Civil and Political Rights, which states that criminal liability is limited to clear and precise provisions. Hence, if States use vague definitions of terrorism, this might be used as a means to cover peaceful acts or to limit certain political oppositions (UNHCHR, 2008), threatening the rights of individuals.

Establishing such a definition is not a way to punish acts that would be otherwise left unpunished, but it is a way to define those acts which need a stronger police and judicial international cooperation and to reinforce the symbolic power of substantive criminal law (Symenidou-Kastanidou, 2004).

2.1 Domestic Perspectives of Terrorism

Definitions of terrorism and terrorist organizations vary across states, leaving room for different interpretations on what to consider that a terrorist act is, and to appoint a particular actor or organization as terrorist. Thus these definitions are crucial to establish something or someone as a terrorist threat and designations will vary depending on legal delimitations of these concepts.

As a consequence, some legal definitions of "terrorism" or "terrorist act" are very much criticized. In some cases, governments establish vague or ambiguous descriptions that can lead to broad understandings of what terrorism is or should be. In other cases, states construct lists of acts that can be considered as terrorist, including attitudes or performances that fall far from what the UN General Assembly or the Security Council have stated as terrorism. While there is no single definition of terrorism under international law, most of them are centred in the use of violence and the political ends, and the most widely accepted one – even though it is still non-binding today – is that of Resolution 1566 of the Security Council. Therefore, in this section we will overview some of these controversial interpretations and the reasons why they have been reproved, analysing the elements on which they are constructed, and comparing them to the definition of Resolution 1566. To this end, I have selected some domestic definitions and classified them according to the extent to which are written according to the definition given in the aforementioned Resolution.

2.1.1 *Closer* Approaches to the International Definition of Terrorism

Some of the definitions at the domestic level which more truthfully imitate that in international law are those of the United Kingdom, for instance, and even that of organizations such as the European Union.

Starting with the first, the United Kingdom's definition of terrorism can be found in Article 1(1) of the Terrorism Act 2000. It is established that terrorism is either a threat or action designed "to influence the government or an international governmental organisation or to intimidate the public or a section of the public, and the use or threat is made for the purpose of advancing a political, religious, racial or ideological cause". Subsection 2 continues as follows:

> (2) Action falls within this subsection if it –
> (a) involves serious violence against a person,
> (b) involves serious damage to property,
> (c) endangers a person's life, other than that of the person committing the action,
> (d) creates a serious risk to the health or safety of the public or a section of the public, or
> (e) is designed seriously to interfere with or seriously to disrupt an electronic system.

Although the definition is still found within the 2000 Act, the Terrorism Act of 2006 sought to extend a list of offenses such as glorifying terrorism or distributing terrorist publication (Setty, 2011). From 2000 onwards, the British parliament has passed several Acts in the field of terrorism, all of them significantly influenced by the 9/11 attacks and the 7/7 bombings in London (European Parliament, 2017). Although the definition of terrorism remains the same, in these subsequent Acts, new powers have been given to the police beyond those related to ordinary crime.

The European Union's definition would also fall within this section. It is somehow closely related to the September 11 attacks. Shortly after these events on the Twin Towers in New York, the European Commission published a Framework Decision on Combating Terrorism (2002/475/JHA) (hereafter "Framework Decision"). This legislation, which was published in 2002, was made in order to harmonize the treatment of terrorist attacks at the domestic legislation of Member States. Article 1 reinforces this idea that the acts described within the Article (points *a* to *i*) are defined as offences under national law.

It is in this first Article where the definition of terrorism given by the EU is found. It establishes that those acts that "seriously damage a country or an international organisation where committed with the aim of (1) seriously intimidating a population, or (2) unduly compelling a Government or international organisation to perform or abstain from performing any act, or (3) seriously destabilising or destroying the fundamental political, constitutional, economic or social structures of a country or an international organisation" are terrorist offences so long as they are deemed to cause at least one of the nine points described in the second part of the Article. Hence, if these three acts are committed intentionally, they will be considered terrorist attacks; thus, the element of intention must be present for the basis of the existence of a terrorist offence (Borgers, 2012).

In 2017, the Framework Decision was replaced by the Directive on Combatting Terrorism[14] and its paragraph (5) states that offences related to foreign terrorist fighters and terrorist financing should be addressed more comprehensively by Member States due to the evolution of the terrorist threat and offenses relating to this topic. In this sense, another descriptive act was added to the 9 that were previously described in the Framework Decision of 2002. The new letter (i) now includes illegal system and data interference. Besides this change and the alteration of the order of the definition, the content of this remained basically the same.

2.1.2 *Extended* Approaches to the International Definition of Terrorism

The United Kingdom's definition of terrorism has influenced those of Canada, Singapore, Israel, and Australia, among others (Walker, 2013; Ananian-Welsh and Williams, 2014). Looking at the latter case, under Australian law instead of defining the word terrorism they define "terrorist act".[15] This definition includes an *action* or *threat of action* where:

(a) the action falls within subsection (2) and does not fall within subsection (3); and
(b) the action is done or the threat is made with the intention of advancing a political, religious or ideological cause; and

14 Directive (EU) 2017/541 of the European Parliament and the Council of 15 March 2017 on combating terrorism and replacing Council Framework Decision 2002/475/JHA and amending Council Decision 2005/671/JHA.

15 Section 100.1 of the Australian Criminal Code Act 1995.

(c) the action is done or the threat is made with the intention of:
   (i) coercing, or influencing by intimidation, the government of the Commonwealth or a State, Territory or foreign country, or of part of a State, Territory or foreign country; or
   (ii) intimidating the public or a section of the public.

This definition, although inspired by that of the UK, has some differentiations. One of the first things to stand out from this definition is that it does not include those acts causing deaths or bodily injury, which are in fact two of the most common elements of most terrorist definitions. The acts described in the Australian provisions are characterized to coerce, influence, or intimidate the government or the public, but there are no specific descriptions on the measures taken to reach these goals.

Martin Scheinin, the former Special Rapporteur on the promotion and protection of human rights and fundamental freedoms, reported in 2006 on the counter-terrorist measures and the protection of human rights in Australia.[16] Among other criticisms, he urged to reconsider the broad definition of "terrorist act", as it did not distinguish properly the difference between a terrorist conduct and an ordinary criminal conduct.[17] He also argued that there was no element of intention,[18] which is essential when talking about terrorism as already stated by the Security Council, and that the Australian definition also includes "acts not defined in the international conventions and protocols relating to terrorism".[19]

Another country to introduce to this category is France. The French definition of terrorism is found in Article 421–1 of the Criminal Code, and it consists on a list of acts that are considered as terrorist, whether they are committed individually or collectively, and as long as their purpose is "seriously to disturb public order through intimidation or terror". Hence, we can already find a difference here between the UK's definition and that of France, which is that the latter does not mention the purpose lying behind the attacks. More concretely, it does not indicate whether there is a political, religious, or other type of goal, and it only states that there is an intention to create "intimidation or terror".

16 *See* the 14 December 2006, Report of the Special Rapporteur on the promotion and protection of human rights and fundamental freedoms while countering terrorism on Australia (A/HRC/4/26/Add.3).
17 *See* para. 16 of the Report.
18 *See* para. 27 of the Report.
19 *See* para. 15(b) of the Report.

Amongst the offences listed in this Article there are murders, kidnappings, abductions, extortions, the production of explosives, hijacking of planes and vessels, etc. The following Articles have also included other actions such as the financing a terrorist organization in any way. However, a more controversial provision is found in 421–2-1, which determines that "The participation in any group formed or association established with a view to the preparation, marked by one or more material actions of any of the acts of terrorism provided for under the previous articles shall in addition be an act of terrorism". This formulation is vaguer than the others and may lead to indiscriminate arrests and detentions of suspects.[20] Another problematic stipulation is that related to introducing substances liable to imperil human or animal health into French territory (be it the atmosphere, ground, soil, food or waters).[21] This type of "ecological terrorism" can also be disputed because of its vagueness and lack of further specific description. The French case, with its addition related to "ecological terrorism" is an example of a definition that has been brought to the domestic level and has reincorporated new elements based not only on national perceptions of terrorism, but also on new contemporary threats that would have not been thought of years ago, bringing new and more modern approaches to the "traditional" international definition of terrorism. Nonetheless, vague and overly broad terms remain, leaving room for the definition of much improvement to be more closely related to that given by the Security Council.

Russia has in its hand a definition which also goes further than that of Resolution 1566. Its definition of "act of terrorism"[22] includes explosions, arsons or other actions to intimidate the population, and also the "infliction of significant property damage". This latter part broadens the scope of application of this Article allowing authorities to take action against what could merely be an altercation or act of vandalism. The definition continues to include "other grave consequences", leaving out the meaning of what should be considered to be "grave" unexplained and opening the room to use this part

20 In this sense, see also the Report of the Special Rapporteur on the promotion and protection of human rights and fundamental freedoms while countering terrorism (A/HRC/40/52/Add.4). She recognized that even though France had a deep experience in managing terrorism through a rule of law-based approach and in respect of upholding human rights obligations in their legal framework, challenges remain, such as those related to definitions of "terrorism" and "apology for terrorism" found in the Strengthening Internal Security and the Fight against Terrorism (SILT) law, as she maintained that they remain "overly broad and ambiguous".

21 Article 421–2-2 of the French Criminal Code.

22 Article 205, Chapter 24, of the Criminal Code of the Russian Federation.

of the definition to a wide range of acts that would usually be left out of what is thought to be terrorism. All these actions, according to Article 205, must have "the intention to influence the taking of a decision by authorities or international organisations" or the threat to do so.

A far more troublesome conceptualization of terrorism is that of Zimbabwe,[23] which would be considered a type of definition that goes far beyond the elements that are established in Resolution 1566. Their national description of terrorism reads as follows:

> (1) Any person who, for the purpose of
> (a) causing or furthering an insurrection in Zimbabwe; or
> (b) causing the forcible resistance to the Government or the Defence Forces or any law enforcement agency; or
> (c) procuring by force the alteration of any law or policy of the Government;
>
> commits any act accompanied by the use or threatened use of weaponry with the intention or realising that there is a real risk or possibility of-
> (i) killing or injuring any other person; or
> (ii) damaging or destroying any property; or
> (iii) inflicting substantial financial loss upon any other person; or
> (iv) obstructing or endangering the free movement in Zimbabwe of any traffic on land or water or in the air; or
> (v) disrupting or interfering with an essential service;
>
> shall be guilty of insurgency, banditry, sabotage or terrorism, whether or not any purpose referred to in paragraph (a), (b) or (c) is accomplished (...)

Even though the preamble of the Zimbabwe's counterterrorism act of 2011 recognizes that "national liberation movements" are not to be considered as part of the law's objects, the law itself does not specifically exempt these groups (HRW, 2012). The preamble goes on to explain that those acts which are part of the exercise of a "legitimate right to national liberation, self-determination and independence against colonialism, or occupation or aggression or domination by alien or foreign forces ... shall not, for any reason, be considered a terrorist activity".[24]

A comparable case to the Zimbabwean one is that of Ethiopia, which can also be categorized as an *extended approach* to the international definition of

---

23 *See* Section 23(1) of the Zimbabwe Criminal Law (Codification and Reform) Act (Chapter 9:23), also known as Act 23/2004.

24 Suppression of Foreign and International Terrorism (Chapter 11:21) Act 5/2007.

terrorism. Section 3 of the Proclamation No. 652/2009 (Anti-Terrorism Proclamation) of Ethiopia establishes a list of acts that can be considered as terrorist attacks.

> Whosoever or a group intending to advance a political, religious or ideological cause by coercing the government, intimidating the public or section of the public, or destabilizing or destroying the fundamental political, constitutional or, economic or social institutions of the country:
> 1) causes a person's death or serious bodily injury;
> 2) creates serious risk to the safety or health of the public or section of the public;
> 3) commits kidnapping or hostage taking;
> 4) causes serious damage to property;
> 5) causes damage to natural resource, environment, historical or cultural heritages;
> 6) endangers, seizes or puts under control, causes serious interference or disruption of any public service; or
> 7) threatens to commit any of the acts stipulated under sub-articles (1) to (6) of this Article;
>
> is punishable with rigorous imprisonment from 15 years to life or with death.

As Human Rights Watch recognizes (HRW, 2012), the definition within this law is so broad that it could be used "to prosecute a wide range of conduct far beyond the limits of what can reasonably be considered terrorist activity". Clauses such as (4), (5), or (6) can be used discretionarily to detain people in a wide array of circumstances, not being considered as anything close to terrorism in other jurisdictions or in international law. The broad application of case (6) can lead to condemning actions such as peaceful demonstrations obstructing traffic as terrorism. Likewise, the understanding of causing "serious damage to property" is too vague and may be interpreted as to qualify a wide range of acts as terrorist.

Ethiopia has created a terrorist narrative that controls critical speeches both on digital and traditional media (Workneh, 2019), making it hard for those opposing to the government to make critiques and participate in the political discourse. To sum up, it seems appropriate to maintain that Ethiopia has an overly broad definition of terrorism that can easily be used to condemn conducts that should not be considered within the conceptualization of terrorism.

2.2 Principal Critiques to the Concept of Terrorism

In the absence of a common universal definition of "terrorism", for the purpose of this thesis, the definition that will be used to refer to this phenomenon will be that of the Security Council Resolution 1566. As it has been outlined before, this is the most global and widely accepted definition in use today; thus, it seems appropriate to agree to take this as the most proper definition during the following lines.

Needless to say, having a common definition of terrorism is useful and necessary for States to develop solid cooperation measures, focusing specially on reinforcing the police and judicial sectors. And furthermore, terrorists take advantage of any legal differences in the treatment of terrorism between States, making it even more necessary to frame a legal definition of terrorism and to offences relating to it.

Symenidou-Kastanidou (2004) argues that the formulation of special offences shows that the intention to define terrorism is not only a matter of strengthening police and judicial cooperation, but instead it also "connotes mainly a desire to use the symbolic power of substantive criminal law". In this sense, she points out three main goals that States follow when making use of this definition: (a) *the manifestation of an illusion of potential safety*, (b) *the enhancement of their authority through the legislative activity*, and (c) *the legalization of special anti-terrorist measures that are being planned or suggested or have already been put into effect, and that have a negative impact on human rights*. Hence, the intention of the State in defining terrorism is the first element to take into consideration when analysing these type offences and their grounds.

There is also an element to take into consideration, which is related to the varying forms of terrorism. For instance, Walter Laqueur (1999) suggests that the character of terrorism has changed through history, and he talks about "old" and "new" terrorism. Old terrorism would be the kind of terrorism that strikes only selected targets, while new terrorism is that which is indiscriminate and seeks to cause casualties to largest extent possible. He argues that terrorist acts have changed not in terms of their demands, but in relation to the destruction they seek to cause and the "elimination of large sections of the population". This terror has evolved "from being a means to an end, to becoming the end in itself" (Morgan, 2004). Following Laqueur's definitions, Matusitz (2012) explains that terrorism has changed because there has been a "paradigm shift". The paradigm – as he defines as "a way of interpreting the world which has been accepted by a group of people and that can be useful for politicians and thinkers to design policy agendas" – this worldview – has changed, and this paradigm shift has also changed the dynamics of terrorism.[25] These evolving perceptions of terrorism throughout time have taken many transformations and facets, which have in turn complicated the establishment of a proper definition, making it much harder to find a complete definition of terrorism as such.

And what is more, since September 11, many states have changed their approaches to counter terrorism, and what was usually strictly a matter of criminal law, has now become replaced in much part by the use of military means (Murphy, 2011). Many oppose to this modus operandi and reproach that taking this view may mean a threat to human rights. Nevertheless, those supporting the military model contend that criminal law is not enough to fight against the terrorist threat.

Authors such as Hardy and Williams (2011) argue that one of the main concerns with domestic definitions of terrorism is related to the principle of legality.[26] They argue that the principle of legality has to comply with two different senses. On the one hand, the principle is linked to the Latin maxims *nullum crimen sine lege* ("no crime without a law") and *nulla poena sine lege* ("no punishment without a law"). The second one is that which refers to the compliance with human rights treaty obligations.[27] Thus this principle is linked to the obligation of states to specify crimes in advance using language that is sufficiently precise, unambiguous, and narrowly focused on the prohibited conduct, and which is strictly construed and not extended by analogy (Duffy,

---

25 To read more about the evolving nature of terrorism and its current forms, see John Murphy on "International Law in Crisis: Challenges posed by the new terrorism and the changing nature of war" and Paul Wilkinson's work "Terrorist Targets and Tactics New Risks to World Order", where he develops the idea that there are different factors which shows that terrorist attacks are more indiscriminate today, such as the saturation of media images of the consequences of these attacks, the fact that attacking civilians also means lowering risks for themselves, and changing political perceptions to the "vengeful and hard-life fanatic" perspective.

26 In this sense, Article 15 of the International Covenant on Civil and Political rights is especially relevant since it is the one which codifies this principle, as affirmed by the International Commission of Jurists (*Legal Commentary to the ICJ Berlin Declaration: Counter-Terrorism, human rights and the rule of law* 16, pp.72–74 (2008), the Special Rapporteur on the Promotion and Protection of Human Rights While Countering Terrorism, Martin Scheinin (*Protection of Human Rights and Fundamental Freedoms While Countering Terrorism*, 42, General Assembly, UN Document A/61/267, 16 of August 2006), and the United Nations Office of the High Commissioner for Human Rights (*Digest of Jurisprudence of the UN and regional organizations on the protection of human rights while countering terrorism* 63, UN Document HR/PUB/03/1, 2003).

27 Further development of the relationship between counter-terrorism measures and their impact on human rights will be developed in Chapter 3.

2009). Otherwise, imprecise and overbroad definitions, very commonly adjudicated by states to the definition of terrorism nationally, may be in breach of the principle of legality and might lead to increasing the risk that governments target, supress or prosecute individuals, associations, or opponents to the government in general who have no real connection to terrorist activity; arbitrarily detaining individuals; and other negative actions associated with abuse of power.

All this debate surrounding the definition of terrorism perpetuates an atmosphere of a lack of certainty both at the national and international levels. The way in which states perceive and face severe national security threats is what defines terrorism domestically, and how they apply these definitions in practice. The lack of a comprehensive definition at the global level has opened the room to deviate from human rights principles and treaties and the rule of law and has led to overbroad and vague definitions which are many times associated with military action. To fight the terrorist phenomenon, it is imperative to enact laws that adjust to the current needs to counter terrorism based on examination and scrutiny, considering the weight of the human rights implicated, legal protection, and the rule of law to ensure that the definition of terrorism is found to apply.

As will be shown in the following chapters, the ambiguity and politicization of both "refugee" and "terrorism" has enabled states to expand security narratives in ways that compromise refugee protection. This definitional fluidity is not simply academic, it has real-world consequences, allowing governments to frame asylum seekers as potential threats and to justify restrictive measures under the guise of national security. Understanding these conceptual foundations is therefore key to grasping how and why refugees are increasingly treated as security risks.

The definitional ambiguities discussed in this chapter – both around who qualifies as a refugee and what constitutes terrorism – are not merely technical or theoretical. They provide the legal and discursive space through which states can shift migration governance from the domain of humanitarian protection to that of national security. This definitional flexibility has enabled the growing trend of framing refugees as potential threats rather than protected subjects. As the following chapters will show, it is precisely this intersection, the one between legal uncertainty and political opportunism, the one which allows securitization narratives to emerge and expand. Understanding how these categories are constructed is therefore crucial to understanding the broader puzzle this book addresses: how and why refugees have become entangled in security discourses across diverse geopolitical contexts.

References

Agamben, G. (1998) *Homo Sacer: Sovereign power and bare life* (D. Heller-Roazen, Trans.). Stanford: Stanford University Press. (Original work published 1995).

Agamben, G. (2005) *State of Exception* (K. Attell, Trans.). Chicago: University of Chicago Press.

Aleinikoff, T. A. (1995 / 2003) 'State-centered refugee law: From resettlement to containment', *Michigan Journal of International Law*, Vol. 14(1).

Alpes, M., Tunaboylu, S. Ulusoy, O. and Hassan, S. (2017) 'Post-deportation risks under the EU-Turkey Statement: What happens after readmission to Turkey?', Migration Policy Center, Issue 30.

Ananian-Welsh, R. and Williams, G. (2014) 'Normalisation and spread of anti-terror laws in Australia', *Melbourne University Law Review*, Vol. 38, pp. 362–408.

Betts, A. (2009) *Protection by persuasion: International cooperation in the refugee regime*. Ithaca: Cornell University Press.

Betts, A., and Collier, P. (2017) *Refuge: Transforming a broken refugee system*. London: Allen Lane.

Bigo, D. (2002) 'Security and immigration: Toward a critique of the governmentality of unease', *Alternatives: Global, Local, Political*, 27(1), 63–92.

Bigo, D. (2011) 'Freedom and speed in the enlarged European area: Identity and the distortion of liberalism' in V. Guiraudon and C. Joppke (Eds.), *Controlling a new migration world* (pp. 31–49). London: Routledge.

Borgers, M. J. (2012) 'Framework Decision on combating terrorism: Two questions on the definition of terrorist offences', *New Journal of European Criminal Law*, Vol. 68.

COE (2017) 'War and terrorism', Council of Europe. Available at: https://www.coe.int/en/web/compass/war-and-terrorism.

Crawley, H. and Skleparis, D. (2018) 'Refugees, migrants, neither, both: categorical fetishism and the politics of bounding in Europe's 'migration crisis', *Journal of Ethnic and Migration Studies*, Vol. 44(1), pp. 48–64.

Crenshaw, M. (1981) 'The causes of terrorism', *Comparative Politics*, 13(4), 379–399.

De Genova, N. (2005) *Working the boundaries: Race, space, and "illegality" in Mexican Chicago*. Durham: Duke University Press.

Duffy, H. (2009) *The "War on terror" and the framework of international law*, UK: Cambridge University Press.

European Parliament (2017) 'EU and Member States' policies and laws on persons suspected of terrorism-related crimes', Committee on Civil Liberties, Justice and Home Affairs, Directorate General for Internal Policies of the Union, PE 596.832.

Gerver, M. (2018) *The Ethics and Politics of Asylum: Liberal Democracy and the Response to Refugees*. Cambridge: Cambridge University Press.

Gibney, M. J. (2004) *The ethics and politics of asylum: Liberal democracy and the response to refugees*. Cambridge: Cambridge University Press.

Goodwin-Gill, G. S. (2014) *The International Law of Refugee Protection*, The Oxford Handbook of Refugee and Forces Migration Studies, UK: Oxford Handbooks.

Halsall, P. (1997) 'Maximilien Robespierre: On the Principles of Political Morality, February 1974', Fordham University.

Hamlin, R. (2014) *Let Me Be a Refugee: Administrative Justice and the Politics of Asylum in the United States, Canada, and Australia*. Oxford University Press.

Hamlin, R. (2021) *Crossing: How We Label and React to People on the Move*. Stanford University Press.

Hardy, K. and Williams, G. (2011) 'What is "Terrorism"? Assessing domestic legal definitions', *16 University of California, Los Angeles (UCLA) Journal of International Law and Foreign Affairs*, Vol. 77.

Hathaway, J. C. (2007) 'Why Refugee Law Still Matters', *Melbourne Journal of International Law*, 8(1), pp. 89–103.

Hoffman, B. (2017) *Inside terrorism* (3rd ed.). New York: Columbia University Press.

IDMC (2017) 'Global Report on Internal Displacement', Internal Displacement Monitoring Centre.

Jubany, O. (2017) *Screening Asylum in a Culture of Disbelief: Truths, Denials and Skeptical Borders*. London: Palgrave.

Laqueur, W. (1999) *The New Terrorism: Fanaticism and the Arms of Mass Destruction*, Oxford University Press.

Lentini, E. (1985) 'The Definition of Refugee in International Law: Proposals for the Future', *Third World Law Journal*, Vol. 183.

Llobet, M. (2008) 'Terrorismo y "guerra" contra el terror: límites de su punición en un Estado democrático', Doctor in Philosophy Thesis, Pompeu Fabra University.

Malkki, L. H. (1995) 'Refugees and exile: From "refugee studies" to the national order of things.', *Annual Review of Anthropology*, 24, 495–523.

Matusitz, J. (2012) *Terrorism and Communication: A Critical Introduction*, London: Sage Publications.

McAdam, J. (2012) *Climate change, forced migration, and international law*. Oxford: Oxford University Press.

MEDAM (2017) 'Sharing responsibility for refugees and expanding legal immigration: 2017 MEDAM Assessment Report on Asylum and Migration Policies in Europe', Mercator Dialogue on Migration and Asylum.

Millbank, A. (2000) 'The Problem with the 1951 Refugee Convention', Parliament of Australia, Research Paper 5 2000–01.

Morgades, S. (2010) 'La protección de los demandantes de asilo por razón de su vulnerabilidad especial en la jurisprudencia del Tribunal Europeo de los Derechos Humanos,' *Revista de Derecho Comunitario Europeo*, n.37, pp.801–842.

Morgan, M. (2004) 'The Origins of the New Terrorism', *ProQuest Central*.

Murphy, J. (2011) 'International Law in Crisis: Challenges posed by the new terrorism and the changing nature of war', *Case Western Reserve Journal of International Law*, Vol. 44.

Pirjola, J. (2008) *Shadows in Paradise –Exploring Non-Refoulement as an Open Concept*, UK: Oxford University Press.

Human Rights Council (2019) 'Report of the Special Rapporteur on the promotion and protection of human rights and fundamental freedoms while countering terrorism, Visit to France', (A/HRC/40/52/Add.4).

HRW (2012) 'In the Name of Security. Counterterrorism Laws Worldwide since September 11', Human Rights Watch.

Rahman, Mahbubur (2024) 'Statelessness -the Root Cause of the Rohingya Crisis-Needs to Be Addressed', 9 July. Available at: https://newlinesinstitute.org/state-resilience-fragility/statelessness-the-root-cause-of-the-rohingya-crisis-needs-to-be-addressed/.

Rapoport, D. C. (2001) 'The four waves of modern terrorism' in A. Cronin and J. Ludes (Eds.), *Attacking terrorism: Elements of a grand strategy* (pp. 46–73). Washington, D.C.: Georgetown University Press.

Richardson, L. (2006) *What terrorists want: Understanding the enemy, containing the threat.* New York: Random House.

Scharf, M. (2001) 'Defining terrorism as the peace time equivalent of war crimes: a case of too much convergence between international humanitarian law and international criminal law?', *ILSA Journal of International and Comparative Law*, Vol. 7, pp. 391–398.

Schmid, A. P. (2012) 'The Revised Academic Consensus Definition of Terrorism', *Perspectives on Terrorism*, University of Leiden, Vol. 6(22,) pp. 86–87.

Schmid, A. P. (2011) *The Routledge Handbook of Terrorism Research*, London and New York: Routledge.

Setty, S. (2011) 'What's in a name? How nations define terrorism ten years after 9/11', *University of Pennsylvania Journal of International Law*, Vol. 33(1).

Symenidou-Kastanidou, E. (2004) 'Defining Terrorism', *European Journal of Crime, Criminal Law and Criminal Justice*, Vol. 12(1), pp.14–35.

Stern, J. (2003) *Terror in the name of God: Why religious militants kill.* New York: Ecco/HarperCollins.

Triandafyllidou, A. and Mantanika, R. (2017), 'La emergencia de los refugiados del Mediterráneo: Evaluación de las respuestas de política de la Unión Europea', *Revista Migración y Desarrollo*, Vol.15(28).

UN (2019) 'Chapter V: Refugees and Stateless Persons', United Nations Treaty Collection, Available at: https://treaties.un.org/Pages/ViewDetailsII.aspx?src=TREATY&mtdsg_no=V-2&chapter=5&Temp=mtdsg2&clang=_en#top.

UNHCHR (2008) 'Human rights, Terrorism and Counter-terrorism', Fact Sheet No. 32, Office of the United Nations High Commissioner for Human Rights.

UNHCR (2006) 'Master Glossary of Terms', UN High Commissioner for Refugees.

UNHCR (2010) 'Introductory Note by the Office of the United Nations High Commissioner for Refugees', Text of the 1951 Convention Relating to the Status of Refugees, UN High Commissioner for Refugees.

UNHCR (2017) 'A guide to international refugee protection and building state asylum systems', Handbook for Parliamentarians N°27, Inter-Parliamentary Union and the UN High Commissioner for Refugees.

UNHCR (2024) 'Statelessness around the world', UN High Commissioner for Refugees. Available at: https://reporting.unhcr.org/global-appeal-2024/focus-areas/stateless ness.

Walker, C. (2013) 'The Reshaping of Control Orders in the United Kingdom: Time for a Fairer Go, Australia!', *37 Melbourne University Law Review*, Vol.143.

Walters, W. (2004) 'Secure borders, safe haven, domopolitics', *Citizenship Studies*, Vol. 8(3), pp. 237–260.

Workneh, T. W. (2019) *Counter-terrorism in Ethiopia: manufacturing insecurity, monopolizing speech*, School of Communication Studies, Kent State University.

CHAPTER 2

Theoretical Underpinnings of the Securitization of Migration

This chapter explores the theoretical foundations of the securitization of migration, with particular attention to how these dynamics affect refugees, a group legally entitled to international protection but increasingly framed as a threat. Drawing from critical security studies and international legal theory, the chapter uses securitization theory to explain the shift from protection to control in migration governance. While securitization has often been applied broadly to migration, this chapter revisits the concept through a refugee-focused lens, laying the groundwork for the case studies that follow.

Since the September 11 attacks and subsequent acts of terrorism, migration has become closely associated with national security agendas, especially in Western states. Migrants, including refugees and asylum seekers, have been portrayed as threats to public safety, cultural cohesion, and increasingly, national security. Refugees, in particular, now find themselves governed not as rights-bearing individuals, but as potential risks, despite their protected legal status under international law. The framing of refugees as political and security challenges is not new; as Zolberg et al. (1989) showed, refugee movements have long been entangled with state interests, sovereignty, and international stability. In fact, refugee movements have long been understood by states as political and security challenges rather than purely humanitarian phenomena, given their links to conflict, regime instability, and international relations (Zolberg et al., 1989). In this sense, this tension lies at the core of the book's central puzzle: how and why states justify the exceptional treatment of refugees through security-based frameworks.

This chapter contributes to that inquiry by examining securitization theory and its critiques, with a specific focus on the refugee context. It demonstrates that securitization is not simply a policy reaction, but part of a broader structural transformation in migration governance, one that normalizes exceptional measures and erodes long-standing protection norms. It is structured as follows: the first section outlines the concept of securitization and its core elements; the second reviews major critiques of the theory; the third examines how securitization operates within legal frameworks; and the final section explores how securitization extends beyond the law through discourse and practice.

 | HTTPS://DOI.ORG/10.1163/9789004704527-004

1 The Concept, Factors, and Actors of Securitization

Securitization is understood to be the process of integrating non-security issues "into a security framework that emphasizes policing and defence" (Bourbeau, 2014) as a consequence of securitizing speech acts (Messina, 2014). Or, as put by Waever, "it is by labelling something a security issue that it becomes one" (Waever, 2004). Through securitization, extraordinary measures are applied in order to protect from a particular threat. This concept is not to be confused with that of the politicization of immigration, which refers to making the subject of immigration from restricted networks and bureaucracies to the public arena.[1] This process can be neutral and even lead to positive benefits. However, that of securitization, as we will discuss in the following lines, is most of the times neither of them.

Many would think that it is after September 11 that this phenomenon appeared, but most scholars agree that the so-called "war on terror" strengthened an already existing concept of securitization. That is, migration policies already provoked certain insecurities and uncertainties at the domestic and international level, but 9/11 further legitimized the security rationale that has prevailed in Europe since the late 1970s (Karyotis, 2011; Chebel d'Appollonia, 2012). As a consequence, it seems appropriate to affirm that the securitization of migration is an "old phenomenon" (Nagtegaal, 2011) that has not been created in the 21st century but has rather reborn. However, for the purposes of this book, the analysis will be in the latest wave of securitization, which is the one that started with the events of September 11.

Following the logic of the Copenhagen School, the political elite *deliberately* connects issues related to migration to those related to terrorism so that the public fear on immigration exploits and is then able to transfer immigration out of the realms of conventional politics to the domain of emergency politics (Messina, 2014; Boswell, 2009). In other words, the construction of situations as problems is useful for politicians, as manage them in ways they would otherwise not be able to (Edelman, 1991; Bigo, 2002). For Roe (2004) successful securitization is based on three elements: first, the capacity of the actors to make socially effective claims about threats; second, the forms of these claims so that they are recognized and accepted; and third, the factual factors or events which they are referring to.

Some authors place special emphasis on this first element referring to the actors of securitization. They argue that the construction of a security frame

1 To read more on this subject see: Bourbeau, P., 2011, *The Securitization of Immigration: A Study of Movement and Order*, London, UK: Routledge.

does not depend so much on the perception of the issue as a threat, on the fact that because it is presented by the political elite as such (Buzan, Waever and Wilde, 1998; Karyotis, 2011). These elites in power are the ones defining the existing risks in a determinate period of time, while also selecting the means through which these threats must be neutralized (Estevens, 2018). Therefore, elites persuade the public with their best resources so that an issue is perceived as an existential threat that needs of security action to be controlled, marginalizing other alternative responses (Van Dijk, 1993). In other words, securitization takes place when elite actors "inject *low politics* public policy issues into the domain of *high politics* by adopting the rhetoric of existential threat" (Messina, 2014); thus, successful securitization is based on the intersubjective establishment of an existential threat (Roe, 2004). Accordingly, a topic becomes securitized not because of its nature or potential threat, but because it is conferred this image by the political elite, so that the public has the perception that it needs of a special and extraordinary response in order to be overtaken. Once the claim is widely accepted, the issue can be transferred from conventional politics to emergency politics. This can in turn dangerously be used as a governmental technique that can give any issue the category of a security one. In the words of Waever (1995):

> Security is not of interest as a sign that refers to something more real; the utterance *itself* is the act. By saying it, something is done (as in betting, giving a promise, naming a ship). By uttering "security", a state-representative moves a particular development into a specific area, and thereby claims a special right to use whatever means are necessary to block it.

It is interesting to study the approach taken by Balzacq (2005) who studies the possibility of considering securitization from a strategic and pragmatic approach instead of seeing it as a speech act. If following this view, he argues, we must then also analyse the contextual and non-linguistic clues such as physical gestures or the social context. We should then also study other implications when analysing securitization discourses, since the element of the speech act as such would not be the only one to consider, but other factors such as the actor's capabilities, the ontology of their interactions and the social field in which the discourse takes place also takes force. This leads to a much deeper analysis, since this discourse is important for its grammatical and syntactical rules of the language, and for the contextual elements such as analogies and metaphors that move emotions and reach more deeply into the audience. But so is the power position of the actor, her social identity and her capacity to target the audience are considered. If considering all of these elements together, securitization becomes a meaningful procedure as a whole, and all of its parts are relevant and equally affect the probability of success of the message being sent. Concurrently, the pragmatic approach of securitization, as opposed to one of universal pragmatics (speech act), shows that securitization is a strategic practice which seeks to determine "the universal principles of an effective communicative action of security" (2005:192).

Thence in practice, securitization is largely based on power and the capacity to build something as a social and political threat (Taureck, 2006:3). But if that is the case, is it then certain that many – if not most – security threats are built on unmanageable and incoherent decisions? As put by Aradau (2001), securitization becomes a technique used by the political elites to create a sudden rupture in the ordinary life of a particular society by "fabricating an existential threat" or, in other words, it is a mechanism that seeks to create fear by "a mythical replay of the variations of the Hobbesian state of nature". If the reasoning behind securitization is that it is depends on power and capacity, then we should be thinking on strategies to determine who is a legitimate actor to securitize, and if he or she is following a legitimate goal. We should then have a more restrictive view of securitization.

Security policies, and thus securitization, have to do with exceptional cases – and thus exceptional measures – of considerable and major threats affecting society. As Aradau and van Munster (2007; 2009) show, exceptionalism increasingly operates through preventive and risk-based governance, normalizing extraordinary control measures within ordinary administrative practices, including asylum procedures. That is why it is then preferable to solve issues through diplomacy and trade, since these situations are normatively preferable to a security reality (Waever, 1995). Since the optimal situation is the latter, when we find ourselves having securitized an issue, it is preferred to desecuritize it so that it loses this restrictive and exceptional nature to go back to ordinary politics (Waever, 1995; Buzan, Waever and Wilde, 1998). In this sense, Bourbeau and Vuori (2015) are of the opinion that "active desecuritization efforts can be made to block the escalation of a contention" (2015:14). As an example, they study the posture of the People's Republic of China since the late 1970s in avoiding other actors' securitization threshold. The country realized that a threat reputation would sabotage their intentions of becoming a great power; thus, the political moves of the authorities were based on avoiding security responses. The Chinese approach has been to bring all their international activities to the economic, social, and political sectors, instead of treating them as national security concerns. A clear example of a political strategy to desecuritize problems before they can be taken to the security sphere.

Nevertheless, the treatment we have given to migration in the past years is not the same case. On the contrary, the securitization of this field has been a response to different elements – such as massive refugee flows, the incapacity of the West to respond to them, to terrorism, etc. – which have led to an increase of speeches linking migration to national security. As Bigo (2014) argues, mobility governance increasingly relies on risk profiling, transforming refugees into suspect populations governed through surveillance and anticipatory control rather than protection. And since security has expanded to converge the meaning of international and internal security, migration has been deeply affected by the claim that politicians and security professionals make that they are only responding to "new threats requiring exceptional measures" (Bigo, 2002).

Discourses linking migration to terrorism have not only proliferated but have also consolidated the perception of migration as a threat to both social and cultural identity (Toğral, 2011). The securitization of international terrorism led by the elite in the US, for instance, is an example of how new security policies pushed the promotion of human rights, environmental sustainability and human governance to the sidelines of the international security agenda (Charrett, 2009). In this sense, a question that arises is that of the reasons behind the aim to securitize migration. It seems that most scholars agree that Western politicians engage in this kind of discourses that link migration to a security threat for self-interested political reasons and/or in order to increase and enhance the legitimacy of their privileged positions (Karyotis, 2007; Messina, 2014). The securitization discourse legitimizes the application of emergency measures and other non-conventional measures that in a normal situation would be hard to implement. And when the public widely accepts something as a security threat, these measures are considered as necessary to combat the potential threat and maintain national security. Furthermore, it also represents a chance for the political elite to reinforce collective identification and generate "greater loyalty and patriotism by defining a particular issue as a common threat" (Boswell, 2007), and this works particularly well with migration, since the "issue" we are referring to is in regard to people with different cultures and values, disconnected from the national identity. Altogether, as Messina (2014) emphasizes, it matters very much whether decision makers act *purposefully* when linking migration to security.

In the particular case of refugees, Hammerstad (2014) highlights that they have increasingly been constructed as security concerns even though international refugee law formally frames them as persons in need of protection. This tension produces a governance logic in which protection and control coexist uneasily, rather than one displacing the other, resulting in the treatment of refugees as exceptional subjects who test the limits of state sovereignty. Within this framework, humanitarian protection is progressively reinterpreted through logics of risk management, whereby refugees are assessed in terms of potential danger, credibility, and governability rather than vulnerability alone. Crucially, this reframing does not operate solely at the domestic level but is embedded in wider policy and discursive environments that shape how refugee movements are interpreted and governed across different political spaces.

Building on this, it is also important to consider the level at which securitization occurs, whether national, regional, or international. While much of the discourse is driven by national political elites speaking to domestic audiences and implementing exceptional measures within their own borders, the securitization of migration does not occur in isolation. It is increasingly embedded in broader regional and international frameworks, where policies and narratives are shared, diffused, and reinforced across jurisdictions. Understanding these multiple levels is essential to grasp the full scope of how migration – and particularly refugee movements – has become entangled in global security agendas.

Within the Copenhagen School there is the concept of *security constellations*, which refers to patterns that exist in the overall social structures of securitization (Buzan, Waever and Wilde, 1998). This concept refers to security issues that take place mostly at the national level, but which have an effect at the regional level. In the case of India and Pakistan, for instance, their rivalry is situated in the context of the Cold War above, and religion and ethnic divisions below (Buzan and Waever, 2009). Furthermore, Buzan and Waever (2009) also use the concept of *macrosecuritizations*, to refer to those referent objects higher than those at the middle level, and thus have a wider international scope. Macrosecuritizations put together multiple lower-level securitizations and identify a common existential threat that needs an exceptional measure in response. These securitizations are placed above the state and national level and put together lower-level security issues within the larger framework, consolidating them as global threats to security. Due to their nature, any reaction will have to compromise liberal values and will be considered securitization, but these actions are justified since they are widely accepted as global security threats affecting civilization. Buzan (2008) puts as an example the Global War on Terror and the events following 9/11, projected by the US as a macrosecuritization.[2]

---

2 For further discussion on this subject see: Buzan, B., 2004, *The United States and the Great Powers: World Politics in the Twenty-First Century*, Polity; Buzan, B., 2006, *Will the 'global war on terrorism' be the new Cold War?*, International Affairs, Vol.82(6); Buzan, B., and Waever,

At the same time, scholars have highlighted several problems associated with macrosecuritizations. Because security threats are often first perceived at the national or subnational level, actors may project local concerns onto the international stage, leading to what Laclau (1996) calls the problematic vagueness of ambitious universalisms. This overlapping of securitization levels means that domestic security concerns can be elevated into global narratives, sometimes without sufficient justification. For instance, since the Global War on Terror, most Western countries – along with Russia, China, and India – have treated international terrorism as a shared global threat. The appeal of constructing macrosecuritizations lies in their potential rewards: they can reinforce legitimacy and leadership, justify the application of exceptional measures at the expense of rights, and facilitate the formation of international alliances (Buzan and Waever, 2009). The US campaign against Al-Qaeda and the broader Global War on Terror are prime examples of this dynamic, demonstrating how a shift in national security strategy can reshape the international agenda as well (Buzan and Waever, 2009).

Understanding how such large-scale security narratives are constructed and justified requires a closer look at the theoretical foundations of securitization itself. The next section introduces the Copenhagen School's framework, which provides the conceptual tools to analyse how issues like migration and refugeehood become framed as existential threats demanding exceptional measures.

2 The Debate on Securitization in Current Literature

The concept of securitization was first introduced by Ole Waever in the mid-1990s and more fully developed in *Security: A New Framework for Analysis* (Buzan, Waever and Wilde, 1998). Since then, it has been agreed upon and further analysed by other scholars[3] but it has also been subject to debate. Some authors[4] have argued that the security approach developed by the Copenhagen School is problematic and some question whether there is in

O., 2009, *Macrosecuritisation and security constellations: reconsidering scale in securitisation theory*, Review of International Studies, Vol. 35, pp. 253–276; Buzan, B., Waever, O. and Wilde, J., 1998, *Security: A New Framework for Analysis*, Boulder: Lynne Reinner.

3 Some of the most remarkable ones are the works of Barry Buzan, Ole Waever and Jaap de Wilde.

4 In this sense see, for instance, Boswell, C. (2007), Chebel d'Appollonia (2012) and McDonald (2008).

fact a securitization of migration today. I will now overview both critiques, starting with that on the concept of securitization.

Security is, for the Copenhagen School, a subjective construction. As stated previously, securitization theory is based on the idea that security is built from a speech act, that alone by uttering 'security' something becomes security (Waever, 2004; Floyd, 2007). It is, in sum, an intersubjective construction – it does not depend on an "objective" threat – and is initiated by the speech acts of political actors, which ultimately serves to justify the application of exceptional measures. The idea then is to show how through securitization, politicians and decision-makers stimulate arbitrarily the perception of something as a threat, and thus make awareness that national security policies are not founded naturally (Knudsen, 2001).

A different conceptualization of security is given by the Paris School.[5] According to these theorists, security is construed according to a series of routinized practices rather than specific speech acts (McDonald, 2008). For both schools, the conception of security is critical in the sense that they do not consider security as a material condition, but it is instead built according to social and political practices (Buzan, Waever and Wilde, 1998). Nonetheless, they differ in the ways they interpret these practices, since the Paris School's understanding is more pragmatic and pays closer attention to the security practices and particular tools that allow for a subject to be transformed and thus securitized (Naumann and Schiele, 2016). Hence instead of only focusing on the political discourses, securitization should, according to them, be based on practices such as those related to surveillance and border control.

Besides the different perceptions of security within security studies, it is also useful to stand out those critics of securitization.[6] McDonald (2008) has argued that the securitization framework is narrow for different reasons. On the one hand, it is narrowed in its *form*, as he argues that the actors on which the Copenhagen School authors have centred the form of the security discourse is basically that of the political elite, excluding other forms of representation as, for instance, images and videos of other "key securitizing actors" such as the media. He also highlights that the aforementioned concept of securitization is based on a particular moment in time instead of constructing securitization over time through various processes and representations, thus being limited in regard to its *context*. Lastly, he argues that the framework of

5 *See* Bigo, D. (2002), *Security and immigration: Towards a Critique of the Governmentality of Unease*, Alternatives 27 (Special Issue), pp. 63–92.

6 See Messina (2014), Chabel d'Appollonia (2012), Boswell (2007) for examples on scholars who stand that there is no objective evidence constituting the existence of the securitization of migration.

securitization is also narrowed in *nature*, as it defines security in terms of threats and dangers instead of considering security as normative goals and core values.

Balzacq (2005), on the other hand, and as explained in the previous section, critiques the focus on the speech act, arguing that the speech act approach reduces security to a conventional procedure and that, on the contrary, securitization should be seen as a strategic practice that occurs when certain circumstances take place. Hence it is "context-dependent" in the sense that the "psycho-cultural disposition of the audience and the power that both speaker and listener bring to the interaction" are more determinant than the speech act, is crucial.

Different authors have also studied the political and media discourses of different countries and have come to the conclusion that there is no such hard evidence showing that there is in fact an intention by the political elite to securitize migration. However, it must be noted that Loescher was among the first to systematically analyse refugee movements as issues of international security, highlighting their potential to affect regional stability, interstate relations, and internal political order (Loescher, 1992).

Examples of these debates on the securitization of migration can be seen by Chebel d'Appollonia (2012), who affirms that even though there is evidence that securitization has occurred in a number of cases, neither the United States nor European countries substantially changed their policies after the 9/11 attacks, and instead they only reinforced existing measures. Boswell (2007) further argues that while there is some evidence that securitization of migration is happening, there is no reason to believe that politics will be "driven exclusively by an interest in encouraging public unease or introducing more stringent security measures".

Although agreeing with Copenhagen scholars that securitization is manifested through speech acts, it is nonetheless materialized – and completed – only when specific public policies and legal come into play. Consequently, the speech act is the previous step to the process of securitization, but this is not concluded until it is formalized through specific changes in the law or policy fields. According to this idea, the following definition of securitization given by Buzan (1983), as claimed by the Copenhagen School, would be completed this way:

> Securitization is the process by which ostensibly non-security issues, such as immigration, are transformed into urgent security concerns as a result of securitizing speech acts *and its formalization through the development of new or reframed laws and policies.*

3 Securitization and the Law

While securitization is often associated with moments of emergency and exceptional rhetoric, refugee securitization frequently unfolds through routine administrative and legal practices, making it less visible but more durable. Rather than remaining confined to speech acts, securitization becomes embedded in law, policy, and institutional procedures that govern asylum and migration (Hammerstad, 2014).

There are, according to Lavenex (2001), two approaches relating these two fields of study: the realist approach, which perceives migration as a threat to national security, and the liberal policy frame, which has a more humanitarian perspective and treats migration considering above all the protection of human rights. The selection of one of the security frames is extremely important to build a process by which the State enacts laws and policies in the field of migration, as this frame will be the standard way to define an issue within the security framework. Some analysts conclude that it is the realist approach what has driven the securitization of migration at the expense of human rights and humanitarian considerations (Geddes, 2003; Huysmans, 2006; Karyotis, 2011).

But the securitization of different social issues such as migration is in fact a "failure" to deal with issues through "normal politics" (Buzan, Waever and Wilde, 1998). Bringing these issues to the emergency arena, requiring of extraordinary security responses, can endanger the protection of the human rights of refugees. And securitizing actors, typically political elites, should have a sense of responsibility with their discourses linking migration to national security.

It is important in this sense to also refer to the "internationalization" of the securitization of this sector, since it is no longer a phenomenon that takes places only nationally, but it has also been externalized. Boswell (2003) also recognized that member states of the EU have exported migration control instruments such as those relating to border control, not only to the EU level, but further beyond. She gives different arguments to explain this. Firstly, these were exported to sending and transit countries, and secondly, future member states were obliged to accept the Schengen *acquis* into their legislation (such as stringer border control and asylum policies). Another element of externalization comprises instruments facilitating the return of asylum seekers and illegal migrants to third countries, as well as other readmission agreements and provisions on safe third countries of transit. Thus, securitization, as much as it has been debated, it is in fact a phenomenon that is happening at the international arena and concerns states at the globally.

These measures to securitize migration can take place in different sectors – and I will also give examples in the following section – but one of the ways in which securitization is channelled is through the legislative process, which I will develop at this point. The securitization of migration through the law is what it is known as the "institutionalisation of securitization" (Dück and Lucke, 2019). Enacting new laws and changing existing ones are examples of how this process can take place. It is then clear than this securitization goes beyond the "discursive practice" and it materializes in a set of heterogeneous practices (Aradau, 2001). The securitization of migration has actually been perceived in a wide range of areas, one of them being, for instance, border policy. The case of the United States is quite clear. Donald Trump acceded to presidency with the repeated message throughout its campaign to build a wall across the US–Mexican border and stop illegal migration from entering the United States. Although many have argued against it, the Trump administration called strongly in its favour from the very beginning and on January 25, 2017, he signed an executive order ("Border Security and Immigration Enforcement Improvements") to include plans to militarize the border and demanding the construction of a wall along the more than 3000-kilometre border.

The European Union, on its side, has also participated in the dynamics of constructing walls to bolster border control. The Schengen agreement of 1985 already introduced measures calling on States to reinforce external borders as part of the requirements to become part of the European Union's area of free movement. And after the 9/11 attacks, the EU also announced new actions to securitize its borders. The 2003 European Security Strategy ("Europe in a Better World") established a relation between globalization and local security, and although migration as such was not mentioned, border control was a relevant part of the new strategies (Ruiz and Brunet, 2018).

In the case of refugees, securitization does not eliminate refugee protection regimes but transforms how they operate, embedding security rationales within asylum procedures, border controls, and status determination processes (Hammerstad, 2014). As Guild (2009) similarly argues, security has become a dominant organizing principle of migration law, reshaping asylum systems in ways that blur the boundary between protection and control and render refugees subject to exceptional legal treatment. Refugees are thus increasingly governed through logics of risk assessment, credibility evaluation, and manageability, rather than vulnerability alone, a shift that normalizes surveillance, detention, and administrative exclusion within systems formally designed for protection (Mountz, 2010; Aradau and van Munster, 2007). This incorporation of security logics into refugee governance also facilitates the blurring of boundaries between asylum and crime control, enabling refugees and other migrants to be regulated through increasingly punitive legal frameworks. As Guild (2009) notes, the growing alignment between migration law and security policy enables punitive measures originally designed for criminal justice to be extended to refugees and other non-citizens.

As a result, migration is thus frequently linked to crime, and increasingly punitive laws have been spread throughout in the past years. In the United States, for instance, the criminalization of immigration has lately been reconsidered to the point where a "criminal alien" has been redefined using "increasingly stringent definitions and standards of 'criminality' that do not apply to U.S. citizens" (Ewing, Martínez and Rumbaut, 2015). This allows for US immigration laws to create more "criminal aliens" and for these to be detained and deported in larger numbers as well. Furthermore, post-9/11 policies were introduced as part of the fight on the "war on terror" and in relation to immigration as part of a wider effort to enhance national security (Ewing, Martínez and Rumbaut, 2015).

In fact, only eleven days after the 9/11 attacks, the Office of Homeland Security was created, and its first director appointed. This office, which became a stand-alone cabinet-level department in 2003, was designed to oversee and coordinate national security strategies "to safeguard the country against terrorism and respond to any future attacks".[7] This bureau, also in charge of citizenship and immigration services, has enacted new anti-terror legislation and other related policies (Dücke et al, 2019). The Uniting and Strengthening America by Providing Appropriate Tools Required to Intercept and Obstruct Terrorism (USA PATRIOT) Act of 2001, the Homeland Security Act of 2002, and the Enhanced Border Security and Visa Entry Reform Act of 2002 are examples of some of the laws that were enacted and which "illustrate the accelerating criminalization of the immigration system" (Miller, 2005). Moreover, not only do they establish a link between crime and migration, but they also make a tighter connection between terrorism and migration. As Miller argues, the relationship between criminal law and immigration law was strengthened after 9/11, and specially to those who had not passed through the criminal justice system such as asylum seekers and undocumented immigrants. Let's remember that the PATRIOT Act in particular allowed federal officers to apprehend and detain "non-citizens on immigration grounds without legal review and without public disclosure of the specific charge for a period of seven days, or for a maximum of six months if the case is deemed a national security risk" (Coleman, 2007).

7 https://www.dhs.gov/creation-department-homeland-security.

Another legal area in which migration has been linked to security concerns is that of nationality and citizenship. Some countries have enacted laws by which persons with dual nationalities who have engaged in terrorism can be removed their citizenship. This is the case of Australia, which introduced the Australian Citizenship Amendment (Allegiance to Australia) Act 2015 to the Australian Citizenship Act 2007 allowing removal of Australian citizenship in these cases. Human rights organizations contested the new provisions alleging that international human rights law requires that any limitation on rights – including citizenship – must be reasonable, necessary and proportionate, three requirements that according to them are not met in these amendments. Involuntary removal of citizenship is a very serious matter, and the new provisions are in clear detriment of the rights of refugees. Unfortunately, other countries such as Italy have followed the same path and amended national legislation allowing the revocation of citizenship in the same circumstances (see Art. 14 of the 2018 Decree Law[8]). In the context of refugee law, such measures risk undermining the foundational principles of the 1951 Refugee Convention, as refugees may be subjected to disproportionate surveillance and detention practices in the name of national security.

These developments are particularly consequential for refugees, who are meant to be protected under international law, yet are increasingly subsumed into general migration frameworks shaped by security concerns. Legal regimes that do not distinguish between irregular migrants and refugees enable the use of restrictive measures – such as detention, surveillance, or revocation of status – even for those entitled to protection. Embedding security logic in law thus erodes the normative clarity of refugeehood and enables states to prioritize control over rights.

4 The Nexus between Refugees and Security Studies

According to Floyd (2011), the moral legitimacy of securitization can be assessed using a three-part framework inspired by just war theory. First, there must be an existential threat: one that genuinely endangers the survival of a referent object. Not all perceived threats meet this standard. To qualify, the aggressor must have both the intention and the capability to cause harm. This distinction between real and perceived threats is crucial, especially when securitization is used to justify exceptional legal measures. Refugees, for instance, are often subjected to the same surveillance and control frameworks as

8 "Decreto-Legge 4 ottobre 2018, n. 113" which entered into force on 5 October 2018.

irregular migrants, despite their legal entitlement to protection. This conflation erodes the normative basis of refugeehood and normalizes exceptional treatment.

Second, the referent object must be morally legitimate, meaning it must promote human well-being. Floyd defines this in objective terms, grounded in liberal democracy, autonomy, and human rights. Security claims must therefore be evaluated against whether they support or undermine these foundational principles.

Third, the security response must be appropriate and proportionate to the threat. It should reflect the actual capabilities of the aggressor and be carried out with sincerity. If the securitizing actor's actions deviate from their stated justifications, this calls into question the legitimacy of the move. Floyd refers to this as the gap between the "securitizing move" and the actual "security practice" (Floyd, 2011:433). This is especially relevant when securitization is directed at refugees, whose treatment often reflects political expediency rather than real necessity. Examining whether these three criteria are fulfilled helps determine whether refugee securitization is ethically and legally justifiable.

Since the Geneva Convention relating to the protection of refugees 1951, its protocol, and the development of customary law, the principle of non-refoulement has become a weakness of border control and a risk to the integrity of national security systems (Guild, 2009). The State no longer has the power to reject a refugee under international law, even with the massive entries of irregular migrants that we have seen in recent years into Western States. This principle categorically prohibits States from returning refugees to any territory where their security might be jeopardized, yet this principle stands in sharp contrast to state practice today (Donnelly, 2017:256). Western countries have regarded the forced migrant, the refugee, as an important security threat. As Guild (2009) explains:

> The forced migrant becomes the one individual (other than citizens) who has a right in international law to breach the security of the border. Thus the forced migrant is the individual who must be kept as far as possible from ever arriving at the border.

As explained by Bello (2017), security threats today are based on *potential* threats and *perceived* threats. We have already seen what a perceived threat it according to Floyd, and its distinction from a real one. It seems evident that the element of perception is important indeed, but as Bello argues, and along with the line of differentiating what a *real* threat is, today we are dealing more with potential threats, that is, those which are characterized by their unpredictability. The clearest example is the terrorist threat, which we never know precisely when, where, against what or who will take place. And while years ago we were more used to seeing terrorism as a phenomenon taking place at the national level – Euskadi Ta Askatasuna (ETA) in Spain, the Irish Republican Army (IRA) in Ireland, and the Brigate Rosse in Italy, for instance – today it is distinguished for being international; we have seen, for instance, ISIS attacking countries in different continents and against different civilian objectives.

Refugee flows can affect security at different levels. Individually, the security of irregular migrants and refugees can be endangered both during the displacement and at the destination country. Not only do they face risks by trying to cross borders illegally in order to not be caught by the police, but they often have to rely on criminal groups such as smugglers to find alternative and more dangerous ways to leave their country and find a way to get into another. National security is also affected by migration in the sense that some countries may perceive the arrival of large numbers of people as a threat to their political stability, economic well-being, public order, and cultural and religious values. At the international level, these migration flows can also lead into tensions between States and their bilateral relations and regional stability (Lohrmann, 2000). Again, what migration governance through security shows is that the latter operates as a powerful justificatory framework that legitimates exceptional legal measures in migration governance, even where such measures undermine established legal safeguards and procedural guarantees for refugees (Guild, 2009).

In fact, securitization theory is linked to the interaction between the securitizing actor and its audience. And if that is the case, designating something as a security issue can be done in a wide range of sectors of social life (Balzacq, Léonard and Ruzicka, 2016: 496). As long as something poses a vital threat to the community, may this threat pertain or not to the military domain, the issue can become securitized. As explained before, migration may be subject to this securitization in a variety of ways; from discourses of the political elite and mass media, to enacting new laws, public policies, and other security measures. In this section, the point is not to conduct a deep analysis of the wide array of securitization initiatives that can be found across the globe, as this will be done in another chapter, but this section can serve to detail the existing signs and evidence of this phenomenon and the reasonings behind them. To this end, a set of grounds to securitize migration have been collected in order to understand the reasoning behind the actors that securitize migration. I have divided them as "threats" which fall into six different areas: (1) threat to national identity, (2) threat to the economy, (3) threat to the welfare state, (4) threat to bilateral relations, (5) threat to the public order, and (6) threat to national security. Acknowledging that the differentiating line between some of these factors may blur, and that areas like the welfare state and the economy of the country are very much interconnected in the way we understand today's societies, I have decided to put them independently to emphasize that migration can be considered as a distinctive "threat" based on arguments referring to particular elements of the organization of the state. Thence it interesting to study each of these factors individually to examine to what extent they can become an independent case in favour or against the securitization of migration.

Firstly, securitization is a response to the threat that migrants – and refugees – pose to the **national identity** of a society.[9] Nowadays, social and political integration of refugees within host societies is a challenge, and multiculturalism collides with the idea of nationalism and the conservation of the local cultural identity. Supporters of the first confront with those seeking to preserve the latter, and permanent migrant settlement are looked on to be undermining the collective identity. During the 1990s many Western societies embraced multiculturalism, accepting different cultures as an enrichment to society and as a mark of a truly liberal democracy. However, 9/11 has led to the portrayal by some of migration and cultural diversity as resulting in fragmentation and to the undermining of national security (Browning, 2017).

In Switzerland, for instance, political discourses against migration and towards the protection of Swiss national identity have raised progressively throughout the last years by using the *Überfremdung*'s concept in public debates to refer to "a foreign overpopulation threatening the Swiss identity" (Riaño and Wastl-Walter, 2006). In the United Kingdom politicians have also used the campaign's discourses to claim that the "uncontrollable" flow of refugees should be stopped as it has become a security threat to the UK due to its magnitude, putting an emphasis on the protection of UK's welfare programmes. Campaigns like these are those such as "Vote Leave, Take Control" (Vote Leave, 2016). Karyotis (2012) collected different examples by the Greek media where they treated a number of high-profile criminal incidents involving foreigners which contributed to rising negative stereotypes image

9 See the discussion in Huntington, S., 1996, *The Clash of Civilizations*, Simon & Schuster. In his book, for instance, he talks about the discourses that link multiculturalism and social disintegration. Migration is perceived as a danger to national tradition and societal homogeneity against the preservation of western civilization.

of migration in the country and reinforced the already prevailing video that migration and crime are related.

Even worse is the case for refugees residing in a territory with ethnic divisions. When there is an ethnic conflict and the society is fragmented, it is even harder to accept a foreigner from another culture who may add to the already existing cultural confrontation. For many people, religious beliefs and practices are a fundamental part of their life and it is what defines their cultural identity, thus being inseparable from social existence. And this is part of the citizens of the country and those immigrants coming from abroad. This cultural clash may not be troublesome in some countries, but it can be a risk in those countries with ethnic, religious, or cultural conflicts. Nationals may see their languages, values, norms and customs challenged with the arrival of immigration, and even more if part of the population – like ethnic or religious minorities – already saw them at risk. If immigrants, including refugees, are not successfully integrated in the hosting society, instability is more likely to happen, and this is more aggravated in fragile societies. All in all, this threat to the identity of the country is perceived as a societal security threat. Thence more than a threat to the integrity of the nation and its territory, it is a threat to the society of the country.

Secondly, migration can be seen as a **threat to the economy**. Immigrant movements have increased in the past decades, as many migrants are looking for better economic opportunities far from their countries of origin. However, it is not rare to see negative opinions in the media and during social gatherings accusing immigrants of "stealing the jobs" of nationals. But do they really steal these jobs? During Trump's presidential campaign, one of his promises was that he would implement new immigration policies to improve the US economy and job market, contributing to the belief that immigrants were stealing jobs from Americans. However, most argue that this idea is not what happens in reality, since most undocumented workers often do the jobs many natives are not willing to do. But adding up to this, during a period of recession, this antipathetic view of immigration is widely spread throughout, leading to a disapproval and negative consciousness towards migrant communities. The perception of immigrants as an economic burden may develop in an unfavourable reaction from the citizens towards them. This, in turn, affects their integration into the new society, as they are seen as an unwanted competence that takes the job opportunities of the nationals and which take an unfair advantage of public goods.

Refugees are affected by these perceptions and can also be perceived as a threat to the economy depending on the existing political regime. While one of the things that is implied with globalization is the movement goods, services, and capital, but also of people across borders, the motivations of migrants and the institutional constraints within one's country is what ultimately determines this movement of peoples. Another element to take into consideration when talking about these movements is the type of political regime of the country. Most may think that democracies are the ones receiving more migrants, and that these are coming from non-democratic countries. However, a study by Breunig, Cao, and Luedtke (2012) shows that democratic regimes accommodate fewer immigrants than autocracies and that more people emigrate from democracies than from autocracies. What is more, it is in most liberal democracies where there is a higher anti-immigration feeling, probably because other types of regimes are able to grant fewer rights to foreign workers since they are less concerned with civil rights, but also because they have more flexible labour markets. That is why many looking for jobs go to autocracies, since these offer more guest worker programmes and because those ruling the country are less constrained by popular xenophobic demand. On the other side, these types of regimes are less likely to allow their citizens to leave the country but instead try to retain them. As the authors of this study say, "At the individual level, the search for economic well-being trumps any aspiration for the political freedoms offered by democracy. At the macro-level, it is important to recognize that democracies tend to block entry and allow exist, while non-democracies tend to block exist and allow entry".

At the same time, the interests on migration of the governments are what may determine migration as a threat or not. As it has been discussed, it seems that in non-democratic regimes immigration does not have such a bad outlook. Immigrants go to these countries looking for job opportunities and their priority is to improve their economic stability, and the rules of the country are interested in increasing their economic profits, while not having to accede to granting civil rights. On the other hand, the viewpoint of liberal democratic regimes is that the arrival of migrants may mean the scarcity of social and economic benefits for its nationals, and thus they are more likely to perceive the arrival of immigrants as a threat. All in all, the political regime is another factor to take into consideration when talking about migration movements and when considering migration as a threat, as depending on the type of political regime we are dealing with, views on migration will differ.

Thirdly, and connecting to the previous point, migration is also perceived as a **threat to the welfare state**. And in periods of economic recessions and of higher unemployment rates when there is more scarcity, immigrants are discerned as the competitors of nationals on the fight of social goods. Some locals see them as illegitimate actors having no right to access national social assistance. And when all of these circumstances are put together, an issue like migration is successfully securitized and the application of extraordinary measures is justified to make sure the national population is protected. Instead of facing migration as a human rights question that should be resolved through human rights instruments, it is turned into a security problem that needs to be resolved through security policy to protect the state. And with exceptionalism[10] – the application of exceptional measures – political elites can further their interests and give grounds for the undermining of civil liberties (Aradau and van Munster, 2009). As Karyotis (2011) puts it, "securitization does not create a safer society but one that lives in permanent fear from real or perceived threats". Instead of protecting and strengthening a country, it breaches its already existing harmony.

Examples of this securitization of migration can also be found in New Zealand, where they are sometimes presented as a burden to the national housing market and as contributing to the higher rates of crime. In this sense, it is interesting to see the collection of articles by Salahshour (2017), who studied the ways in which migration was treated in political discourses and the print media. She found that, in some cases, there was a dehumanization of migrants as they were presented with similes and comparisons with non-human entities; there was also an important "immigrants-as-a-threat-discourse"; and other associations of refugees as being needing of support, of integration, and of weak or no particular use to society. In sum, they are shown as a threat to the livelihood of locals.

A similar study, but focusing on Indonesia, is made by Lee (2017), who stands that while there used to be a positive representation of Indochinese refugees in the period of 1975–1996, new generations of forced migrants are now being portrayed negatively and framed as security threats. This, he argues, may be due to securitization moves made by specialized agencies in the country. And while there used to be a politization of migration before, there is now securitization within the treatment of new cohorts of migrants. Like these, there are many other examples on the ways politicians and the media have worsened the image of the migrant and on how migration has been securitized.

Fourthly, migrants – but more concretely refugees – can also be perceived as a threat to the host country in regard to the **bilateral relations** established with the country of origin. Weiner (1992) explains that there are different reasons why bilateral relations can be endangered when there are refugees in-between. He argues that when refugees are opposed to the regime of their

10 For more on the theory of exception see Schmitt, C., 1996, *The Concept of the Political*, by Tracy B. Strong. Chicago: University of Chicago.

country and it is recognized that there is a well-founded fear of persecution, the host country is somehow accusing the country of origin to engage in persecution, and so it is saying that there is a justification to be morally opposing to the regime. Thus just the granting asylum can create a more hostile relationship between the two. He exemplifies this case with the US Congress debate in January 1990 on whether Chinese students should be permitted to remain in the US because of the possible persecutions that could face in China. Hosting this debate was seen by the People's Republic of China as an "interference" in its internal affairs.

Worst is even the case of supporting these incoming refugees against the regime of their country of origin, as this bitters even more the relationship between States. Weiner gives the examples of the United States and its active support to Cuban refugees against the Castro regime at the Bay of Pigs; when India gave arms to the Bengali "freedom fighters" in the fight against the Pakistani military; when Pakistan, Saudi Arabia, China, and the United States reinforced Afghan refugees with arms to force Soviet troops to leave Afghanistan, and so on. It is clear, then, that when host countries actively support refugees in their fight with the country of origin, they become a tool of interstate conflict. Hence, the way in which governments assess and respond to one another's intentions in these cases can potentially represent the level of possible clashing between the two.

Fifthly, it is a way to reduce threats to **public order**. In this sense, the link that some political groups and media establish between crime and migration increase migration and challenge the integration of migrants within the host country.[11] The perception that migrants are more frequently involved in drug trafficking, thefts and robberies, armed aggressions, or terrorism has been strengthened not only since 9/11 but also since the terrorist attacks in 1995 by Algerian extremist on French soil (Lohrmann, 2000). The involvement of some immigrants in criminal activities has led to using prejudicial stereotyping in public debates connecting immigration with criminal threats. Adjudicating security connotations related to terrorism and international crime to the area of migration is now more common than ever. This, in turn, means that decision and policymaking in the area of asylum is moving away from human rights to the security field. In fact, asylum seekers are more vulnerable to detention as irregular entrants and as long as they do not have safe and

11 Some scholars have called the attention to the fact that migration (including refugees and asylum seekers) is being connected to terrorism, drugs, crime, border control security, etc. For more on this, see Bigo, B., 1996, *Police en reseaux. L'expérience européenne*, Paris: Presses de Sciences Po; Rudge, P., 1989, Kumin, K., 1999, *An Uncertain Direction...*, Refugees Magazine, No. 113.

legal routes to seek asylum, they will continue to be seen as potential threats with no real guarantees (Costello and Mouzourakis, 2016). It is thence important to highlight that when the elite and this mass media refer to migration, most times they do not distinguish, for instance, between refugees, illegal migrants or economic migrants, blurring them all into a single policing-repression scheme (Statham, 2003; Karyotis, 2011). Words like "migrant", "foreigner" and "refugee" are now connected to security and are powerful signifiers in contemporary Europe (Huysmans, 2000; Greimas and Courtés, 1993), which can be referred to as the cause of many problems, even though they were not connected to migration before. Migration is simply presented as a danger "to public order, cultural identify, and domestic and labour stability" (Huysmans, 2000).

Last but not least, migration can also be perceived as a threat to **national security**, and here one must make special reference to the terrorism threat. Since 9/11, the Bali bombings or the Mombasa and Kenya attacks, there has been a linkage of national security to a borders-related issue. Especially relevant is the first, as it created a precedent which transformed the association of the foreigner with terrorism. And this has led to conducting immigration controls as a form of protection from terrorism. What is interesting in this sense is the fact that check controls are not so much based on nationality, but on ethnicity and religion (Guild, 2007).

After the 9/11 attacks, migration has been more often treated as a security threat by the West, being Muslim communities those which have more often been perceived as such. New political and media discourses have led to a new security agenda based on the securitization of Islam in many Western countries, and it has been challenging for these countries with an important number of Muslim immigrants to respond to 9/11 and other terrorist attacks without damaging the functioning of democracy and multiculturalism. According to Magen (2018), even though the West has faced a clear intensification of terrorist attacks since 9/11, liberal democracies are less prone to terrorist attacks than other regime types. Groups like the Islamic State in Iraq and Syria, Boko Haram, and al-Qaeda affiliates have perpetrated attacks in fragile states and have recruited adepts throughout.

Until recently, however, the idea was the opposite. Many scholars believed that democracies were more likely to be subject to terrorist attacks because of different reasons. One of them is related to the easiness of movements and the openness of liberal democracies. Another is also directly linked to the freedoms of press and communication which guarantee that discourses reach wide audiences. The third and last argument is that electoral competition and institutional design heighten the likeliness of suffering a terrorist attack.

He continues explaining that this perception changed in the mid-1990s, when scholars believed that democratic openness allowed for grievances and injustices to be publicly addressed. This in turn meant that similar attitudes could be cut from the ground before they lead to bigger extremisms. Recent studies defend that the higher the quality of the democracy and the more civil liberties are guaranteed, the less likely it is for that country to suffer terrorist incidents (Magen, 2018). Contrarily, countries like Bahrain, Iran, Kuwait, Somalia, South Sudan, and Sudan, among others, had in 2013 multiplied by more than seven thousand percent the likelihood of suffering terrorist attacks than in 2002.

As said in the previously in this thesis, the G8 made of terrorism a transversal threat affecting the international agenda and NATO now deals with global terrorism and mass migration. Furthermore, in meetings of the G8 several nations have brought migration to the table to discuss it as a security threat. Interestingly, Bigo (2006) argues that most government of liberal democracies put "their own security beside the security and freedom of the individual".

In addition, the governance of terrorism through risk is characterized by preventive action oriented towards an uncertain and potentially catastrophic future, combined with expansive surveillance practices that operate at the limits of knowledge. As the use of technologies such as biometrics expands, entire populations are increasingly subjected to regimes of suspicion, decoupling security intervention from concrete evidence. In this context, the anticipation of irreparable harm legitimates indefinite detention and control measures based on potential rather than proven threat. Risk governance thus gives rise to forms of prudentialism that distribute responsibility across society, encouraging citizens to remain vigilant and to participate actively in security practices (Aradau and van Munster, 2007).

All of these potential threats are presented as such by the elite, and perceived as such by the society, considering the previous existing values and circumstances of the country. Hence migration can be seen as a threat to the economy or the welfare state in a country, but as a threat to national identity in another. It is usually a combination of different threats, but there can be one that sticks out among the others given the historical, political, and social context of the particular country. What has been outlined here are the potential views that an actor can give to migration to consider it a threat but depending on the context and circumstances of a state, one or a combination of some will predominate among the others. Table 2.1 summarizes all of these potential factors that have been analysed and which can place migration as a security threat:

TABLE 2.1 Potential threats

Potential threat	Justification/rationalization	Example
To national identity	Clash between multiculturalism and nationalism. Nationals may see their languages, values, norms, and customs challenged with the arrival of immigration. The priority is the preservation of the national cultural identity.	The case of Switzerland where political discourses have raised the need to protect national identity towards immigration ("*Überfremdung*'s).
To the economy	Migration as an economic burden, associated with the scarcity of social and economic benefits for its nationals. Dependant on the political regime.	The repeated message that immigrants are stealing the jobs of nationals. This idea has been repeated throughout, including Trump's presidential campaign.
To the welfare state	Immigrants as illegitimate actors using social goods and accessing national social assistance. Intensified feeling/threat when the country is in economic recession.	Political ideas considering the migrant community as a burden to the national housing market as seen in New Zealand.
To bilateral relations	Especially when there are refugees involved. If supporting these refugees, the host country can be seen as accusing the country of origin to engage in persecution and, in some cases, to be opposing to its political regime.	The debate in the United States on whether to allow Chinese students to stay in the country. This was perceived as a hostile move by the People's Republic of China.
To the public order	Connecting crime and migration. Frequently seen in areas like drug trafficking, thefts and robberies, armed aggressions, and terrorism.	Public messages from politicians and the media connecting migrant groups to crime and security issues. This is now commonly seen in many Western countries.
To national security	Association of the foreigner with terrorism. New political and media discourses have led to a new security agenda based on the securitization of Islam, specially seen in the West.	Many of today's security agendas are based on the securitization of Islam. This has been the case of the United States and European countries.

Overall, the ideas linking migration to security threats have aggravated the general public perception of the refugee community. Immigration attitudes vary across countries, but it seems fair to assert that the perception of immigration by the West has been generally negative for many years now (Freeman, 1997). And what is more, a report by the IOM (Esipova et al., 2015) found that the most negative region towards immigration is Europe, holding the highest numbers (52%) of people who would like the quantity of refugees in their countries to decease. This does not mean that in all European countries the image for or against immigration is the same, as every case is different, but in the case of Great Britain and that of the Russian Federation – who are one of the largest populations in these countries in the larger Europe region – are particularly negative. The report also highlights that the strongest predictor of the view of the country on immigration is very much dependant on the country's economic situation. Thus when there is a favourable economic situation, the citizens seem to be more likely towards welcoming refugees.

The rise of nationalist political parties and the voter support for right-wing parties it is very visible today; from Germany, where the Alternative for Germany (AfD) has become the largest opposition of the government; to Spain, where Vox became the third biggest force in the parliament (BBC, 2019). Matteo Salvini's leader of the League in Italy has gained popularity for its anti-immigration policies and has also been known for actively refusing to help rescue ships, barring their entrance by closing Italian ports. The rise of right-wing and extremist movements is, of course, not only due to their views on migration, but it is also about concerns on globalization, the perceived need to reinforce national identities, and so on. However, they all refer to migration and are keen on taking stricter and harsher measures to control it.

Nonetheless, even though populist parties address a wide range of topics as any other, it is their attitude towards immigration what has given them more votes in the past years, or what it is the same, those who support these parties mostly do so because of their anti-immigration feelings. But it is also interesting to point out that it is not that people's attitudes towards migration have suddenly changed, but it is a combination of factors what has led to the rise of far-right parties specially in Europe. Rooduijn (2020) further develops this idea and describes three reasons to explain why these political parties have gained force. On the one hand, they have learnt to mobilize their voters. They learnt to present certain issues in a better way and a through what seems to be a more "moderate" way of saying things, while backing up a radical political programme with radical ideas. Second, there has been an emancipation of voters, who are not stick to voting the same political party over the years as they used to do before. Now the voter has become more floatable and is moving through a variety of options that were not there before. And third, migratory movements, the refugee crisis, terrorist attacks, and the Brexit have all become circumstances that have brought the topic of migration to the forefront of every European media outlet. We are all used by now of hearing about immigration news, opinions, and discussions. Thence it is not that the people's opinion on migration has changed, it is that migration has become a much more relevant topic, which has made it more important for the citizen to vote according to his or her migratory perception.

And this public opinion on migration is important for a variety of reasons. One of them, as it has been outlined previously, is that if the majority of the population agrees on the existence of a security threat, then the application of exceptional measures to counter terrorism is justified, which in turn can lead to infringing basic rights, weakening civil liberties safeguards. This can mean that authorities can get into the private sphere of the citizens, but it can also mean that the rights of vulnerable groups, such as refugees, are even more endangered. On the other hand, this capacity to go beyond ordinary policing powers can also lead to using certain measures against political adversaries.

When analysing the conflict that migration can arise in international security and considering this as another "justification" to securitize migration, one has to bring in mind that migration today is a global phenomenon that cannot be only kept within national borders, but which is in fact touched upon and faced in every region of the world. Irregular migration flows and large refugee movements (more recently known as the "refugee crisis" in Europe) can lead to tensions between origin countries from the one side and destination and transit countries on the other. The latter are concerned about finding ways in which the first can control the departure of its nationals from its territory, and these countries of origin are in turn using irregular emigration as a negotiation card to force destination countries to make political, commercial and other economic concessions (Lohrmann, 2000). Tensions of this kind have arisen in different regions: between the Albanian Government and the European Union or between the US and Mexico. A clear exemplification of this securitization as an international phenomenon is namely that the G8 has made terrorism and transnational organized crime as one of the transversal threats at the top of the agenda and NATO also treats "global terrorism" and "mass migration" within their concerns (Bigo, 2006).

These representations in media, political rhetoric, and foreign policy shape how refugees are perceived and govern how they are treated. Even where legal definitions promise protection, the prevailing narrative often casts them as risks to sovereignty, security, and public order. This gap between legal norms and securitized perceptions is at the heart of the puzzle this book seeks to address.

These dynamics matter because they erode the legitimacy of refugeehood itself. When refugees are governed not as individuals fleeing persecution but as generalized risk factors, the legal categories underpinning the international refugee regime begin to dissolve. This chapter has shown how securitization theory helps us explain that shift – not as an accident of policy, but as a deliberate discursive move with structural consequences.

Although written before the emergence of securitization theory, Loescher's analysis anticipates later debates by demonstrating how security concerns shape state responses to refugees in ways that may conflict with humanitarian obligations (Loescher, 1992). As the discussion in this chapter has shown, securitization is not only a matter of legal classification or state policy; it is also a discursive and symbolic process. The framing of mobility as a threat, whether through associations with terrorism, cultural change, or economic instability, sets the stage for how different categories of migrants are treated.

Refugees, although defined in international law as persons in need of protection, are increasingly subsumed into these narratives of risk and exception. They are increasingly reframed as potential threats through the same discursive mechanisms applied to irregular migrants, undocumented individuals, and foreign nationals. This reframing undermines not only individual rights but the normative foundation of the refugee regime itself. This dissonance between legal entitlement and political framing is central to the puzzle this book investigates: how and why states construct refugees as potential threats, and what this reveals about deeper shifts in the global governance of migration. Understanding this paradox is essential to analysing the spread of exceptional migration governance across different national contexts, a central concern of the chapters that follow.

Returning to Floyd's (2011) three criteria for just securitization, the refugee case raises significant moral and legal dilemmas. Even if one accepts the premise that migration may pose societal challenges, treating refugees – a group recognized as vulnerable and protected – as embryonic threats contradicts the spirit of international protection. The proportionality and sincerity of security responses are often questionable, especially when speech acts do not match actual policy, or when securitizing actors rely on exaggerated claims of danger to justify restrictive laws.

References

Aradau, C. (2001) 'Migration: The Spiral of (In)Security', *E-journal*.

Aradau, C. and van Munster, R. (2007) 'Governing Terrorism through Risk: Taking Precautions, (Un)Knowing the Future', *European Journal of International Relations*, Vol. 13(1), pp. 89–115.

Aradau, C. and van Munster, R. (2009) *Politics of Catastrophe: Genealogies of the Unknown*. London: Routledge.

Aradau, C. and van Munster, R. (2009) 'Exceptionalism and the 'War on Terror', *British Journal of Criminology*, Vol. 49, pp. 686–701.

Balzacq, T. (2005) 'The Three Faces of Securitization: Political Agency, Audience and Context', *European Journal of International Relations*, Vol. 11(2).

Balzacq, T., Léonard, S. and Ruzicka, J. (2016) 'Securitization' revisited: theory and cases', *International Relations*, Vol. 30(4), pp. 494–531.

BBC (2019) 'Europe and right-wing nationalism: A country-by-country guide', *BBC News*, 13 November. Available at: https://www.bbc.com/news/world-europe-36130006.

Bello, V. (2017) *International migration and international security. Why prejudice is a global security threat.* Routledge.

Bigo, D. (2000) 'When two become one: internal and external securitisations in Europe', in Kelstrup, M. and Williams M., *International Relations Theory and the Politics of European Integration*, New York: Routledge.

Bigo, D. (2002) 'Security and immigration: Toward a critique of the governmentality of uneas', *Alternatives: Global, Local, Political*, Vol. 27(1), pp. 63–92.

Bigo, D. (2006) *Migration and Security issues*, Manuscript.

Bigo, D. (2014) 'The (In)securitization Practices of the Three Universes of EU Border Control', *Security Dialogue*, Vol. 45(3).

Boswell, C. (2003) 'The 'external dimension' of EU immigration and asylum policy', *International Affairs*, Vol. 79(3), pp. 619–638.

Boswell, C. (2007) 'Migration Control in Europe after 9/11: Explaining the Absence of Securitisation', *Journal of Common Market Studies*, Vol. 45(3), pp. 589–610.

Boswell, C. (2009) 'Migration, Security and Legitimacy: Some Reflections', in Givens, T. E., Freeman G. P. and Leal D. L., *Immigration Policy and Security: U.S., European, and Commonwealth Perspectives*, New York, New York: Routledge.

Bourbeau, P. (2014) 'Migration, exceptionalist security discourse, and practices', in *Handbook on Migration and Security*, UK: Edward Elgar Press.

Bourbeau, P. and Vuori, J. (2015) 'Security, Resilience, and Desecuritization: Multidirectional Moves and Dynamic', *Critical Studies on Security*, Vol. 3(3), pp. 253–268.

Breunig, C., Cao, X. and Luedtke, A. (2012) 'Global Migration and Political Regime Type: A Democratic Disadvantage', *British Journal of Political Science*, Vol. 42(4), pp. 825–854.

Browning, C. S. (2017) 'Security and migration: a conceptual exploration', in Bourbeau, P., *Handbook on Migration and Security*, UK: Edward Elgar Publishing Limited.

Buzan, B. (1983), People, States and Fear: The National Security Problem in International Relations, Chapel Hill, NC: University of North Carolina Press.

Buzan, B. (2006) 'Will the 'global war on terrorism' be the new Cold War?', *International Affairs*, Vol. 82(6), pp. 1101–1118.

Buzan, B. (2008) 'A Leader Without Followers? The United States World Politics after Bush', *International Politics*, Vol. 45, pp. 554–570.

Buzan, B., and Waever, O. (2009) 'Macrosecuritisation and security constellations: reconsidering scale in securitisation theory,' *Review of International Studies*, Vol. 35, pp. 253–276.

Buzan, B., Waever, O. and Wilde, J. (1998) *Security: A New Framework for Analysis*, Boulder: Lynne Reinner Publishers.

Charrett, C. (2009) 'A Critical Application of Securitization Theory: Overcoming the Normatie Dilemma of Writing Security', *International Catalan Institute for Peace.*

Chebel d'Appollonia, A. (2012) 'Frontiers of Fear: Immigration and Insecurity in the United States and Europe', Cornell University Press.

Coleman, M. (2007) 'Immigration Geopolitics Beyond the Mexico-US Border', Antipode 39, No. 1.

Costello, C. and Mouzourakis, M. (2016) 'Refugee law and the securitisation of asylum', *Journal of Common Market Studies*, Vol. 54(3), pp. 629–646.

Council of the European Union (2003) 'European Security Strategy – A secure Europe in a better world', General Secretariat of the Council of the European Union.

Donnelly, F. (2017) 'In the Name of (de)Securitization: Speaking Security to Protect Migrants, Refugees and Internally Displaced Persons, *International Review of the Red Cross*, Vol. 99(1), pp. 241–261.

Dück, E. and Lucke, R. (2019) 'Same Old (Macro-) Securitization? A Comparison of Political Reactions to Major Terrorist Attacks in the United States and France', *Croatian International Relations Review*, No. 84, pp. 6–35.

Edelman, M. (1991) *Pièces et règles du jeu politique*. Paris: Seuil.

Esipova, N., Ray, J., Pugliese, A. and Tsabutashvili, D. (2015) 'How the world views migration', International Organization for Migration. Available at: https://publications.iom.int/system/files/how_the_world_gallup.pdf.

Estevens, J. (2018) 'Migration crisis in the EU: developing a framework for analysis of national security and defence strategies', *Comparative Migration Studies*, Vol. 6(28).

Ewing, W., Martínez, D. and Rumbaut, R. (2015) 'The Criminalization of Immigration in the United States', Special Report, American Immigration Council.

Floyd, R. (2007) 'Towards a consequentialist evaluation of security: bringing together the Copenhagen and the Welsh Schools of security studies', *Review of International Studies*, Vol. 33, pp. 327–350.

Floyd, R. (2011) 'Can securitization theory be used in normative analysis? Towards a just securitization theory', *Security Dialogue*, Vol. 42(4–5), pp. 427–439.

Freeman, G. (1997) 'Immigration as a Source of Political Discontent and Frustration in Western Democracies', *Studies in Comparative International Development*, Vol. 32(3), pp. 42–64.

Geddes, A. (2003) *The Politics of Migration and Immigration in Europe*, London: Sage.

Greimas, A. J. and Courtés, J. (1993) *Sémiotique. Dictionnaire raisonné de la théorie du langage*, Paris: Hachette.

Guild, E. (2009) *Security and Migration in the 21st Century*. Cambridge: Polity Press.

Hammerstad, A. (2014) 'The securitisation of forced migration' *in* E. Fiddian-Qasmiyeh, G. Loescher, K. Long and N. Sigona (eds.), *The Oxford Handbook of Refugee and Forced Migration Studies*. Oxford: Oxford University Press.

Huysmans, J. (2000) 'The European Union and the Securitization of Migration', Journal of Common Market Studies, Vol. 38(5).

Huysmans, J. (2006) *The Politics of Insecurity: Fear, Migration and Asylum in the EU*, London: Routledge.

Karyotis, G. (2007) 'European Migration Policy in the Aftermath of September 11: The Security-Migration Nexus', *Innovation: The European Journal of Social Science Research*, Vol. 20(1), pp. 1–17.

Karyotis, G. (2011) *The fallacy of securitizing migration: elite rationality and unintended consequences*, Security, in Insecurity and Migration in Europe, Farnham, pp. 13–30.

Karyotis, G. (2012) 'Securitization of Migration in Greece: Process, Motives and Implications', *International Political Sociology*, Vol. 6, pp. 390–408.

Knudsen, O. F. (2001) 'Post-Copenhagen Security Studies: Desecuritizing Securitization', *Security Dialogue*, Vol. 32(3), pp. 355–368.

Laclau, E. (1996) *Emancipation(s)*, London: Verso.

Lavenex, S. (2001) 'Migration and the EU's New Eastern Border: Between Realism and Liberalism', *Journal of European Public Policy*, Vol. 8(1), pp. 24–42.

Lee, A. (2017) 'Forced Migrants, Media, and Securitization: Making Sense of the Changing Representations of Transit Asylum Seekers in Indonesian Print Media', *Journal of ASEAN Studies*, Vol. 5(2), pp. 75–101.

Loescher, G. (1992) *Refugee Movements and International Security*. London: IISS.

Lohrmann, R. (2000) 'Migrants, Refugees and Insecurity. Current Threats to Peace?', *International Migration*, Vol. 38(4).

Magen, A. (2018). Fighting terrorism: The democracy advantage. *Journal of Democracy*, 29(1), 111–125.

McDonald, M. (2008) 'Securitization and the Construction of Security', *European Journal of International Relations*, Vol. 14(4), pp. 563–587.

Messina, A. (2014) 'Securitizing Immigration in the Age of Terror', *World Politics*, Vol. 66(3), pp. 530–559.

Miller, T. (2005) 'Blurring the Boundaries Between Immigration and Crime Control after September 11th', *Boston College Third World Law Journal*, Vol.25(1).

Mountz, A. (2010) *Seeking Asylum: Human Smuggling and Bureaucracy at the Border*. Minneapolis: University of Minnesota Press.

Nagtegaal, K. (2011) 'Security, Insecurity and Refugees in the Netherlands', in Lazaridis, G., *Security, Insecurity and Migration in Europe*, London: Routledge.

Naumann, S. and Schiele, J. (2016) 'Men with Hammers: The Paris School Securitization Theory and the US American War on Drugs', University of Groningen.

Riaño, Y. and Wastl-Walter, D. (2006) 'Immigration Policies and Discourses on Foreigners and the Politics of Identity in Switzerland', *Environment and Planning A*, Vol. 38(9), pp. 1693–1713.

Roe, P. (2004) 'Securitization and Minority Rights: Conditions of Desecuritization', *Security Dialogue*, Vol. 35(3), pp. 279–294.

Rooduijn, M. (2020) Immigration attitudes have barely changed – so why is far right on rise?, *The Guardian*, 2 March. Available at: https://www.theguardian.com/world/2020/mar/02/immigration-attitudes-have-barely-changed-why-far-right-on-rise.

Ruiz Benedicto, A. and Brunet, P. (2018) 'Building Walls: Fear and securitization in the European Union', Centre Delàs d'Estudis per la Pau, Report No. 35.

Salahshour, N. (2017) 'Representation of Immigrants in New Zealand Print Media: A Critical Discourse Analysis', Doctor of Philosophy Thesis, Victoria University of Wellington, New Zealand.

Statham, P. (2003) 'Understanding the Anti-Asylum Rhetoric: Restrictive Politics or Racist Publics?', *Political Quarterly*, Vol. 74(1), pp. 163–177.

Taureck, R. (2006) 'Securitization theory and securitization studies', *Journal of International Relations and Development*, Vol. 9, pp. 53–61.

Toğral, B. (2011) 'Convergence of Securitization of Migration and 'New Racism' in Europe: Rise of Culturalism and Disappearance of Politics', in Lazaridis, G., *Security, Insecurity and Migration in Europe*, Farnham Surrey, UK: Ashgate.

Vote Leave (2016) 'Why Vote Leave' Vote Leave Take Control. Available at: http://www.voteleavetakecontrol.org/why_vote_leave.html.

Waever, O. (1995) 'Securitization and Desecuritization', in Lipshutz, R. D., *On Security*, Columbia University Press, pp. 46–86.

Wæver, O. (2004) 'Aberystwyth, Paris, Copenhagen: New Schools in Security Theory and the Origins between Core and Periphery', Montreal: ISA Conference, March.

Weiner, M. (1992) 'Security, Stability, and International Migration', *International Security*, Vol. 17(3), pp. 91–126.

Van Dijk, T. (1993) 'Societal Security: the Concept', in Buzan, B., Waever and Lemaitre, P., *Identity, Migration and the New Security Agenda in Europe*, London: Pinter.

Zolberg, A. R., Suhrke, A. and Aguayo, S. (1989) *Escape from Violence: Conflict and the Refugee Crisis in the Developing World.* New York: Oxford University Press.

CHAPTER 3

Understanding the Process

In the previous chapters, we have been studying the concept of securitization in the case of refugees and its applicability on today's legal and political systems of different countries from different regions around the globe. This has been useful to become aware of the increasing development of norms and public policies connecting security matters to migration-related issues. There has been a tendency in the past years to interlace both areas, and the establishment of this link has arisen because of various reasons.

Once a theoretical approach has been established, it is now time to see how this applies in practice. This chapter explores how international legal norms concerning migration and security are created, institutionalized, and diffused across jurisdictions. While many of these norms originate in counterterrorism, border management, and immigration control efforts, they increasingly extend to refugees and asylum seekers – individuals who, in principle, are entitled to international protection. By tracing how norms shape the securitization of mobility, the chapter shows how legal frameworks contribute to the erosion of protection standards and the reframing of refugeehood through a security lens. This shift is not merely conceptual, but it has concrete effects on how legal systems classify, manage, and exclude individuals. The refugee, once a figure of protection, is increasingly governed through tools designed for risk prevention and border enforcement. Understanding this transformation is crucial to the book's core puzzle: how and why refugeehood has become entangled in the global security apparatus.

While this chapter explores migration securitization generally, particular attention must be paid to the case of refugees: individuals who, despite their entitlement to international protection, are increasingly subjected to the same logic of suspicion and control. Their inclusion within broader migration securitization strategies reflects a deeper erosion of the legal and normative framework that once distinguished refugees from other categories of migrants. Understanding this shift is critical to grasping the transformation of refugeehood under security-based governance.

 | HTTPS://DOI.ORG/10.1163/9789004704527-005

1 *Why* Is Migration Securitized? Identification of the Main Interests Used to Justify These Practices

The Copenhagen School has described securitization as an intersubjective and socially constructed process from a rhetorical perspective. This definition includes a securitizing actor and an audience, the first placing a threat to a particular object affecting the latter. To study securitization, then, it is necessary to analyse and interpret the goals and interests of the securitizing actor when trying to protect us from the potential threat. The role of the security analyser is therefore to answer a set of questions, as expressed by Charrett (2009), "Has the securitizing actor managed to mobilize support? Who is the audience and what are the facilitating conditions? Have extraordinary actions been taking? And what might be the impact of such securitizing acts on other units?" We have already focused on the securitization of migration theory in the previous chapter. It is now time to move the investigation from the vision of the particular situation of every state, to that involving the international society as a whole.

Finnemore argues that state interests are defined not by the result of external threats, but by "internationally shared norms and values that structure and give meaning to international political life" (1996). Thus interests are construed through social interaction. Her point is that not all state interests are defined by domestic politics – although they are indeed a determinant factor – but they are also articulated by the international society of which they are part. As this society evolves over time, normative developments adapt progressively, and state interests and their behaviour also shift to coordinate the with changes of social interaction. State interests are thus in part subject to changes in international society.

What are the interests then of the international society? According to the first point of Article 1 of the UN Charter, one of the main United Nations' purposes is "to maintain international peace and security". Thence we understand that international security is a priority for the international society, and basic to maintain international order. There are many security concerns today within the international arena, from the environmental crisis to the development of chemical weapons. We have already mentioned some of the main global problems of today's world and acknowledge terrorism as one of them. While we may also see the massive displacement of populations as a global threat, it is different linking it to terrorism, than looking at it from a humanitarian perspective. Can we think of migration as an international security problem affecting the international society? Can it be considered a shared global "worry" or "problem"? Is it a threat affecting common international goods or common interests? In sum, what are the reasons to securitize migration?

Migration is indeed one of the 21st century's biggest concerns, but not because of its debatable connection to terrorism, but because mass migration flows appear because of unstable, fragile and totalitarian governments. While security concerns may include broad categories of migrants, refugees present a specific contradiction: they are both symbols of vulnerability and perceived vectors of instability. By framing refugee flows as destabilizing, states instrumentalize international norms to justify practices that blur the line between protection and threat mitigation. Among the many justifications for migration securitization, the inclusion of refugees within this framework remains particularly troubling. Although international law sets clear obligations towards those fleeing persecution, securitizing states often collapse the distinction between irregular migrants and refugees. This blurring facilitates legal and discursive strategies that treat even protected individuals as potential threats, undermining the very foundations of the refugee protection regime. We should then se the issue from a human security perspective to ensure and protect these peoples fleeing in search for their personal security instead of perceiving them as a source threatening the stability and security of national governments in destination countries and of the international society.

Still, governments have continuously applied measures to place migration within the security realms. Thence we can start thinking of the securitization of migration as an international practice. It is important to emphasize that even where there is widespread agreement to put an issue within the legal international framework, this can be "hotly contested and compromise will be essential" (Boyle and Chinkin, 2007). It is clear that an issue such as terrorism must be condemned and there is a general willingness to compromise to adopting measures to prevent it. The United Nations has taken several steps by adopting resolutions and setting up special committees addressing different aspects of terrorism-related concerns. Similar efforts have been taken both at the regional and national levels. From international specialists in the field, to lawmakers, bureaucrats and states' political representatives have participated in adopting such measures. There has been an exchange of information from a wide range of states, organizations, police services and intelligence agencies to discuss potential mechanisms of response to the terrorist threat. Thence it seems evident that there is a wide consensus to condemn terrorism and find a common international framework to resolving this issue.

But why is it so hard to find a coordinate answer to fight the terrorist threat? Why does it seem so hard to find common ground to protect international security? Vurnek, Bengez and Perkov (2018) argue that it is harder to find measures to protect international security than it is to achieve national security because the international system is under protected: "The reasons for this are non-centralized operating systems, insufficiently coordinated and non-centralized data collection systems, data processing and undisclosed use of information on security threats, such as migrants, migrations, and side effects that they cause". With a series of security challenges, international organizations – especially those dedicated to maintaining world security as the UN, NATO, and the SOCE – have made efforts to find solutions, some even transforming and reorganizing themselves with new agencies and departments, but they have still been unable to respond to them.

At this point, it is also compelling to consider Weiner's perspective on the subjective perception of migration as a security issue depending on the country situation and the peoples in this country. Security, he argues, is a social construct with different meanings for different people:

> An ethnically homogeneous society, for example, may place a higher value on preserving its ethnic character than does a heterogeneous society and may, therefore, regard a population influx as a threat to its security. Providing a haven for those who share one's values (political freedom, for example) is important in some countries, but not in others; in some countries, therefore, an influx of "freedom fighters" may not be regarded as a threat to security. Moreover, even in a given country, what is highly valued may not be shared by elites and counter-elites. The influx of migrants regarded as radicals may be feared by a monarch, but welcomed by the opposition. One ethnic group may welcome migrants, while another is vehemently opposed to them. The business community may be more willing than the general public to import migrant workers. (Weiner, 1992:103)

The discussion on what is a *real* or a *perceived* threat is an infinite one. And if we acknowledge that the interpretation of what security is differs from one another it is much harder at times to divide the line of what is real than what is not. Then what do the countries analysed have in common? If they have all securitized migration to some greater or lesser degree, then they must have all perceived migration as a real security threat, although the reasons between them may differ. As explained before, the reasons to securitize migration are due to various perceptions of threats: a threat to the national identity of the country, to the economy and/or the welfare state, to bilateral/international relations, to the public order and to national security. It is within this perception of threat that the figure of the refugee is problematically absorbed. Although refugee movements are often caused by the very forms of violence and insecurity that securitization aims to prevent, states increasingly treat them as liabilities rather than subjects of legal obligation. This contradiction lies at the heart of contemporary refugee governance.

The reason some states focus on one of these potential threats or another is shaped by a set of influencing factors, from the country's past history to its current situation. Historical events, such as South Africa's Apartheid period, the continuous entrance of Indonesian migrants in Malaysia for decades, or the large quantity of foreign workers in Saudi Arabia since the 1930s are part of the reasons why for some countries can be perceived as better or worse. In the last case, for instance, Saudi Arabia has become increasingly dependent on foreign labour, which has made of migrants a necessary workforce for the country. On the other hand, South Africa holds a xenophobic racial history along with the increasing entrance of Zimbabwean migrants since the 1990s. Malaysia, from its part, has also seen a massive entrance of Indonesians in the country – including refugees-. All of these elements of their recent history have contributed to shaping a particular view of migration within these territories.

Besides this historical approach, another element influencing the perception of migration as a security threat is the quantity of the migrant population, not only in the past, but in the current moment. The so-called "European refugee crisis" was marked by the massive entrance of refugees into European borders starting in 2015. The EU migration system was unable to cope with such large numbers of asylum applications and refugees spreading throughout the Union, collapsing both the EU and national migration services.

The United States has also had a long close history with migration, being the same country built in itself from peoples from other lands. However, the acceptance and integration of refugees in the country has changed a lot in the past decades. Even though it has been considered a nation of immigrants, attitudes and laws on immigration have switched from passing the first law on US citizenship to white people through the Naturalization Act of 1790, to banning the entrance of Chinese immigrants through the Chinese Exclusion Act of 1882. But it is with World War I that xenophobic attitudes arise; first, by tackling Asian countries in particular through the Immigration Act of 1917, and then limiting the number of allowed migrants in the country with the Immigration Act of 1924. More recently, the Trump administration issued the "Protecting the Nation from Foreign Terrorist Entry into the United States" two executive borders, which banned immigration from six majority-Muslim countries (Chad, Iran, Libya, Syria, Yemen, and Somalia), as well as North Korea and Venezuela (History, 2018).

The previous history of the country with immigration, the quantity of migrants entering the country, the economic situation in which it is going through, and so on. All of these are elements which somehow explain the perceptions of some countries towards migration, as well as their interests. Going back to the US case, the Chinese Exclusion Act was passed after 30 years of continuous and steady flow of Chinese workers emigrating to the United States. The Immigration Act of 1917 is designed to tackle Asian immigrants after xenophobic feelings arise due to World War I. The Immigration Act of 1924 favours Northern and Western European immigration while limiting that coming from Southern, Central and Eastern Europe (History, 2018). Mexican labour force is encouraged in the US during the 1940s and 1950s due to labour shortages during World War II, but it is not today when the message that "they are stealing US jobs" is being echoed. All these legal developments have responded to the interests of the country in a particular given time, thence immigration feelings are shaped by the combination of a multiplicity of elements, past and present.

Are there interests to protect then or are there strategic tactics to follow? Or, considering that the perception of security threats can be subjective to some extent, can it be a combination of both? It seems appropriate to say that, in some cases, certain practices to securitize migration in fact follow a particular strategy from a government to regain control over migration. In other cases, it can also be the case that the perception by some of migration as being linked to terrorism can cause some governments to find it necessary to establish certain security measures to frame immigration. It will then depend on the particular case to determine whether the securitization of migration is a tactic or a protection movement. Whatever the case, though, the debate on whether it is justified doing so is a different on.

2 *Who* Is Driving This Transformation? The Actors Involved

Refugees, in particular, are increasingly designated as securitized "objects" not for what they do, but for what they represent: uncontrolled entry, demographic change, or geopolitical entanglement. This symbolic power makes them disproportionately vulnerable to securitizing moves, regardless of their legal status or actual threat.

Migration movements have proved to be a matter of concern for many countries around the world and even for the international society, since we can find mass migration movements in almost all regions in the world and thus affecting many countries – be it as origin, transit or host countries. Furthermore, the international terrorist threat also illustrates how necessary it is to find a global solution to fight against terrorist groups and to prevent their attacks. The movements of peoples and goods is a key component of our interconnected and interdependent world, thence it is also basic to address these issues within the international legal field to find a common legal ground which binds all states equally. Refugees are frequently caught in the crossfire of these efforts. Security institutions often treat all forms of cross-border mobility as potential vectors of terrorism, leading to systems where refugees must pass through the same scrutiny and suspicion as irregular migrants, despite the fact that their movement is protected under international law. This misalignment reveals how refugee protection is being eroded by security-first logic.

In order to understand how these dynamics become embedded in law and policy, we must turn to the process of global norm creation. Having explored the broader context in which new norms arise – particularly the perceived threats posed by migration and terrorism –we now turn to the actors involved in creating these norms. Identifying who sets the normative agenda allows us to analyse how specific legal frameworks are developed, and what their consequences are. In this chapter, we address three core questions: Who is making these norms? How are they doing it? And what outcomes do these processes produce?

First and foremost, we obviously have the state. This can actually be understood to be compound by a diversification of actors and departments. At an organizational level, we could consider as being part of the process of norm creation in this area not only the President's Office,[1] but also the Foreign Affairs Department, the Department of Home Affairs (or Internal Affairs), and the Defence Department. In some countries these may be mixed or be independent from one another.[2] In some cases, the Department of Home Affairs will also be responsible for all migratory-related issues, in other cases, there will be an independent Ministry for doing so.[3] They may all collaborate at some point in making sure that their interests and goals are safeguarded. Finding a common ground at this point is not the most difficult of issues, since the government usually shares a common view and thus works towards achieving the same

1 This can also be known as the Prime Minister's Office, Department of the Prime Minister, and other similar titles.

2 In the United States, the government counts with the US Department of State (with the head figure of the Secretary of State), taking care of carrying out the President's foreign policies.

3 This is the case, for instance, of Australia, where the government has a Ministry for Immigration, Citizenship, Migrant Services and Multicultural Affairs.

goals. What is different though is to satisfy the demands of other political parties not being part of the government. Thus there is an interplay within governmental institutions where debates of different opinions on, for instance, immigration laws, can be much heated.

In more sensitive scenarios, we can also find extremist right-wing parties throwing into these different views on migration and its relation to security, and rising controversies. We have also seen some of the discourses of parties like the National Rally in France, presenting migration as the source of terrorist attacks; the entrance in Parliament of VOX in Spain; references of refugees and asylum seekers in Germany as an “invasion of foreigners” by the Alternative for Germany; or the continuous politicization of immigration and Islam by the Party for Freedom in the Netherlands. In fact, in the latter case, the party has repeatedly accused immigration from Islamic countries of profiting from the Dutch welfare state and causing a negative impact on the national economy and disrupting the cultural life. And more importantly for our case, through social media and other means it has connected Islamic migration as a source of violence and danger everywhere. Outside of Europe, other parties like the Canadian Nationalist Party have also irrupted in the political scenario, claiming for maintaining the demographic majority of white people in the country, deporting all illegal migrants, including refugees, and so on.

However, today there are also many other participants in these debates besides those part of the political elite. There are also international organizations, from international to regional ones, involved in the securitization of migration. As a regional example a clear case is that of the European Union. We have analysed different instruments like the European Agenda on Migration of 2014, which introduced hotspots to register and control incoming refugees and asylum seekers as well as to reinforce border control. It has also created new entities like the European Coastguard which was set up to provide border security against “all kinds of threats”. Refugee boats have been considered as one of these threats to European security. The involvement of the NATO, though, is another example of the well-established linked between security and migration. This organization has included terrorism and mass migration as part of their main concerns in their defence agenda. EU Operations like EUNAVFOR Sophia, whose mission is to identify and capture vessels used by migrant smugglers and traffickers have been highly controversial, and they have counted with the cooperation of EU Member State authorities, EUROPOL, FRONTEX, the European Asylum Support Office (EASO), and EUROJUST. But naval missions have also been directed by the NATO. NATO, after Germany, Greece, and Turkey asked for its intervention, also sent warships to the Aegean Sea to conduct “reconnaissance, monitoring and surveillance of illegal crossings in the stretch of sea between Turkey and Greece" (Drent, 2018).

These are just a couple of examples of measures which show how migration has been brought to the security field and is treated as a national and even international security threat. Not only have states taken the necessary steps to pass laws and public policies controlling migration and increasing border surveillance, but they have also worked together to coordinate their forces in fighting against illegal migration and making sure that their borders are kept secure and away from those trying to enter them, even though doing it as asylees. The terrorist threat has not only contributed to increasing fear against the immigrant and refugee population, but it has also been used to justify the approval of measures furthering in the control and prevention of immigration. With the excuse that terrorist fighters are sometimes hiding between migration flows, new technologies on surveillance measures have been used to identify and check refugees during their trips to reach the land of Western countries.

But let's not forget that within today's international order there are not only states and international organizations, but transnational corporations and other powerful enterprises are also participating in shaping the interests of governments and of the international society as a whole. The role of these enterprises in the field of security is utterly important. And that is precisely the reason why it is key to focus more specifically on them to explain what is exactly the role that they play in shaping international norms related to security and migration.

The protection of European borders has been put at the forefront of the European agenda, with important increases in the funding of this sector. As noted by Akkerman (2018a) it is striking that in a time where the EU has had to deal with the Brexit and an unfinished economic crisis, the European Commission still proposes to triple the funding for borders, migration, and asylum with wide consensus. What is more, I would add to his comment that, again, borders, migration, and asylum go hand by hand, since it seems that dealing with refugees and asylees is intrinsically linked to border control, and not to their safeguard.

In fact, between December 2014 and June 2018 EU and member states' officials have had dozens of interviews, conferences, roundtables, and fairs with the European Organisation for Security (15 times), the AeroSpace and Defence Industries Association of Europe (29 times), Airbus[4] (131 times), Leo-

4 Airbus is a global leader in the defence sector and the largest defence supplier in Europe. Besides manufacturing commercial aircraft and helicopters, it also develops combat aircraft and military communications, intelligence, and surveillance.

nardo[5] (25 times), and Thales[6] (18 times) (Akkerman, 2018a). Members of these arms companies also participate as experts on border security in the drawing up of EU reports and make concrete proposals which later on have been framed as EU immigration policies. This has led to the approval and setting up of the wide border monitoring system EUROSUR and the establishment of a European border guard (Akkerman, 2018a) which, in turn, have generated a market of more than 17 billion euros between 2014 to 2016 (ODI, 2016). If this were not enough, another sign of how this industry has expanded the market is the budget allocated to the EU border agency Frontex, which has gone from just 6 million euros in 2005 to 254 million in 2017 (Delle Femmine, 2017). On top of that, Leonardo (formerly known until 2017 as Finmecannica) Thales, and Airbus are three of the top four European arms traders, selling in the Middle East and North Africa, where many refugees come from.

The walls to separate Spain from North Africa placed between Ceuta and Melilla and Morocco were backed up by Spanish companies Indra and Dragados. The costs of these walls have been said to be of 72 million euros between 2005 and 2013, and the Spanish coastal surveillance system SIVE of about 230 million between 2000 and 2008 (Delle Femmine, 2017). In a freer Europe after the fall of the Berlin Wall where a new era seemed to begin, we are now closing our doors to refugees. Akkerman (2019) is the one to ask, "Who killed the dream of a more open Europe?", and the answer he gives is clear: "One group has by far the most to gain from the rise of new walls – the business that build them". All in all, it seems clear that the industry is one of the few beneficiaries from the refugee crisis.

Thence the interplay between governments and private entities is key in understanding today's processes of global norm-making. As Bloom described (2014), the "privatization across all stages of migration occurs in some form in all global regions and leads to a relocation of migration control and delegation of key functions". Thence there seems to be an international pattern adjudicating – at least partially – the control of migration to the hands of private actors.

In December 2017, the Italian government redeployed part of its troops in Iraq and Afghanistan to North Africa to stop migration; and the French government also wanted to increase its military presence in Niger to fight against the so-called war on terror. In addition to this, governments from origin coun-

---

5 The Leonardo S.p.A. is an Italian company designed to advance in the development of defence technology for air, land, sea, and cyber security.

6 The Thales Group is a French multinational company serving in various security sectors, including aerospace, ground transportation, digital identity security, and defence security.

tries are praised by Western states when they apply harsher measures to restrict refugee flows (i.e. the same way that Niger did through its northern city of Agadez). In fact, collaboration between origin and destination countries has reached bilateral agreements, but so has the European Commission. Collaboration between the EU and its member states individually with third countries has taken place in terms of accepting deported persons, training of police and border officials, developing biometric systems, and donations of helicopters, ships, and other vehicles, as well as surveillance and monitoring equipment (Akkerman, 2018b).

It is clear then that the role of governments is indeed key in developing international laws and policies in any matter, but their interaction with private enterprises has also become a huge part of today's negotiations in security affairs. As stated by Davitti (2019:53), "Private Military and Security Companies do not merely provide border security and migration control services. They frame, shape and entrench militarized responses within the European Agenda. They contribute to the framing of irregular migration as a security threat which can only be addressed through emergency-driven military responses – and, conveniently, the same services that they provide. Thus, they irreversibly shape European migration policies and accelerate the securitization of the EU border".[7] In setting up EU priorities in defence and security they are contributing to framing irregular migration as a security threat, in other words, to reinforcing practices that lead to a securitization of migration. With terrorist attacks leading to increasing reliance on security technologies and thus on security companies, we are seeing a translation of the War on Terror into a "War on Immigrants" (Kumar, 2020).

Another very relevant and active actor participating in the process of securitizing migration and thus contributing to the creation of global norms is mass media. As we have seen in previous chapters, media outlets in occasions have used language diminishing the immigrant community and even accusing refugees of the terrorist threat. We have seen examples of these media discourses in relation to news media in Australia, the Czech Republic, Malaysia, and New Zealand. Acknowledging the important impact that the media has on public

7 To see similar conclusions on this subject, see Chris J. (2017) 'Market Forces: The Development of the EU Security-Industrial Complex', *Transnational Institute*. Available at: https://www.tni.org/files/publication-downloads/marketforces-report-tni-statewatch.pdf; Akkerman, M (2016) 'Border Wars. The arms dealers profiting from Europe's refugee tragedy', *Transnational Institute*. Available at: https://www.tni.org/files/publication-downloads/border-wars-report-web1207.pdf; and Akkerman, M (2016) 'Border Wars II. An update on the arms industry profiting from Europe's refugee tragedy, *Transnational Institute*. Available at: https://www.tni.org/files/publication-downloads/borderwars-issuebrief-web.pdf.

opinion, it is crucial to be aware of the messages they send because many times they will contribute to giving a bad image of the immigrant population of the country, including that of refugees, which worsens the public perception of migration, hinders a positive integration of immigrants, and thence is part of increasing measures securitizing of migration.

And on top of that, and of course also linked to the impact that the media and politics have on the public opinion, there is also civil society actively participating in the international political life, and here we can specifically refer to civil associations but also to the citizen as an individual. NGOs such as the Red Cross, Human Rights Watch, and Amnesty International participate monitoring and reporting abuses and making sure that international laws are complied with, or even lobby for their change. Whether organized in groups or acting on their own, citizens are the ones voting on elections for their governments and campaigning for and against political parties since they are the ultimate subject for which laws and policies are addressed to. According to Hammerstad (2012), citizens are also a securitizing actor. He argues, for instance, that South Africans living in the most disadvantaged areas and where there are more Zimbabwean refugees living are also where acts of intolerance take place, creating widespread public disorder to achieve some policy recognition. They are subject to them, and thus they are also the ones in favour or against them. And this also applies to the international arena, and especially if we consider today's globalized world as an interconnected one, in which we all are somehow part of the international community.

To sum up what has been explained in this section, I have divided all of the actors mentioned above in a table following different categories based on their intensity or degree of involvement in the process of norm-making in the field of security and migration. The levels of implication have been synthetized as high, medium, and low, having either direct or indirect impact. Thence in the first category, we can find those actors with a high and direct degree of involvement, also known as the "promoter". Most of the times, the state will most likely be engaged in this position since it is the government the one approving laws and policies of their interest. But depending on the state or the moment in which we are making this analysis, the position of different actors will vary. Therefore, it is also possible that the promoter is found on civil society but that at a later stage it has a less relevant involvement causing its position to pass onto a lower category and having a low-direct participation. Thence it must be noted that this is a generic table, but more accurate definitions are very much dependant on the specific country being studied and depending on the phase of construction of the particular norm at stake. While in general, it is clear that the implication of the state understood as the government is usually high since it is a driving actor and in many occasions, the main actor securitizing migration as it is the one approving laws and policies in this and other fields, the situation of other players such as international organizations is very much likely to change according to the particular geographic space. For instance, as it has already been exposed, the role of the European Union in moving forward certain legislative developments that favour specific sectors makes it an actor that has a much higher level of involvement that other regional international organizations like for instance, the Association of Southeast Asian Nations (ASEAN), or bigger ones like the United Nations. Thence the role of international organizations will be very much dependant on each organization.

The second category is formed by what I have found in "supporters". The difference between this and the third category – that of "followers" – is their level of implication. While both have a direct involvement in the development of a particular norm securitizing migration, the first is more actively participating than the second, which is a mere interested part but without taking any major steps to influence the process. Falling between the two categories there can be actors like, for instance, the opposition of the government. I have specifically referred to extreme right-wing parties since these are the ones having a much clearer intention to securitize migration than those being on a leftist side. However, it will be very much country-dependant the role and implication of these parties according to the parliamentary representation they might possess. Other actors that could suit these two categories would be international organizations, private entities, or even civil society. Again, the clash between groups can be more or less evident depending on the particular situation of the specific country. Private entities can be the very early promoters of a norm and can even participate in its design, which will be later on enforced by the state. The passing of responsibility from one actor to another and their level of involvement can then vary along the phases of construction of the norm.

In general, the role of civil society in the field of the securitization of migration is more likely to fall within the third category. Not because of the lack of presence of civil society organizations advocating for the rights of refugees, for instance, but because of their low level of implication in actively securitizing migration. Since most of these bodies try to defend the rights of the most vulnerable groups in society, they are not participating in the securitization of migration, but on the contrary, calling for the de-securitization of the sector. As in every case, there are civil society organizations in favour of securitization measures, and even though they are not political associations, they sometimes lean towards certain right-wing political parties. Whatever the case or their preference, the implication of civil society does not have such a relevant impact on the making of these laws and policies in the area of migration and security, which other players do in fact have.

From a different perspective, there are also the fourth and fifth categories, that of the persistent objector and general contenders, are characterized for having a more indirect involvement. I have found unnecessary to divide this indirect implication within high, medium and low since the nuance between them is not so strong. That is also the reason why I have also highlighted whether the implication of these actors is direct or indirect. With "direct" implication I am referring to the willingness to securitize of migration. This can be due to a variety of reasons: to re-gain control over a specific area, to obtain economic benefits, to xenophobic or racist reasonings, etc. On the other hand, "indirect" implication refers to the impact of certain discourses or measures in the securitization of migration, even though it does not willingly want to achieve this end. Here, the different between the persistent objector and the general contender is that the first is, as the same word connotes, continuously disputing the measure, while the latter is only arguing against it during particular moments of the process and without as much intensity as the persistent objector.

Mass media is the clearest example of this case, since it does not actively participate in the approval of such measures, but some of its discourses indirectly contribute -and in many cases, very strongly- to the development of a negative perception of migration and creates a collective imaginary where migration is perceived as a threat. Mass media can at times have a high level of implication while at others a much lower one, depending on the specific media outlet, its interests, its influence and its relationship with the government (depending, of course, on the form of government of the country). Table 2 summarizes the proposed typology of actors according to the intensity of their involvement.

TABLE 3.1 Intensity of involvement by actor

Typology of actors	Intensity of involvement
First category (promoter)	Direct-High
Second category (supporter)	Direct-Medium
Third category (follower)	Direct-Low
Fourth category (persistent objector)	Indirect-High
Fifth category (general contenders)	Indirect-Low

These are the main actors taking part in drawing one direction or another to certain parts of the international political agenda. They are all responsible to some extent in the way we treat common global issues like climate change and sustainability, the protection of human rights and the fight against poverty, the development biotechnologies, dealing with international migration, and providing international security. In tackling these and other issues, we need to be aware of the importance of international law as the source to find common ground and to establish basic rules while finding potential solutions. International law is essential in a globalized world, and that is why it is so crucial that the evolution of international norms and the processes to make them adapts to the changing conditions of today's international order. The debate around the international normative approximation of terrorism has demonstrated that it is key to be able to adapt to current international concerns, and the international community has at times shown its incapability to cope with the pressure to reach global and effective agreements on both migration and terrorism.

3 *How* Are They Doing It? Characteristics of the Processes and Outcomes

In the aftermath of the 9/11 attacks, the War on Terror started, and it was endorsed with the subsequent Madrid and London Bombings of 2004 and 2005 respectively. The involvement of defence companies to provide security to the citizens led to the development of technological innovations on the one side, and new legal instrument from the other. The narrow relationship between public and private interests – the first being represented by the state and regional bodies such as the EU, and the others by security and defence companies, lobbying consultancies, and other similar private actors – has tightened even more in the past years. But the question is how has this happened altogether?

As it has already been explained, there are several reasons why a government would like to re-gain control over a subject when it feels it has lost it, such as what happened during the refugee waves at the beginning of the refugee crisis. There are also several reasons why they want to refrain them from entering their territories, from economic, social to national security motives. The terrorist threat has been an important addendum seeking to further control migration, and terrorism has become the main priority in most national security agendas. Thence protecting from the terrorist threat has been put at the forefront of most national and international strategies. To reinforce this idea, security states have resorted to defence and security companies, and these have been astute in asserting their dominance in the field through their technical expert opinions in every negotiation process and by perpetuating the insecurity narrative about the figure of the migrant (Kumar, 2020). They have developed a wide and complex range of border technologies and perimeter security systems, communication and identification systems (aircraft, drones, biometrics systems, command and control schemes, screening and scanning mechanisms, etc.), information technology systems, and other types of surveillance, tracking and tracing technologies to control goods, vessels, trucks, aircraft, and peoples. These measures have in turn represented a change in national and international security policies. These companies have thence framed, shaped, and entrenched militarized responses further contributing to securitizing migration (Davitti, 2019).

All these methods frame the refugee as a de-politicized and technologically manageable threat (Kumar, 2020), and instead of considering them as vulnerable groups seeking for a safe refuge and thus leaning towards the Refugee Convention, the refugee is seen as a security threat from which we have to protect ourselves. At the same time, if there is technological failure or inefficiency which leads to the death of refugees or to their entrance into Western territory, this is seen as a reason to reinforce security technologies and promote their further advancement. This also means that refugees will be more likely to take even more dangerous routes (Lutterbeck, 2006). As explained by Kumar (2020):

> We witness the emergence of a selective-mobility regime which, on the one hand, smoothly facilitates trade and tourism but simultaneously sorts and filters the illegal and illegitimate and severely shrinks the protection space on the other. This selective-mobility regime stands in contradiction to the protection space afforded by the Refugee Convention read along with other relevant treaties and conventions as it frames a refugee along the migration-security nexus who must be controlled, managed, categorised and sorted as "desirable" or "undesirable" (Bigo and Guild, 2005:234) making migration control a viable and profitable enterprise.

The actors responsible for reinforcing security technologies and constructing this particular view of the refugee have been non-state, private actors. As we have already seen, they do provide not only resources but also services of expertise which help shape new migratory and security frameworks. The proliferation of actors (public and private, national and international) involved in restrictive policy implementation has led to an externalization and privatization of migratory and border control management. In the case of refugees, the securitizing actor often invokes not direct threats, but symbolic and cultural fears: strain on welfare, erosion of national identity, or potential radicalization. This illustrates how securitization can target protected groups without invoking conventional security discourse – a central paradox explored throughout this book.

Liberal states have overcome certain constraints by including private, local, international, and supranational agents which enlarge the migration playing field and make use of state functions. It is important to highlight that states can transfer such powers and responsibilities precisely because of how important it has become to the citizen to secure themselves from the terrorist threat and to secure the country from external – immigrant – irruption in their society. Security is powerful enough to motivate voters to transfer the control of some of their basic rights and freedoms in exchange for a greater sense of security in front of the refugee and terrorist threats. As argued by Lahav (2003), the control of this security can then be assigned to non-State actors in the name of law and order, and contractors from the private sphere like transport companies, health care services, and shipping carriers among many others endure a privatization of the regulation in the sector. Private carriers and agencies become, in part, agents of the State while they are ensured business, trade, and labour.

We already have an international legal framework tackling different aspects of migration, and not only is it interesting to analyse whether this structure has been ampliated, but to see what kind of sources have been incorporated. We need to keep in mind that although international migration law is fixed in customary and treaty law, soft law has also been used to develop material in this field. In the past years, many nonbinding instruments have been used to treat migration issues and foster international cooperation, showing how migration governance involves a variety of actors besides the state, at the international, regional, and bilateral levels (Chetail, 2017). Thence in the field of migration, different types of sources are used to construct the entire body of international migration law. The fact that legal instruments in this field are captured in treaty law, customary international law, and soft law shows its heterogeneity and cross-cutting character. While positivism, expressing international norms in a written manner, seems fundamental to attain international actors to comply with certain basic norms, we must think of migration as a global phenomenon in an era when new ways to construct international norms are at play, thus in a time when migration law might also be subject to certain changes, even in the way it is constructed.

In regard to terrorism, there have also been international legal developments in the field, which have been especially emphasized more recently after 9/11. However, international law has long addressed terrorism. Boyle and Chinkin (2007) make a brief summary of the evolution of international instruments on terrorism. Holding that first references to the subject date back to the International Conference for the Unification of Penal Law after World War I. The League of Nations subsequently sought to suppress this activity by setting up a committee of experts to draw up a convention (the 1937 Convention for the Prevention and Punishment of Terrorism), although this failed to come into force (Boyle and Chinkin, 2009). Most of the earliest conventions on international terrorism were adopted by the International Civil Aviation Organization (ICAO) and International Maritime Organization (IMO); they were mostly focused on attacks on aircraft and ships in response to events occurred in the 1970s and 1980s. It was not until 1994 that the United Nations through its General Assembly started developing instruments on terrorism more broadly. The first instrument to be approved by the UN was the Declaration on Measures to Eliminate International Terrorism. Later on, an ad hoc committee to prepare the 1997 Convention for the Suppression of terrorist Bombings was adopted, as well as the 1999 Convention for the Suppression of the Financing of Terrorism and the 2005 Convention for the Suppression of Acts of Nuclear Terrorism. These are examples of the progressive legal development of international measures taken in regard to the terrorist threat.

Even so, these authors (2009) also stand that following the September 11 attacks in New York and Washington, the Security Council started taking more resolutions in relation to terrorism. First, by adopting Resolution 1373 of 28 September 2001 (S/RES/1373) which established a comprehensive approach to terrorism applicable to all states (although not defining terrorism as such). Many of the provisions of the Terrorist Financing Convention became obligatory upon all states and to this binding nature the Security Council set up the counter-Terrorism Committee, to ensure that states would comply with these provisions. What is more, Resolution 1373 required member states to change domestic law in order to fulfil the requirements established by this Resolution. Thence for the first time it attributed the capacity to the Security Council to require all UN member states to adapt domestic laws (Scheppele, 2010). Later on, with the Security Council Resolution 1540 of 28 April 2004 (S/RES/1540) on non-proliferation of weapons of mass destruction, new obligations were imposed. These are two examples of institutional responses which have imposed obligations on all states. On the one hand, they have reached their goals of being binding more quickly than through treaty-making processes, and on the other, they made everyone accountable regardless of whether they decide to join the document or not. Describing the evolution of terrorism-related instruments in the words of these authors (2007):

> International legal responses to terrorism illustrates many facets of contemporary international law-making that are discussed throughout the book. It shows how international law evolves both rapidly in response to specific events and more slowly through policy deliberation. It also illustrates the diversity of law-making approaches that international law now offers and that the choice of process depends upon context, political preference and purpose. In addition assessment has to be made as to whether a particular process is law-making, or whether the outcomes of specific deliberations are moral or political recommendations rather than legally binding norms.

Interestingly, many countries adopted similar laws in a very short time reacting to the 9/11 attacks. For the first time in history, countries around the globe reacted to a particular event to protect from the same threat and fight global terrorism. Following a constructivist interpretation of international relations, it is only when states are involved in non-previously constituted situations (in other words, in new situations) that new practices can arise (Wendt, 1995). That is, there can be collective interactions that contribute to constituting new patterns. Global terrorism, or the terrorist threat, is an example of a new situation that states have had to confront by creating new practices internationally (Bello, 2017).

In addition to this, we also count with faster ways to make legal reforms and respond to particular international threats (Scheppele, 2010). Comparative law has also had its part, and countries have been able to see the measures applied in other states, and "borrow" legal ideas from others (Epstein and Knight, 2003). These ideas and legal developments migrate in international space, and, despite having different legal and political systems, they can still be used and placed into another legal systems. As put by Scheppele (2010), "Laws of different countries converge through the movement of legal ideas horizontally from one domestic legal system to another".

If we put together this willingness to learn from certain laws of other nations with the fact that after Resolution 1373 new international legal obligations arose, making binding global security law, we have now a more international approach to security law as ever before. This does not necessarily mean that a clear international response to terrorism exists, since all nations can still have different perspectives on the terrorist threat and may respond differently from one another. We have seen how some prioritize human rights while others play with the interaction between gaining control in detriment of

TABLE 3.2 Strategies by area

Strategies	Examples
Centred in the law	USA Patriot Act of 2001 (United States); Anti-terrorism, crime and security Act (ATCSA) of 2001 (United Kingdom); Immigration Act No. 1154 of 2002 (Indonesia)
Centred in public policy	Operation Sovereign Borders (Australia); EUNAVFOR Sophia (European Union)
Centred in discourse	Discourses given by political parties such as the National Rally (France); Discourse by Korwin-Mikke, leader of the KORWIN party in 2015 (Poland); publications by the New Zealand Herald (New Zealand)
Centred in security technologies	Project Seabilla (an EU-funded research project related to border surveillance conducted by Leonardo S.p.A in 2016);[a] CLOSEYE (EU project to advance in the technological control of external maritime border surveillance); Scenario Based Targeting System (a Canadian system which uses algorithms to assess individuals' levels of risk); Trusted and traveller programmes including biometric entry/exit systems such as Hong Kong's e-channel, Germany's Easypass, and USA's Global Entry.

a European Commission, "EU Research for a Secure Society" (2016), pp. 304–305. Accessed at: https://ec.europa.eu/home-affairs/sites/homeaffairs/files/what-we-do/policies/industry-for-security/docs/security_research_fp7_catalogue_part1_en.pdf.

basic rights. There is, then, a global response to terrorism, and there are, now, more common security legal practices across the globe. It remains to be seen how these will evolve and whether they will end up designing an entire international security framework or not.

To summarize the complexities of the outcomes and processes associated with the securitization of migration I have developed a table in which there are four main strategic areas through which security and migration are brought together and a few examples for each of them. They all superpose one another to some extent, but here the strategies have been divided according to the area in which they are most focused in or centred. The first two have been widely explained, and we have already seen some of the measures related to both law and politics. Thence it is crystal clear that the law and politics are critical in the securitization of migration, with their most common developments including norms and public policies, these being two of the most often outcomes. These are applied at the local, state, regional and international levels and involving a wide range of actors. On the other hand, we also have mentioned the importance of discourses in spreading this general view of the migrant and refugee as being necessarily connected with security. These discourses are usually given by actors who are part of the government, political parties, media outlets, etc. A fourth strategy is that related to security technologies. While migration is presented as a threat, reinforcing certain security technologies has become a justified strategy directed to protecting the citizen. And the citizen agrees to give up part of her privacy or free movement rights, for instance, in exchange of being ensured greater security. Overall, as we have seen, there has been a growing number of surveillance mechanisms and other security related technology developments to further control foreign nationals and the citizens within the territorial borders of a country, and a region. In the following table these categories have been divided including some examples which have been picked and classified as being part of a particular strategic area to securitize migration.

These are just a hand pick of examples of different strategies that can be found worldwide securitizing migration. As we have seen, the result of the process of securitizing migration, in practice, is the creation of new laws and policies, and their reform. We have seen very clearly how nations have passed legislation and public policies tackling migration from a national security perspective. We have seen how Canada created a new class of "Designated Foreign Nationals" to mandate discretionary detention without a warrant to those migrants – and thus also refugees – arriving by sea. We have heard discourses in the US targeting refugees as potential terrorists posing a threat to national security in order to present the entrance of undocumented migrants. In the UK, the 1971 Immigration Act provided deportation powers on national security grounds, but with the approval of the Anti-terrorism, Crime and Security Act (ATCSA) of 2001, the government increased its powers to detain foreign nationals indefinitely and without charge or trial if this person was suspected of being a terrorist. A connection between national security – terrorism, in this case – and migration was more tightly established. In Europe, after the adoption of the 1990 Schengen Agreements, the 1992 Maastricht Treaty and the

1997 Treaty of Amsterdam the distinction between internal and external security disappeared, and it became harder to tell when there was one or another. Furthermore, the ways followed by the EU to develop border control have put immigration at as a threat requiring security response. Both in theory and practice, the EU has connected security to migration more often than not. And these are just a few of the many examples out there linking migration to national security. These national and regional frameworks can give rise to an international global response towards terrorism and migration altogether, they can be the base to set up an international framework on security which departs from the securitization of a particular group, with the negative impact that this can cause to migrants and, more particularly, to even more vulnerable groups like refugees.

4 *Which* Are the Effects of These Norms? The Global Consequences of Framing Security and Migration

In previous chapters we explored the consequences that securitizing migration could have on migration, and specially on particularly vulnerable groups such as that of refugees. While some social consequences will also be explored here, the main idea is to highlight the legal and political effects that norms and policies framing migration from a security perspective can cause on these groups. The perception of migration as a threat has brought the figure of the migrant – and specially those categorized as irregular or undocumented migrants, which often includes refugees – at the forefront of many national security agendas as they are seen as a contemporary security "problem". And even though many destination countries have tried to establish measures to prevent them from entering their territory, these policies have not resulted in a lesser number of arrivals. On the contrary, the effect they have caused has been in the detriment of the situation of these peoples, who have seen their human security unprotected in detriment of the national security where they are trying to seek for a safe haven. These and other related themes will be the main topic of this chapter.

Starting with this rejectionist perception of migration, which considers the migrant as a threat associates it with security is not directed to all migrant groups uniformly. Most of the times, when we talk about migration as a security threat we are referring to particular groups of migrants, those known as irregular or illegal migrants. However, some have also thrown in refugees due to the large numbers of international refugees crossing borders and collapsing national asylum systems of Western states. As it has been repeatedly stated in previous pages, the link between migration and national security has been intensified in periods of economic recession or when terrorist attacks have taken place and one or more of the attackers were of migrant origin. This has led to strengthening border which are no longer a method of defence and protection from enemies but has also become a symbolic frontier separating "us" from "the others" (Da Sousa Santos, 2000; Ferrero, 2017). It has internationalized border issues leading to international cooperation measures of exchange of information, identification, and surveillance. What used to be addressed through national policies has now become feasible outside of the regular state jurisdiction through international cooperation between states in order to increase their own national security but also international security as a whole.

Vietti and Scribner (2013) argue that from a sovereignty perspective, irregular migration is perceived as an attack on the state's sovereignty, which justifies the deployment of immigration officers and frontier guards, as well as the construction of border fences. Under a human security approach, it puts even more obstacles to these peoples in search for protection. It will thence become impossible to sustain mechanisms securitizing migration without harming the security of the refugee. These authors further argue that if providing a framework which responds to the causes of migration instead of their control at the destination country would be helpful to find more rational and humane solutions. In consequence, we should be thinking of strategies that seek to buttress local economies so that people have economic opportunities in their countries of origin and pressuring governments to protect human rights to maximize freedom of opportunity. Instead of being forced to flee, we should make sure that people can exercise their most basic rights and find opportunities in their countries.

Contrary to what some appear to believe, establishing prohibitions and restrictions to migration does not increase national security. A rejectionist approach to refugees causes more damage than the good to national security it seeks to achieve. As explained by Massimino (2017), "ISIS is already exploiting hostility to refugees and other Muslins, using it to validate its clash-of-civilizations narrative". Refugees are pictured to be threats to safety and to be going against European and Western values. The worsening of the image of refugees given by some governments and media outlets presents them as invaders from which we need to protect. The systematic presentation of refugees as a threat to our security has put them at the forefront of many national security agendas and has led to a rise of populist and extremist parties. In reality, the increasing numbers of ultra-right nationalist parties and groups and of their supporters in Europe poses an existential threat to European democracies and to the European Union (Massimino, 2017).

Furthermore, governments and regional bodies – and this is especially clear in the case of the European Union – have shifted the burden to deal with forced migration towards non-state actors in order to "blur" their responsibility with refugees. Their responses to deal with these migratory flows have been directed to the security sphere, with an increased and more technical control of the borders, the militarization of the way we deal with migratory-related issues, and a decrease of the eternalization of human rights (Morgades, 2017). What is more, the administrative routines followed by destination countries, and this is especially clear in the EU case, have added up to this negative perception of refugees. The EU establishes that asylum seekers need to prove their status of refugee; otherwise, they will be expulsed from European territory (European Parliament, 2015). As exposed by Bello (2017:61), the fact that many citizens witness the arrival, detention, and expulsion of these peoples increases prejudice since it is only with the presence of long-term migrants that positive attitudes increase towards newcomers. Short-term migrants and return migration, on the contrary, do not contribute to improving this image. The EU administrative approach to deal with the arrival of asylum seekers is thence not helping towards the integration of migrants in general and, in fact, becomes another setback that derives into increasing this negative perception of migration overall.

We seem to have forgotten that it is not only important to protect the security of the nation as a whole (national security), but we also need to secure that of the individual (human security). According to the 1994 UNDP report, human security is both "freedom from fear" (i.e. threats from war or violence) and "freedom from want" (i.e. poverty, pandemics, etc.). In this report, the UN agency enumerates seven different categories which can lead to human security threats: economic, food, health, environmental, personal, community and political (UNDP, 1994). Failure to protect the individual from one or more of these categories can lead to increasing the vulnerability of already ill-protected groups such as refugees. Economic crises, environmental disasters, and political, religious, or ethnic persecution can all lead to forcing families to leave their homes in search for a safe haven. Internally displaced peoples and refugees are a result of these and other catastrophic events, thus migration results from and can lead to human insecurity.

Thence if we continue focusing on the national security perspective instead of that of human security, we are opening the pathway to militarizing migration, that is, increasing surveillance and border control and allowing the detention and deportation of immigrants. In sum, more restrictive security policies and a more restrictive legal framework. Sadly, a big number of states have gone for this approximation. This has aggravated the situation of immigrants and particularly that of refugees, which have had to search for new and more dangerous routes to reach Western shores, but it has also reinforced a negative perception of migration by nationals of destination countries. It is important to be aware of this antipathetic perception of immigration since many have associated social, economic, and cultural worries with them, and as a result, we have seen rising discrimination and xenophobic rates, a growth of extremist right-wing parties, more restrictive and/or anti-immigration policies, greater difficulties for the integration of migrants, and a more segmented society. As a consequence, what these securitization measures are seeking altogether is not achieved since migrants have not ceased to arrive to Western land. But what is more, they are now facing more risks during their journeys to escape stricter border controls through the market of irregular crossings, such as those in charge of smugglers and human traffickers. Instead, what these dynamics have generated are other long-term social consequences. When refugees are systematically framed as suspect (by media, policy, or political rhetoric) public perception shifts, and the normative framework of protection weakens. What was once an internationally recognized right becomes conditional, revocable, and subordinate to national security narratives.

5 *Where* Can We Find These Norms? The Diffusion of Norms Securitizing Migration

Departing from the previous sections where we have seen how there are different actors, processes and reasons securitizing migration, we have seen that this is no longer a unique or rare practice, but it has instead become quite usual in certain contexts, countries, and regions. If it has spread to different places throughout the globe, it is interesting to see why and to what extent these norms on security and migration have been diffused. Has there been a diffusion of norms securitizing migration, and if so, to what extent and why have them spread to different countries with different characteristics and probably, different interests? Have these norms been applied very similarly, or have they taken different forms depending on the context they are being applied?

States are influenced by their external environment (Jörgens, 2004:257). That is, states and their legal developments are in part a result of transnational influences. In today's globalized world, sometimes the line separating states and their legal frameworks blurs, and while they all have their legal systems existing independently from one another, they influence each other continuously as the fluctuation of information spreads very rapidly and can be accessed almost instantly across the globe. It is even easier to share certain views of a particular conflict when the problem is shared, and even more when the countries are part of the same region.

Thus, if we think of migration or terrorism as a common concern, it is likely that we turn to other nations to see how they have handled similar issues, we may want to cooperate to find a common and more effective solution. And we even might develop norms to regulate threats and acts on these matters. Norms which can affect other nations, be duplicated or imitated by them, or that can even emerge and become part of the international legal system spiralling from these precursory national outcomes. Norm diffusion is, as it has been explained in the previous chapter, a process of imitation or learning (Simmons and Elkins, 2003), and it occurs in the absence of a formal obligation (Jörgens, 2004:252). It is a process which facilitates adopting new norms and which favours new policies since they are already in place in other countries, meaning that one is able to see the success and consequences of their application elsewhere. Norm diffusion becomes evident through the accumulation of individual cases of imitation of the same policy or norm.

Dembinski and Schott (2014) offer a particular view of norm diffusion in which they emphasize the importance of "regional security arrangements", using as examples the cases of the European Security and Defence Policy and the Africa Peace and Security Architecture in relation to the Responsibility to Protect. These authors argue that regional security arrangements are based on each regions' security culture, these being "patterns of agreed statements and established practices carried out by a given regional security organization which define the role, legitimacy and efficacy of particular approaches to protecting values" (Dembinski and Schott, 2014:364). Their idea is that regional security arrangements play a major role in modifying global norms into the local level. There are three main ways to exert the influence of these regional arrangements. Firstly, they shape the reception of emerging global norms at the regional and national level in an *outside-in* transmission process. Secondly, the can opt to reject the global norm through an *inside-out* process of dismissal. And thirdly, and adding the contribution of Amitav Acharya (2009), there can also be a localization of norms, that is, modifying them to make them more adaptable to the local context, instead of just accepting or rejecting them. This is what he calls *pruning*. Evidently, the success of these processes will very much depend on norm entrepreneurs (international institutions, states, civil society organizations, etc.) who will, according to the way they involve themselves into norm-shaping and according to their transnational networks and international support, be more or less likely to accept a norm and, if necessary, adapt it to the particular area where it wants to be integrated.

This perspective might be useful to further contribute to that of the established life cycle of norms. Instead of seeing the diffusion and internalization of norms as a patterned process, we should consider them as a still evolving process through which norms are adapted to the particular local and regional situation of the country. The norm might be contested, or not, within the region, or within the nation. Thence we should no longer see the life cycle of norms and the process of diffusion as being static, but it is a dynamic and context-depending one instead. Crucially, this diffusion of norms affects not only migration control but refugee protection itself. Norms designed for managing irregular migration and counterterrorism are often extended to refugee contexts without distinction. This has led to a global erosion of asylum regimes and legal safeguards, an outcome directly tied to the puzzle this book sets out to explain.

And what is exactly this national or regional context that will ultimately accept, reject, or adapt the global norm? There are a series of elements defining the conditions under which a norm will be integrated within a national's legal framework. Among them, we can think of the values and interests of the particular country – or even government of the country-; its long-standing social values and beliefs; its geographical situation; its historic past and, of course; its present, including recent events that might have taken place and disrupted the normal functioning of the country, may there be related to national security (i.e. terrorist attack), economic stability (i.e. economic crisis), or any other. I have divided all of these factors in three major categories: those related to the values and beliefs of the country; those related to its historic past; and those concerning more recent events and/or the current situation of the country.

When dealing with the first category, I refer to those countries in which, for instance, religious beliefs might become a barrier to accept a particular global norm. This is also the case of those states who do not want to diminish the rights of their citizens embedded in their legal systems to favour a norm focusing on particular aspects of security. Or even the case of those who have more directly attacked particular religious or ethnic groups because of the widening of immigration, because of the origin of major criminal offenses, or other similarly applicable situations. An example would be that of Western countries who have seen growing number of arrivals of immigrants from Muslim origin and in order to prevent them from entering their countries, they have publicly and continuously tackled immigrant groups of Muslim origin, including refugees, and dealt with them as a security issue. Wolffe and Moorhead (2016) summarize this in a clear and thoughtful way:

> Like "religion", "security" also proved to be in many ways an ambiguous and contested concept. It should first be noted that the issues raised in the previous two sections have substantial implicit relevance, given that perceptions that "religion" is a threat to "security" are often rooted in partial, polemical and Western-centric understandings of its character and significance. An obvious example is the drawing of a simplistic connection between Islamic belief and the radical and violent actions of a small minority of Muslims, a perception that fuels Western Islamophobia, which in turn stimulates Islamism in the Muslim world. In these polarised constructions of the religious "other" lie perceptions of substantial threats to global security.

In relation to the second category, here we can find countries that because of their historical past are resentful to integrate certain security norms within their national legal systems. Historical experiences can foster a security culture within a country or region hindering the integration of foreign normative initiatives. African states, for instance, have a security culture of non-interference regarding external actors. This is due to their past colonization experience, which has left Africans overtired of outside interventions (Dembinski and Schott, 2014).

And third but not least, recent events also define the willingness of a country to enact certain security norms that would have otherwise not been applied before. The clearest example is that of terrorist attacks which, as we have seen, have unchained a series of legal developments nationally and internationally to protect from the terrorist threat. Some of these norms would not have been applied should not these events had taken place, since at times some basic rights and freedoms have as a consequence been diminished (i.e. freedom of movement, privacy rights, etc.). Interestingly, if these events had not occurred, these laws would not have been passed since they would have conflicted with the first category that related to the values and beliefs of the country, which would include the importance of the protection of certain values and rights.

As we move into the case studies, it becomes clear that many of the security norms discussed here, including those governing border surveillance, refugee status determination, detention, and cooperation with third states, are applied not only to migrants but also to refugees. This is significant because it demonstrates how norms originally developed for managing irregular migration or combating terrorism become embedded in refugee governance. Through this process, refugees are no longer treated exclusively as rights-holders in need of protection, but as potential threats whose presence must be screened, managed, and deterred. Norm diffusion thus plays a central role in the global reframing of refugeehood as a security issue, the very puzzle this book seeks to unravel.

In the next chapters, we will explore the 'what, who, how, when, where, and why' of these norms across different countries. This analysis will help determine whether norms securitizing migration have been widely developed at the global level, and how they have influenced – or been shaped by-national, regional, and international legal frameworks. It will also allow us to assess where these norms stand in their life cycle, the paths they have followed, and the consequences they have produced. Building on this theoretical and contextual groundwork, the following chapters turn to specific legal sources to examine how securitization-related norms are produced, codified, and diffused. The aim is to understand how far the securitization of migration, and particularly of refugees, has become embedded in law, and to identify the stages these legal developments have reached within different systems.

To offer an international perspective, the cases of South Africa, the European Union, and the United States have been selected. This selection will be useful to analyse the cases of countries/organizations in a different stage. To study the situation of the development of norms on the securitization of migration, it will be interesting to see the scenario of South Africa as a state in a preliminary stage, that of the EU as an intermediate stage, and the one of the US as an advanced one. Moreover, the European Union will offer an insight of an international organization, which can in turn influence the creation of new norms or the modification of existing ones of Member States.

The cases of the EU and the United States, being powerful actors in today's international order, will contribute to providing a more definite approach since the recompilation of information on the debates preceding the creation of these norms and their subsequent evolution will be more accurate due to the higher number of sources that can be found from them. South Africa, from its side, will be a good example of a developing country of a major economic and political power within Africa, and thus amplifying the geographic scope of analysis of this research by studying cases from three different regions and continents in the world.

For each of these actors, there has been a selection of different legal and policy sources which will hopefully positively add to the analysis of the situation of the international securitization of migration and therefore determine whether there are any existing patterns nationally which can contribute to affirming that new norms or frameworks are emerging and being shaped internationally.

References

Akkerman, M (2016a) 'Border Wars. The arms dealers profiting from Europe's refugee tragedy', *Transnational Institute*. Available at: https://www.tni.org/files/publication-downloads/border-wars-report-web1207.pdf.

Akkerman, M (2016b) 'Border Wars II. An update on the arms industry profiting from Europe's refugee tragedy', *Transnational Institute*. Available at: https://www.tni.org/files/publication-downloads/borderwars-issuebrief-web.pdf.

Akkerman, M (2018a) 'How the security industry reaps the rewards of E.U. migration control', *News Deeply*, 5 June. Available at: https://deeply.thenewhumanitarian.org/refugees/community/2018/06/04/how-the-security-industry-reaps-the-rewards-of-e-u-migration-control.

Akkerman, M (2018b) 'Expanding the Fortress. The policies, the profiteers and the people shaped by EU's border externalisation programme', *Transnational Institute*. Available at: https://www.tni.org/files/publication-downloads/expanding_the_fortress_-_1.6_may_11.pdf.

Akkerman, M. (2019) 'The Business of Building Walls', *Transnational Institute*. Available at: https://www.tni.org/files/publication-downloads/business_of_building_walls_-_full_report.pdf.

Acharya, A. (2009) *Whose ideas matter? Agency and power in Asian regionalism*. Ithaca, New York: Cornell University Press.

Bello, V. (2017) *International Migration and International Security. Why Prejudice Is a Global Security Threat*, New York: Routledge.

Bigo, D. and Guild, E. (Eds.). (2005). *Controlling Frontiers: Free Movement Into and Within Europe*. Ashgate.

Bloom, T. (2014) 'The Business of Migration Control: Delegating Migration Control Functions to Private Actors', *Global Policy*, Vol. 6(2), pp. 151–157.

Boyle, A. and Chinkin, C. (2007) *The Making of International Law*. Oxford: Oxford University Press.

Charrett, C. (2009) 'A Critical Application of Securitization Theory: Overcoming the Normative Dilemma of Writing Security', *International Catalan Institute for Peace*, Working Paper No. 2009/7. Available at: https://ssrn.com/abstract=1884149.

Chetail, V. (2017) 'The Architecture of International Migration Law: A Deconstructivist Design of Complexity and Contradiction', *American Journal of International Law*, Vol. 111, pp. 18–23.

Chris J. (2017) 'Market Forces: The Development of the EU Security-Industrial Complex', *Transnational Institute*. Available at: https://www.tni.org/files/publication-downloads/marketforces-report-tni-statewatch.pdf

Da Sousa Santos, B. (2000) *Crítica de la Razón Indolente. Contra el desperdicio de la experiencia*. Bilbao: Editora Desclée de Brouwer.

Davitti, D. (2019) 'The Rise of Private Military and Security Companies in European Union Migration Policies: Implications under the UNGPs', *Business and Human rights Journal*, Vol. 4, pp. 33–53.

Delle Femmine, L. (2017) 'The lucrative business of securing Europe's borders', *El País*, 14 August. Available at: https://english.elpais.com/elpais/2017/08/08/inenglish/1502192834_823925.html.

Dembinski, M. and Schott, B. (2014) 'Regional security arrangements as a filter for norm diffusion: the African Union, the European Union and the responsibility to protect', *Cambridge Review of International Affairs*, Vol. 27(2), pp. 362–380.

Drent, Margriet (2018) 'Militarising migration? EU and NATO involvement at the European border', *Clingendael Spectator*, Vol. 72.

Epstein, L. and Knight, J. (2003) 'Constitutional borrowing and nonborrowing', *International Journal Constitutional Law*, Vol. 1(2), pp. 177–324.

European Parliament (2015) 'Migrants in the Mediterranean: Protecting Human Rights' *Directorate General for External Policies*. Available at: https://www.europarl.europa.eu/RegData/etudes/STUD/2015/535005/EXPO_STU(2015)535005_EN.pdf.

Ferrero, R. (2017) 'Los principales retos de la gobernanza de las migraciones. El binomio migración y seguridad a debate' in *Monografías 152. Las migraciones internacionales, percepción y realidad. Un análisis desde la perspectiva de la seguridad*, Escuela Superior de las Fuerzas Armadas.

Finnemore, M. (1996) *National Interests in International Society*. Ithaca: Cornell University Press.

García, C., Pareja, P. and Rodrigo, A. J. (2019) 'La creación de normas globales: entre el cosmopolitismo soft y el resurgir de Westfalia', ORBIS Working Paper, Vol. 08.

Hammerstad, A. (2012) 'Securitisation from below: The relationship between immigration and foreign policy in South Africa's approach to the Zimbabwe crisis', *Conflict, Security and Development*, Vol. 12(1), pp. 1–30.

History (2018) 'U.S. Immigration Timeline', History.com, 14 May. Available at: https://www.history.com/topics/immigration/immigration-united-states-timeline.

Jörgens, H. (2004) 'Governance by diffusion: implementing global norms through cross-national imitation and learning', in Lafferty, W. M., *Governance for Sustainable development. The Challenge of Adapting Form to Function*. Cheltenham: Edward Elgar, pp. 246–283.

Kumar, R. (2020) 'The role of security and defence companies in EU migration and border control and the impact on the protection of the rights of refugees, migrants and asylum seekers', Office of the High Commissioner for Human Rights. Available at: https://www.ohchr.org/Documents/Issues/Mercenaries/WG/ImmigrationAndBorder/kumar-submission.pdf.

Lahav, G. (2003) 'Migration and Security: the Role of Non-State Actors and Civil Liberties in Liberal Democracies', paper prepared for the *Second Coordination Meeting on International Migration*, Department of Economic and Social Affairs, Population Division, UN, New York 15–16 October.

Lutterbeck, D. (2006), 'Policing Migration in the Mediterranean', *Mediterranean Politics*, Vol. 11(1), pp. 59–82.

Massimino, E. (2017). *Statement before the U.S. Senate Committee on the Judiciary, Subcommittee on Border Security and Immigration, hearing on "The Effects of the Refugee Ban on National Security and Foreign Policy."* Human Rights First. February 7, 2017

Morgades, S. (2017), 'Migraciones forzosas y la Unión Europea: la gestión de los flujos como cuestiones de seguridad' in Quero, J., Abegón, M. and Morgades, S., *Origen, trayecto y destino la gestión de las migraciones forzosas contemporáneas como desafió a la seguridad en Oriente Medio, en el Mediterráneo y en Europa*, ORBIS Working Paper, Vol. 6.

ODI (2016) 'Refugees and migrants taking hidden routes as Europe spends at least €17 billion on borders and deterrents', Overseas Development Institute.

Prantl, J. and Nakano, R. (2011) 'Global Norm Diffusion in East Asia: How China and Japan Implement the Responsibility to Protect', *International Relations*, Vol. 25(2), pp. 204–223.

Scheppele, K. L. (2010) 'The International Standardization of National Security Law', *Journal of National Security Law & Policy*, Vol. 4, pp. 437–453.

Simmons, B. A. and Elkins, Z. (2003) 'The globalization of liberalization: Policy diffusion in the international political economy', Paper prepared for delivery at the workshop 'Internationalization of Regulatory Reforms: The Interaction of Policy Learning and Policy Emulation in Diffusion Processes', Berkeley, CA, 24–25 April.

UNDP (2014) 'Human Development Report 1994: Dimensions of Human Security Technical Report', *United Nations Development Program*. New York: United Nations Development Program.

Vello, B. (2017) 'Migraciones, Seguridad Nacional y Seguridad Humana: un nuevo modelo migratorio para luchar contra el prejuicio como reto a la seguridad global' in *Monografrías 152. Las migraciones internacionales, percepción y realidad. Un análisis desde la persepectiva de la seguridad*, Escuela Superior de las Fuerzas Armadas.

Vietti, F. and Scribner, T. (2013) 'Human Insecurity: Understanding International Migration from a Human Security Perspective', *Journal on Migration and Human Security*, Vol. 1(1), pp. 17–31.

Vurnek, D., Bengez, A. and Perkov, M. (2018) 'Security aspects of migrations', *Acta Economica Et Turistica*, Vol. 4(2), pp. 121–214.

Weiner, M. (1992). Security, stability, and international migration. *International Security*, 17(3), 91–126.

Wendt, A. (1995) 'Constructing International Politics', *International Security*, Vol. 20(1), pp. 71–81.

Wolffe, J. and Moorhead, G. (2016) 'Religion, Security and Global Uncertainties', Report from a Global Uncertainties Leadership Fellowship, The Open University.

PART 2

Case Studies

CHAPTER 4

The Securitization of Refugees in the European Union

This chapter examines how the European Union has responded to refugee flows through an increasingly securitized and externalized migration governance model. While much of EU policy language refers to "migration" broadly, the measures adopted often have direct and disproportionate effects on refugees and asylum seekers, groups entitled to protection under international and EU law. By tracing the shift from asylum to security, this chapter explores how the EU has reframed refugee movements not as humanitarian challenges, but as political threats requiring deterrence, control, and external management.

In this case, one of the main instruments dealing with migration, and which will also serve as a good example of a measure securitizing refugees, is the Return Directive 2008/115/EC. The chapter will thus start with an exhaustive exploration of this Directive – both the first text and the recast approved in 2018 – and its most contentious parts. In the second part, an analysis of the overall initiatives which have been approved at the EU level will follow, including the New Pact on Migration and Asylum. This will be useful to provide a global overview of some of the measures approved, their impact in the external dimension of EU policy. This will, in turn, be useful to show the direction taken by the EU when dealing with refugee flows and provide a more accurate picture of securitization of refugees in the region and see the extent to which these measures have affected the migrant population.

1 The 2015 'Refugee Crisis' in the European Union

The term 'European refugee crisis' appeared in April 2015, when five boats sank in the Mediterranean Sea while trying to reach European shores. There was an estimated death toll of 1,222 people out of 2,000 of those who were in the boats (Baerwaldt, 2018). In 2015 the number of refugees travelling to Europe also increased more sharply, and thus the media, and everyone else, started paying more attention to the growing refugee flows.

The term 'crisis' has thus been used to describe the large amounts of refugees arriving to Europe in a short period of time. At the start of this so-called "refugee crisis" there were over one million refugees crossing the Mediterra-

 | HTTPS://DOI.ORG/10.1163/9789004704527-006

nean to get to European shores; more than 370,000 in 2016 and 185,000 in 2017. In 2018 numbers kept lowering down, and only a bit more than 140,000 made their way to Europe (UNHCR, 2019). Even though the numbers have largely decreased, we are still talking about a crisis. Betts and Collier (2018) argue that in the case of Europe, this is not a crisis of numbers, which is what most think, but instead it is a crisis of trust. This is due to the perception of many Europeans that their leaders have no real plan for handling these migration flows, which are out of control.

Therefore, we should consider whether this crisis is about the refugee flows themselves or about the European Union migration system, which has not been capable of dealing with this flood. On the one hand, receiving systems in Southern European states failed, and on the other, Northern European states have failed to support them. The absence of rule of law in the admission of migrants and of integration policies has undermined public confidence in their authorities' management criteria, and this in turn has fuelled populists' movements with radical ideas. They untruthfully talk about the socioeconomic impact that immigration causes in their countries and in some cases the use of fake news is also the source of their discourses. Calling a disturbance a crisis can be a means to justify radical action, and this is what populist parties are doing to justify their actions (Liukas, 2018).

But what is more, this refugee crisis has also been called many times the "European refugee crisis", when 40 per cent of the 60 million displaced people worldwide come from the Arab region, and mainly Syria. Many of Syrian refugees have fled to Lebanon and Jordan, also overflowing their national systems and taking even larger numbers of refugees than Europe. Thus, it seems that when we see our own countries being over flooded by massive flows of refugees, we have a crisis, and what politicians have done most times has been to turn their back around and try to refrain them from entering European territory. But refugees are still there, and they are still fleeing their nations to go to neighbouring countries or to cross land or sea to leave further away, even though the EU has closed deals with countries of origin and transit to not let them go through EU borders.

May it be a crisis of numbers or a crisis of trust with the authorities' management with these numbers, there is in fact a crisis when refugees are massively leaving their homes seeking for protection somewhere else. What is important is not to forget that a refugee crisis is a human crisis, and behind the numbers and statistics there are people in despair searching for safety for themselves and for their families.

2 The Return Directive 2008/115/EC

The Directive 2008/115/EC on common standards and procedures in Member States for returning illegally staying third-country nationals (hereafter Return Directive) was approved in June 2008 by the European Parliament under the co-decision procedure by 369 votes to 197 and 106 abstentions. The main purpose of the Directive is to lay down a set of rules and procedures for all Member States on the return of illegal immigrants within the Union. Although every state can still decide whether it wishes to regularize or deport an immigrant found within its territory, the goal of this EU legislation is to be applied once this decision has been taken to establish periods of custody, re-entry bans, and other similar regularizations. For the first time at EU level, the Directive established mandatory return decisions, the preference for voluntary return, the mandatory issuance of entry bans along with return decisions, procedural safeguards in these processes, and grounds for pre-removal detention (European Parliament, 2019). Let's see in more detail each of these requirements.

The Directive states that once the decision to deport an individual has been adopted, there is first a voluntary departure period from seven to thirty days in which, if the deportee does not leave the country, a removal order will be issued. If this order is issued by a judicial authority which believes that the individual might abscond, the person can be placed in custody for a maximum period of six months, extendable by a further of twelve months. In addition to this, if the person does not leave the country during the voluntary period, she can then be forbidden to entry for up to five years, or longer if she presents a threat to public safety.

It took three years to agree on the text, a fact showing how complex the negotiations were. Some of the contentious parts of the Directive concerned the personal scope of the directive, the period of voluntary departure, re-entry bans, detention, procedural rights, and the situation of children (European Parliament, 2020). It is interesting to highlight in this sense that the United Kingdom and Ireland have not opted-in into this area of EU law and have preferred to do the same when it comes to the enforcement of this Directive. In the case of the United Kingdom, for instance, arguing that the Directive does not establish a sufficiently strong returns regime (European Parliament, 2008a).

According to the Slovenian Interior Minister Dragutin Mate speaking on behalf of the Council Presidency-in-Office, the part which was more difficult to agree on was that on legal aid, as there was a multiplicity of views depending on whether states were near to or far from migratory flows. The diversity of political positions and the debate surrounding the text becomes clearer when seeing the opinion of the representatives of different political groups. While the European People's Party (EPP-ED) supported the Directive and considered it a "firm and decisive step", others like the Party of European Socialists (PES) argued against it because it did not offer adequate human rights protection, or according to Greens/EFA group,[1] the established periods of detention were too long and could harm the mental health of detainees (European Parliament, 2008b).

Other groups have also manifested against it. Hélène Goudin, of Independence/Democracy (IND/DEM) said that "the EU is becoming a Fortress Europe (...) The result of this ban or return will lead to an increase in illegal immigration, more human trafficking and a hatred for the system we are setting up in our western world". Giusto Catania, speaking on behalf of the European United Left/Nordic Green Left (GUE, NGL) made much tougher declarations (European Parliament, 2008b):

> The directive is a disgrace, an insult which aims at ruling out thousands of years of welcoming people, of openness in Europe. It seeks to limit free circulation. We are talking about 18 months not 6 months detention without having committed any crime. Detained in degrading and humiliating conditions as the Committee has seen in various detention centers. This directive is being forced upon us by Governments (...) There is a need to consult wider. People are dying to get into the EU, 12,000 have died over recent years. The Mediterranean is becoming a cemetery. We should not approve this directive.

As Kilpatrick (2019) points out, the same introduction of the legislative text was highly controversial since it introduced very low standards governing the removal of migrants. Debates over the text emerged from the very beginning, with a compilation of signatures from more than 600 NGOs advocating for a stronger protection to the human rights of migrants during the same year the norm came into force. The Platform for International Cooperation on Undocumented Migrants (PICUM) even argued in its 2015 report that "the directive fail to establish a principled policy on return which fully respects migrants' dignity and human rights" adding that "references to human rights in the text are vague and mostly limited to the introduction" (Manieri and LeVoy, 2015:4).

Looking in more detail the reasons why the Return Directive has been so widely criticized we see that, as mentioned above, the detention period of migrants is of 6 months but can be extended for up to a maximum of 18

1 This group is made up of Green, European Free Alliance, Pirate, independent, ecological, and animal welfare members of the European Parliament.

months. This has meant that some countries have decided to change their national law to increase their previous period of detention. This is the case of France which, after the approval of the Return Directive, extended its maximum length of detention of 32 days to a maximum of 45 days after passing Law No. 2003–1119 of 26 November 2003.[2] A similar case is that of Italy, which also extended this custody interval to twelve months in application of the Return Directive, but later on in 2014 moved back to a 90 day period[3] (Manieri and LeVoy, 2015:5). We must keep in mind the text of the Directive states that going beyond the six-month period is only an option foreseen for exceptional cases. And in addition to that, the EU Court of Justice has clarified that these detentions are limited only to instances where immigrants are awaiting repatriation.[4] Thence while the length of the period of detention has been questioned by many human rights organizations, this period has then been used by Member States to justify amplifying the time of custody of their national laws.

With regard to detention, there are additional grounds for detention relating to public order by Article 18(1)(c) and considering also the risk of absconding (Article 6). Member State have used the latter to implement an open-ended list of "objective criteria" through which it was rather easy to find a justification for detention. Judicial dialogue has contributed to narrowing down these lists and ensuring that each case is studied individually and based on substantial grounds, being insufficient the mere fact of illegal stay. For instance, criminal records cannot automatically lead to a risk of absconding but there has to be proof that it can lead to such risk (Cornelisse, 2020).

In 2016, a new Partnership Framework was approved by the Commission in accordance with the European Agenda on Migration, seeking to cooperate with third countries to ensure effective returns based on readmission agreements. These agreements were signed with countries like Gambia, Bangladesh, Turkey, Ethiopia, Afghanistan, Guinea, and Ivory Coast. However, these deals were concluded "in the complete absence of a duly parliamentary scrutiny and democratic oversight (…) [that would] ensure appropriate monitoring through the establishment of legally binding frameworks for cooperation, which can be challenged before courts" (Sargentini 2019) and "in the com-

2 Law 2011–672 of June 16, 2011, on Immigration, Integration and Nationality, published in the country's official gazette on June 17, 2011 (Loi n. 2011–672 du 16 juin 2011 relative à l'immigration, à l'intégration et à la nationalié).

3 This happened after the approval of Law 30 ottobre 2014, n. 161, "Disposizioni per l'adempimento degli obblighi derivanti dall'appartenenza dell'Italia all'Unione europea - Legge europea 2013-bis", (14G00174) (GU Serie Generale n.261 del 10–11-2014- Suppl. Ordinario n.83).

4 Case C-357/09 PPU Said Shamilovich Kadzoev (Huchbarov) v. Bulgaria.

plete absence of duly parliamentary scrutiny and democratic and judicial oversight" (Strik, 2020).

In 2017, a Commission Recommendation called for a stricter interpretation of the Return Directive and urged states to harmonize their approaches on the return of third-country nationals.[5] While different human rights organizations again tried to make the Commission take a step back, the following year the Commission proposed a new Return Directive to turn these recommendations into law (Kilpatrick, 2019). Later on, in September 2018 the European Commission proposed a few amendments to the Return Directive. This Proposal has been criticized for "betraying a shift in the EU's immigration agenda by prioritizing speedy returns, increasing possibilities for the use of pre-removal detention, and limiting judicial scrutiny, thus overlooking important human rights and procedural guarantees developed by European and domestic courts (Moraru, Cornelisse and De Bruycker, 2020). In reaction to the Commission's Proposal, and not having this one conduced an impact assessment, the European Parliament issued a draft Report in early 2019. However, since parliamentary elections were taking place that same year the report was never submitted for voting in plenary.

2.1 The *New* Return Directive 2018/0329/(COD)

On 12 September 2018, the commission published a recast proposal of the Return Directive[6] arguing that it needed to "notably reduce the length of return procedures, secure a better link between asylum and return procedures and ensure a more effective use of measures to prevent absconding".[7] However, and as it has been widely criticized, the proposed recast did not come accompanied by a Commission's impact assessment that would justify any of the changes and additions of the new proposed version of the text. Considering this as the latest version of the Return Directive, I find interesting to study in more detail the controversies it has arisen and the reasons behind them. Doing an analysis on the most contentious Articles of the new Return Direct-

5 *See* Commission Recommendation C(2017) 6505 of 27.9.2017 establishing a common "Return Handbook" to be used by Member States' competent authorities when carrying out return related tasks.

6 Proposal for a Directive of the European Parliament and of the Council on common standards and procedures in Member States for returning illegally staying third-country nationals (recast) A contribution from the European Commission to the Leaders' meeting in Salzburg on 19–20 September 2018 COM/2018/634 final. Available at: https://eur-lex.europa.eu/legal-content/EN/TXT/?uri=COM:2018:0634:FIN.

7 European Commission, COM(2018) 634, explanatory memorandum, 12 September 2018, p. 2.

ive seems appropriate at this point, thus an exploration of the most debatable topics of the Directive will be analysed as follows.

2.1.1 Risk of Absconding

In Article 6 there are sixteen grounds for Member States used to justify detention, and the identification of one of them automatically leads to the surmise of risk of absconding.

Frontex also participated in the negotiations by submitting a non-paper in January 2019, arguing in favour of the proposal, and noting that this would further facilitate the agency's tasks. However, as Kilpatrick (2019:6) highlights, "it approaches the Directive from a clear position that coercion, rather than cooperation, is the preferable route to ensure more effective returns". For example, on the risk of absconding (Article 6) Frontex argued that "the increased number of conditions to identify the risk of absconding is assumed to lead to a higher number of detention cases" which would in turn "increase both the number of returnees identified and those taking part in return operations". Arguing that around 44–57% did not show up on the day of the identification if they were not detainees, having them in detention while the documentation process is concluded would certainly benefit the return operations (Frontex, 2019).

However, in the draft report of the Rapporteur Judith Sargentini on behalf of the Committee on Civil Liberties, Justice and Home Affairs, she argued that this long list of criteria proposed by the Commission includes almost all irregularly staying third-country nationals, meaning that the assessment of the risk of absconding can very likely result in the automatic use of detention measures and compromise the principles of proportionality and necessity (Sargentini, 2019).

2.1.2 Obligation to Cooperate

This obligation embodied in Article 7 is a new addition to the proposal given by the Commission, consisting in individuals having to cooperate with the return procedures being held against them. The consequences of not fulfilling such obligation are not specified. However, according to the list of Article 6, failing to cooperate would be one of the criteria to be considered when assessing the risk of absconding.

Sargentini proposes an amendment in her report on not *obliging* them, but to instead "facilitate cooperation between persons facing return procedures". Moreover, she further argues that Member States should at all stages make sure to inform third-country nationals in a language they understand and in a "concise, transparent, intelligible and easily accessible form" (Sargentini, 2019).

2.1.3 Return Decision

A troubled part of Article 8 is that relating to the moment after a decision not to grant a third-country national refugee status is made. According to the proposal of Article 8(c), after this decision has been made, a return decision must be made also immediately after. Sargentini (2019) argues that this obligation to issue a return decision so rapidly is "disproportionate and counterproductive" and that an amendment to ensure that the rights enshrined in Article 47of the EU Charter of Fundamental Rights should be made. Let's remember that the right to asylum, the principle of non-refoulement, the right to an effective remedy but also the right for private and family life are to be protected and would be endangered if the proposal was left as suggested. Imposing an obligation to issue a return decision immediately after the adoption of a negative decision on an asylum application would "create unnecessary legal ambiguity as regard the asylum seeker's legal status pending an appeal or during the time period for lodging an appeal". She further argues that issuing a return decision would determine that the immigrant is on an irregular status and while she would still have the right according to international protection standards to remain in the country during the time of the appeal procedure – which, very often, are lengthy processes – this Article would create confusion on whether she is, in fact, an irregular migrant or not, what her status then is, and about her right to remain on the territory.

The Greek Ombudsman stated that there is no adequate information offered to third-country nationals about return procedures while they are detained in Greek island hotspots. The fact that no one informs them of their rights means that many do not even consider challenging negative asylum decisions, which in turn leads them to a return order (Kilpatrick, 2019).

2.1.4 Voluntary Departure and Entry Bans

One of the changes in Article 9 on voluntary departure refers to the minimum length of time an individual can stay in the country before he is forced to return. While there used to be a 7-day minimum, the Commission's proposal reframes this obligation to establish instead a 30-day maximum period for voluntary departure. While Member States are free to establish a minimum period in their national laws which some may use to extend to longer time frames beyond the seven days, it can also be the case of some states to decide to establish this period to one or two days if they prefer, making it difficult for individuals to arrange their own voluntary departure. That is why Sargentini clarifies that the text should instead persuade states to establish a minimum of at least to fifteen days for voluntary departure, thus not granting a voluntary departure period might make it difficult for them to comply with this voluntary return before coercive measures are applied and thence "undermine the primacy of voluntary return over forced return" (Sargentini, 2019).

Civil society organizations have reported that Member States do not comply with the provisions established in this Article. In Spain, for instance, it has been denounced that voluntary return is not complied with, most immigrants being subject to executive return orders having had no prior time or option of voluntary return (Manzanedo et al, 2013), forcing the return of asylum seekers and refugees not being able to exercise their rights.

Furthermore, the Council's version of Article 13 on entry bans increases the length of entry bans from five to ten years. And what is more, "if the their-country national represents a serious threat to public order, public security or national security", this period could even surpass the ten years. Imposing lengthy re-entry bans on migrants contributes to the logic of criminalizing migrants and refugees. Thus, instead of establishing long periods forbidding them to re-enter the country, reviews of each case individually should be made in order to establish an appropriate period of time according to the particular case and reasons lying behind her expulsion.

2.1.5 Detention

The proposal also introduces new grounds for detention. While the Return Directive stated that Member States could only keep in detention immigrants in cases of risk of absconding or when "the third-country national concerned avoids or hampers the preparation of return or the removal process", the new text would include in Article 18 cases when this person "poses a risk to public policy, public security or national security". This is a rather ambiguous legitimation of detention since depending on the interpretation authorities give to a particular situation, this can more easily fall within one of these situations and thence the probability of finding sufficient grounds for detaining a person will likely increase.

The proposal has been reinforced by a July 2019 CJEU judgment where the court ruled that the interpretation of this addition relating to third-country nationals posing a threat to public order counts with a big margin of appreciation since authorities "are not obliged to justify that the personal conduct of such national constitutes a real, actual and sufficiently grave threat affecting a fundamental interest in society". Thence the mere existence of a suspicion that a third-country national has committed a crime threatening public order can be sufficient grounds justifying that this person can be considered a risk.[8]

In addition to this, the Commission's proposal would also change the minimum period of detention, preventing states from setting a maximum period of detention of less than three months. This would mean that countries like Spain and Portugal would have to extend their time limits of detention since they were established at 60 days (Kilpatrick, 2019).

Furthermore, countries like Spain are using detention as a primary measure instead of applying it "unless other sufficient but less coercive measures can be applied effectively in a specific case". As reported by Pueblos Unidos (Manzanedo et al, 2013), none of the alternative measures to detention are applied neither by the police nor by judicial authorities. While Spanish Immigration Law establishes measures like periodically reporting to authorities, residing obligatorily in a particular place, passport withdrawal, or any other measure that the judge of the case might find appropriate, authorities nevertheless continue resorting to detention as a priority measure.

As Manieri and LeVoy (2015) have pointed out, "the use of detention for migration purposes involves the deprivation of liberty for the administrative convenience of States and has a very detrimental impact on migrants' human rights, even on refugees, and particularly on children and their families"; thence, they strongly suggest that alternatives to detention should be promoted and adopted in accordance with the Return Directive. The United Nations High Commissioner for Refugees (UNHCR) and the Office of the High Commissioner for Human Rights (OHCHR) organized the first Global Roundtable on Alternatives to Detention of Asylum-Seekers, Refugees, Migrants and Stateless Persons in 2011. Non-surprisingly, the main conclusions made reference to finding alternatives to detention. Arguing that "there is no empirical evidence that detention deters irregular migration, or discourages persons from seeking asylum" and that "seeking asylum is not a criminal act and asylum-seekers should not, as a consequence, be penalized for the act of seeking asylum through detention", these experts argued that imposing penal sanctions to persons who have not committed a crime bestows to criminalizing immigration (OHCHR-UNHCR, 2011).

In addition to this, Article 20 – which used to be Article 17 in the first text – also refers to detention and, in this case, deals with the detention of minors

8 Conclusiones del Abogado General Sr. Giovanni Pitruzella, Case C-380/18. Available at: http://curia.europa.eu/juris/document/document.jsf?text=&docid=216086&pageIndex=0&doclang=ES&mode=req&dir=&occ=first&part=1&cid=2599777.

and families. This Article states in its first paragraph that "Unaccompanied minors and families with minors shall only be detained as a measure of last resort and for the shortest appropriate period of time". Nevertheless, even though as a last resort measure, allowing the detention of children breaches the UN Convention on the Rights of the Child since regardless of their situation, detaining them because of their migratory status or that of their parents breaches the principle of the best interest of the child and it is never justifiable or in their best interest.[9] Furthermore, as established in *Abdullahi Elmi and Aweys Abubakar v. Malta*, parents or legal or customary primary caregivers should also not be detained to protect the best interest of the child.[10] Despite the limitations established in the Directive, 17 Member States have detained unaccompanied children and 19 have detained families with children (Manieri and LeVoy, 2015).

2.1.6 Border Procedure

Chapter 5 is dedicated to border procedure. In Article 22, the Commission proposes that once a decision rejecting an application for international protection taken by virtue of Article 41 of the Asylum Procedures Regulation, there will be no voluntary departure period. In paragraph 4, it is established that only those "holding a valid travel document and fulfilling the obligation to cooperate with the competent authorities of the Member States at all stages of the return procedure" may be granted "an appropriate period for voluntary departure". Furthermore, the following paragraph also states that a period of maximum 48 hours can be granted to appeal against the aforementioned return decision. Paragraph (c) adds that this period will only be suspended if there is a risk of breaking the principle of non-refoulement.

This part of the proposal was highly controversial among Member States. In October 2018, the Austrian Presidency of the Council said that the lines on whether the application for border procedure should be mandatory or not was one of the most challenging parts of the text, although a note by the Romanian Presidency a few months later stated that a large majority preferred it for it to be mandatory, although the matter was still highly controversial (Statewatch, 2018).

---

9 In this sense see: UN Committee on the Rights of the Child, *Report of the 2012 Day of General Discussion on The Rights of All Children in the Context of International Migration*. Available at: http://www.ohchr.org/Documents/HRBodies/CRC/Discussions/2012/DGD2012ReportAndRecommendations.pdf.

10 *See* ECtHR Abdullahi Elmi and Aweys Abubakar v. Malta, Application No. 25794/13 and 28151/13, 22 February 2017.

In Sargentini's draft report, she dismisses the entire article, arguing that establishing a maximum of 48 hours to lodge an appeal is "unacceptable in light of the precarious situation of third country nationals subject to a return decision in border procedures and in detention" since many times they do not have access to legal assistance and interpretation, which would lead to damaging their judicial protection. Furthermore, she also argues that an extension of the maximum duration of detention of 22 months for those whose asylum application has been rejected at the border and are subject to a return's procedure would not ensure an effective return but would instead, and according to research, decrease its chances after 30 or 60 days of detention (Sargentini, 2019).

2.2 Assessment of the Return Directive

In the exploratory memorandum of the renewed version of the Return Directive, it is explained that effective return is a primary objective of the European Union and that "in order to address the key challenges to ensure effective returns, a targeted revision of the Return Directive is necessary to notably reduce the length of return procedures, secure a better link between asylum and return procedures an ensure a more effective use of measures to prevent absconding".[11]

Overall, not only was the Return Directive disputed at the time of approval, but it has also arisen many voices against it after the Commission's proposal and the Council's recast version. As Kilpatrick (2019) says in her analysis of the matter:

> The entire aim of the Commission's proposal is to lower fundamental rights standards in order to increase the number of deportations from the EU, yet there is no evidence that this would make the EU's expulsion system any more effective. Even if this were the case, it would be difficult to argue that such harmful and destructive means – such as the massively-expanded use of detention – could justify the ends. It appears that the Commission and Council favour a recast version of the Returns Directive that would both degrade fundamental rights standards and be ineffective, ignoring potential alternatives and

---

11 *See* the "Explanatory Memorandum" of the *Proposal of the European Parliament and of the Council on Common standards and procedure sin member states for returning illegally staying third-country nationals (recast)* 2018/0329 (COD). Available at: https://www.europarl.europa.eu/RegData/docs_autres_institutions/commission_europeenne/com/2018/0634/COM_COM(2018)0634_EN.pdf.

discarding the progress made by member states in implementing such alternatives in the framework of the existing rules.

She argues that there was no public consultation nor impact assessment studying its potential effects before approving the new Returns Directive, and the result was a text which placed "emphasis on coercion at the cost of cooperation, despite a lack of evidence for the effectiveness of forced removals in increasing the overall number of returns and clear evidence of the harms to health and wellbeing caused by forced removals".

As explained in PICUM's report, "the current emphasis on border control in Europe significantly overshadows the need to address other causes of irregularity, such as inadequate visa and residence policies, administrative failures and difficulties in understanding the complex procedures of residence and work permits" (Manieri, M. G. and LeVoy, M., 2015). Furthermore, the lack of existence of any impact assessment makes it impossible to determine whether the Directive has affected return rates or if there is a need for additional EU action. Still, the need to ensure the protection of human rights of third-country nationals in the EU while ensuring a fair and effective return procedure in light of the Return Directive persists.

The Substitute Impact Assessment published by the European Parliament in February 2019 reached a series of conclusions, which will be exposed below along with a short summary explaining the grounds for each of them (European Parliament, 2019):

1) **There is no clear evidence supporting the Commission's claim that its proposal would lead to more effective returns of irregular migrants:** This first point is based on the fact that the time elapsed between the recommendations (such as the Commission's 2017 Recommendations and the Return Handbook) has been very short to objectively affirm that a revision of the legislative framework was necessary. What is more, the Commission's approach in the new proposed text moves away from acceding voluntary departure to focus instead on enabling more detention measures to Member States. The same recast impact assessment argues that the proposal for the new Return Directive, although mentioning a preference for voluntary departure, hardly proposes any provisions on supporting and facilitating them to instead include several additions increasing opportunities for forced return.
2) **The Commission proposal complies with the principle of subsidiarity, but some provisions raise proportionality concerns** This finding is that related to the proportionality of certain provisions of the revised text. The parts arising concerns are those related to adding a

list of criteria indicating risk of absconding, the limitation of possibilities for voluntary return, those related to entry bans, the inclusion of a new ground for detention based on "public policy, public security or national security", the length of detention of three months, and the overall border procedure. As it has already been discussed, the implementation of such measures would rather limit the possibilities for voluntary return while putting at risk the coordination of asylum and return procedures since it seems that the primary focus is on speeding enforcement return decisions.

3) **The Commission proposal would have an impact on several social and human rights of irregular migrants, including likely breaches of fundamental rights**
This third point on the likeliness to breaching fundamental rights is also an important one to consider. On the one hand, the right to asylum and the principle of non-refoulement could be breached by the adoption of Article 7(1)(d). As the European Parliament states in its assessment, the obligation to lodge a request for obtaining a valid travel document to third countries "encompasses a right to confidentiality and the obligation for the State not to request the asylum seeker to contact his or her home country". Other rights like that to liberty and the likeliness to increase the risk of arbitrary detention are also highly controversial because of the criteria set out indicating risk of absconding (Article 6), and the increase in the grounds for detention (Article 18).

4) **The Commission proposal would generate substantial costs for Member States and the EU**
Articles 9, 14, 18, and 22 would require substantial investments to contract new staff and improve infrastructure to ensure, for instance, the existence of enough detention facilities in all Member States. This would not only mean more national investment but also additional EU costs stemming from monitoring and coordinating agencies across the territories.

5) **The Commission proposal raises questions of coherence with other EU legislation, especially legislation that is pending**
The last point, as explained in more detail in the analysis of Article 22, might not be coherent with Article 41 of the proposed Asylum Procedure Regulation affecting coherence between both return and asylum legislation.

These conclusions were also supported by Tineke Strik, the rapporteur in charge of writing a report on the implementation of the Return Directive on behalf of the Committee on Civil Liberties, Justice and Home Affairs. She argues that many of the measures of the Directive have not been contrasted and might not have a direct impact on increasing the number of returnees but on the contrary, they might even have a counterproductive effect. Firstly, because entry bans may make it less likely that returnees want to leave the Member State and secondly, because the short periods of time available for voluntary leaving the country are actually an added difficulty for them to actually be able to make this return successful. She is also concerned that some rights might be put at stake because of the broad interpretation of certain provisions (i.e. risk of absconding), because of the long periods of detention, and the lack of access to legal aid and interpreters, among others issues that have already been highlighted (Strik, 2020).

Less than a year later, in June 2020, another report was published concerning the Return Directive. In this case it was an Implementation Assessment in which there was a complete evaluation of the implementation of the Return Directive. The first part of this report, written by Katharina Eisele, a summary of the main findings is listed (European Parliament, 2020:17–20). Again, it is accentuated that the risk of refoulement is not fully assessed when contemplating return decisions and that the text's emphasis on prioritizing the effective return of irregular migrants "at all costs" might undermine the human costs involved. Other provisions relating to entry bans and detention are also marked as controversial, adding other conclusions related to the lack of transparency due to the lack of disaggregated and comparable data; the increasement of costs related to making detention possible; and the lack of judicial and democratic accountability because of, for instance, informal agreements. All of these are again contentious measures that need to be reviewed.

And what is more, the Return Directive has been complemented in the following years with strategies and policies that further hardened the EU's approach to migration, and to refugees in particular. This includes agreements with third countries aimed at preventing entry into EU territory or facilitating the return of individuals to their transit states. The Global Approach to Migration and Mobility reflects this intention to deter refugee and asylum seeker arrivals, often in exchange for visa facilitation for nationals of those same third countries. Over time, migration has remained a top EU priority, as reaffirmed in the New Strategic Agenda for 2019–2024, which now couples a preference for skilled labour migration with enhanced border enforcement to limit the entry of refugees and asylum seekers.

In sum, although the Directive formally targets all third-country nationals, in practice affects refugees and asylum seekers by facilitating their expulsion without due consideration of protection needs. The conflation of undocumented migrants and refugees under a unified return regime not only erodes procedural safeguards but also contributes to a broader reframing of refugeehood. By embedding security-based logic into the legal architecture, the Directive transforms individuals entitled to international protection into administrative problems or potential risks to be removed. This administrative conflation of refugees and irregular migrants is a core feature of the securitization process: it collapses the legal distinction between protection and enforcement, enabling the treatment of refugees as deportable threats. This reflects the deeper contradiction within EU law: the coexistence of rights-based protection norms and enforcement-first securitization measures.

3 The EU's Approach on Irregular Migration

In the past years several steps have been taken to deal with refugees. Through different strategies and agreements with third countries, the EU has tried to address the growing numbers of refugee flows, and especially those which appeared after the so-called refugee crisis of 2015. In this section, I will focus on some of the main initiatives that have been approved to address this issue in the hope of drawing an accurate picture of the EU's approach in dealing with refugees and other migrant groups. Thus, while a focus on the Return Directive in the previous section was useful to determine what was exactly that was established in the law, and in a particular law which has shaped the legal framework on migration in the EU, when analysing the political field I will take a different approach. Firstly, because political initiatives are approved more easily and often than legislation, thence counting with a multiplicity of documents defining the EU strategy in the field. Secondly, because analysing these political initiatives altogether will provide a more accurate picture of the steps taken in the past years and the direction and goals followed by the EU.

Thus if we go back a few years, an important document dealing with migration in this millennium was the Global Approach to Migration (GAM). It was established in 2005 and it aimed to address the causes of migration and prioritize the rights of migrants. Thence it was supposed not to be an answer to the security interests of EU states, but instead to focus on the figure of the migrant as a person whose rights needed further protection. It became a tool to cooperate with third states on signing readmission agreements in exchange of visa facilitation agreements, mobility partnerships, etc. Thence the two main ideas under which the programme worked were the cooperation with non-EU countries based on the principle of equality, and the idea that the main intention was to protect the migrant and the refugee (Strik, 2017).

Another Global Approach to Migration and Mobility (GAMM) was presented in 2011, being formally adopted in May 2012 by the Council's Committee of Permanent Representatives. The main aim was to address irregular migration and human trafficking, and to cooperate with third countries to better deal with migration, although the text has been denounced as "a means for the EU to restrict access to its territory and for allowing Member States to use migrants as disposable workers" (Martin, 2012). The M for "mobility" was added to cover all forms of mobility and it has worked as a way of facilitating visas as an incentive for third countries to cooperate in combating illegal migration. Since Member States can decide on short-term visas, this part of the GAMM requires Member States to voluntarily give up their discretion. In practice many have not done so, which in turn means that third countries cannot fully cooperate. That is why European Commission officials have complained that Mobility Partnerships cannot be dealt with because of the unwillingness to cooperate by Member States (Strik, 2017).

It is interesting the comparison that Martin (2012) makes on the evolution of the Global Approach on Migration of 2005 and that of 2011. While in the first integration of immigrants is emphasized for "all areas of importance including labour and socio-economic, public health, cultural and political dimensions", the later text is directed towards temporary works rather than full residents. In this sense, the 2011 approach talks about the need to improve the effectiveness of policies related to the integration of migrants into the labour market of the destination country.

There is broad consensus that GAMM policies seek to fight against irregular migration, which involves mostly refugees and asylum seekers, and ensure the return of these migrants through readmission agreements (Strik, 2017). And while at times these frameworks theoretically want to safeguard migrants' and refugees' rights, in practice and through its implementation this is rather unreal. The prioritization of internal security and border control over the right to seek for asylum or the protection of non-refoulement do not help in improving the protection of third-country nationals but instead their human rights are set aside. The UN Special Rapporteur on the human rights of migrants in 2015, François Crépeau, also expressed his opinion in this sense, pointing out that "the overall focus on security and the lack of policy coherence within the Approach as a whole creates a risk that any benefits arising from human rights and development projects will be overshadowed by the secondary effects of more security-focused policies".

The Committee of the Regions also issued an opinion document[12] in which one of their considerations was to call "for a policy to combat irregular immi-

12 Committee of the Regions, *Opinion of the Committee of the Regions: The Global Approach to Migration and Mobility* CIVEX-V-027, 96th plenary session, 18 and 19 July 2012.

gration which is not based solely on border controls and the interception of migrants on departure, but also on effective legal entry opportunities which are also open to less-skilled workers, taking into account the specificities of the individual Member States".

The Strategic Agenda for the period 2019–2024 has put once again migration policy as one of the priorities to address during these years. The four main goals of the Agenda are to (1) protect citizens and freedoms, (2) develop a strong and vibrant economic base, (3) build a climate-neutral, green, fair, and social Europe, and (4) promote European interests and values on the global stage. Included in the first of these objectives is to develop a fully functioning comprehensive migration policy, calling for deepening cooperation with third countries and reforming the Dublin Regulation to balance shared responsibility (European Council, 2019). Having agreed on a new EU Strategic Agenda for the period of 2024–2029, once again, in the security pillar to build a "strong and secure Europe" (European Council, 2024), a comprehensive approach to migration and border management continue being part of some of the main concerns of the Union.

Once again we see some differences between the way in which migration and refugees were addressed in the latest agenda presented in 2014 and the one published in 2019. While both strategies seek to fight against illegal migration, they are designed to contend unwanted flows of refugees. In the first one the idea was to reinforce skilled labour from third countries, while in 2019, the EU considers the protection of external borders as an absolute prerequisite for the security of Europeans. The asylum and returns policy along with border enforcement is much more reinforced in the latest agenda, although the issue of how to establish a harmonized and comprehensive European policy to address immigration is rather vague (Joannin, 2019).

3.1 New Pact on Migration and Asylum

More recently, the New Pact on Migration and Asylum (hereafter New Pact) has taken the stage. This was one of the flagship proposals of President Ursula von der Leyen in 2020. That same year, the European Commission presented the New Pact as a way to offer a "comprehensive European approach to migration" and which puts in place "a predictable and reliable migration management system". The Commission argued that the Pact will promote faster border procedures, a fair sharing of responsibility and solidarity with flexible contributions, further partnerships with third countries, and boosting a common EU system for returns with a stronger role of the European Border and Coast Guard with a newly appointed EU Return Coordinator (European

Commission, 2020). The New Pact was finally approved by the European Parliament on 10 April 2024, and formally adopted the following month, on 14 May.

The New Pact it consists of a legal framework that establishes consistent rules for all Member States on migration with the aim to "ensure that the Union has strong and secure external borders, that people's rights are guaranteed, and that no EU country is left alone under pressure" (European Commission, 2024). As in the past years countries have taken unilateral and uncoordinated steps to deal with the arrival of asylum seekers, the New Pact seeks to balance the principles of responsibility and solidarity among the Union, including a system of mandatory solidarity to distribute migratory pressure more evenly through a "solidarity pool".

In sum, the New Pact is based on four main pillars. The first pillar is in relation to securing external borders through "robust screening", a migration database, mandatory border procedures, more efficient returns, and a Crisis Regulation providing protocols in emergency situations. Examples of regulations in this first pillar are the Screening Regulation or the Crisis and Force Majeure Regulation. The first pillar designs a pre-entry procedure to offer a rapid examinator of the asylum seeker who arrived at the EU, which is then stored in the European Dactylopscopy (Eurodac) database system. The Crisis and Force Majeure Regulation are a set of rules that will apply in times of sudden and massive arrival of asylum seekers and refugees, as what happened during the 2015 migratory crisis or the COVID-19 pandemic. In these cases, Member States will be allowed to apply harder security measures such as extending the border procedure and detention times for up to 20 weeks. Countries like Germany or NGOs have voiced concerns, arguing that this Regulation could infringe the principle of non-refoulement or, for instance, degrade the rights of children (Liboreiro and Genovese, 2023).

A second pillar is dedicated to the design of faster and more efficient procedures. This is done through clear asylum rules through the Asylum Migration Management Regulation, which determines which is the member state responsible for handling an asylum application. There is also the Qualification Regulation, harmonizing criterial for international protection, or the Asylum Procedure Regulation, establishing obligations for cooperation between countries. The third pillar is on building an effective system of solidarity and responsibility. The main purpose of this pillar is to ensure solidarity among all EU countries when dealing with migration through operational and financial support. One of the rules that have remained is that asylum seekers must apply for international protection in the first EU country of first entry, and this will be the one responsible for deciding on their asylum application. The last pillar is on embedding migration in international partnerships. Through this, the EU continues designing externalization measures to prevent unwanted migration before it arrives to EU territory and to facilitate the return of those entering or staying illegally. This is what the EU calls "preventing irregular departures", which are "strengthened capacities of border management authorities in priority partner countries" (European Commission, 2024). Or "cooperation on readmission", based on ensuring cooperation on return and readmission of migrants – often asylum seekers – to third countries.

Many voices have risen against it. The pact has been described as a "push-back" and criticized "for catering to the priorities of the more conservative and anti-immigrant member states such as Hungary, Poland, and Slovakia" (Kirişci, Erdoğan, Eminoğlu, 2020). It is a pact which will not, according to Home Affairs Commissioner Ylva Johansson, satisfy anyone, adding that "voluntary solidarity is not enough (...) there should be no way for Member State to have an easy way out" (Zalan, 2020).

After its official approval, several organizations have raised concerns on the ways in which the New Pact may harshen the situation of already vulnerable groups such as refugees and asylum seekers seeking protection in the EU. Martin Nyman, senior legal advisor at Civil Rights Defenders, explained after the New Pact came into force that "Every day, brutal human rights violations occur at Europe's borders. The EU's new migration pact will worsen this situation and significantly increase refugees' and asylum seekers' suffering. People will be prevented from seeking and receiving protection from war and persecution" (CRD, 2024). For instance, through the present the solidarity mechanism, states can pay their way out of the responsibility to accept their proportional share of EU asylum seekers, and countries like Sweden have already announced they are open to paying to avoid participating in the reallocation system (Sunderland, 2024). In addition, countries like Poland have refused to take part in any solidarity mechanisms, and it remains to be seen what the EU will do to force countries to comply with their obligations in these cases (González, 2024).

Another criticism is in relation to the reference of "safe third country". A new feature of the New Pact is that allowing member states to return or deport asylum seekers to third countries where they have a connection. That is, if the asylum seeker has spent time in such country before reaching the EU, she may be returned to this country if it is considered a safe third country. The problem is that these countries are not always safe, yet asylum seekers may be returned there despite the risk of human rights violations. An example would be a return to Tunisia, a country that has supported violent and collective expulsions of sub-Saharan Africans to Libya and Algeria (EuroMed, 2023).

In this sense, it is also important emphasizing the ways in which the EU has attempted to externalize the processing of asylum claims in Albania, or border control in Tunisia, Egypt, and Mauritania. Instead of setting higher standards for the protection of the rights of refugees, the new reforms "will put people at heightened risk of human rights violations" (Amnesty International, 2024).

In conclusion, the emphasis lays on measures to capture, identify, contain, return, or detain refugees and asylum seekers through the reinforcement of borders and border externalization and represents the sidelining of humanitarianism and a more robust approach to exceptionalism (Stępka, 2023). In time, the EU seems to continuously base its migratory system on security measures instead of human rights protection. The framing of refugee arrivals as "pressure" on external borders reveals how security logics dominate even in ostensibly humanitarian contexts. Refugees are not treated as rights-holders but as risk vectors: to be processed, surveilled, or deflected.

3.2 The External Dimension of Migration Control

As one can see, there have been several laws and policies over the years trying to address the management of refugees at the European level, from strategies, to agendas, approaches, and pacts. Still, the EU has been unable to find a harmonized and coherent approach to immigration that suits all the interests of Member States, and it has also failed to protect the figure of the immigrant, be it legal, irregular, an asylum seeker, or a refugee. A third country national whose rights should be at the forefront of one's interests since international treaties and conventions establish their human rights and guarantees. Nevertheless, this framework has been used to pass new legislation, adopt new public policies, and reframe national frameworks. In addition, there have also been non-legal initiatives, crucial to understand the development of specific manoeuvres, operations, and actions taken by states.

At the international level, the EU has also looked for cooperation with third countries, as also shown by the application of the Global Approach to Migration and Mobility, a tool to design a framework of external migration and asylum policy. An example of an agreement with another country is that of Turkey, as previously stated in an earlier chapter, through which refugees and asylum seekers who arrived at EU land from Turkey would be return to the latter country in exchange for visa liberalization for Turkish citizens and a payment of 6 billion Euros under the Facility for Refugees in Turkey (European Parliament, 2018). In July 2023, the European Commission also signed a controversial pact with Tunisia to fight irregular migration (European Commission, 2023). In this case, 127 million euros are made available in budget support to the latter country as a response to an increase in boats leaving North Africa and making their way to Europe (Al Jazeera, 2023; Reuters, 2023). These arrangements disregard the specific legal status of asylum seekers and refugees, treating them as logistical problems to be outsourced rather than individuals with rights under international and EU law. In this way, externalization reinforces the perception of refugees as burdens to be managed, not protected.

In fact, a key feature of the EU's approach to dealing with immigration is cooperation with third countries. The Migration Partnership Framework adopted in June 2016 tries to address the "refugee crisis" of 2015 by making agreements with non-Member States. While this was not the first initiative to find agreements on refugee movements, but the tone is very different from previous documents (Clare, 2017). As Lehne (2016) states, "the EU's interests are laid out in brutally clear terms [and] the approach focuses almost exclusively on keeping people out and sending them back". What happens in turn is that the EU's interests are put at the forefront while mentioning the ones of African countries in more general terms. The purpose of these agreements is to cooperate with third countries so that these readmit their nationals in exchange of certain incentives (such as visa facilitation or liberalization, development aid or trade preferences), so that readmission procedures are efficient and enforced. Or they can also be used to strengthen border control at these countries so that potential refugees do not reach the EU in the first place.

The EU provided Ukraine with resources to sign readmission agreements to facilitate returns, and Italy negotiated with the Gaddafi government to prevent migrants from leaving its shores, despite the well-known human rights abuses of this country (Frelick, Kysel and Podkul, 2016). All in all, the refugee crisis led to the EU seeking for externalizing migration related issues, and it sought to shift responsibility towards third countries, especially those transit countries, to refrain potential refugee waves from entering the EU.

The Treaty of Amsterdam allowed the EU to sign readmission agreements with non-Member States, but this practice has raised concerns on the avoidance of judicial and democratic accountability (European Parliament, 2020; Molinari, 2019). However, there have also been informal means of cooperation which have increased the focus on operationalizing returns of irregular migrants, further uplifting doubts.

Furthermore, Frontex – the European Border and Coast Guard Agency – is the main body managing border control efforts in the EU. The agency has been reinforced by a wide set of operations and policies and has a budget that has not stopped increasing since its creation. In 2016, it had a monitoring role in the Aegean Sea,[13] but shortly after it also patrolling Greek and Turkish waters and pushing back boats with refugees back to Turkey.[14] The European Agenda of 2015 and the "Smart Borders" initiative were designed to "saving lives and securing external borders" through cooperation with Frontex. However, surveillance technologies and have since then been used to push back boats to the countries where they departed and thence make sure that they never reach EU land. This has resulted in raising concerns on the vulnerability of human rights of migrants at sea.

Matteo de Bellis, Amnesty International's Refugee Rights Researcher, explains that Frontex uses plans and drones to spot people at sea trying to reach EU land and they alert the Libyan coastguards to take them back to Libya, where they face arbitrary detention and torture on a mass scale (Amnesty International, 2023). Human Rights Watch argues, in the same line, that by following these practices, Frontex is complicit in the abuse of human rights. In addition, Judith Sunderland, associate director at the organization, further argues that "Frontex's rhetoric around saving lives remains tragically empty as long as the border agency doesn't use the technology and information at its disposal to ensure that people are rescued promptly and can disembark at safe ports" (HRW, 2022). Similarly, the illegal pushback from Greece to Turkey and violence against refugees and other migrant groups in Greece has been covered by Frontex, showing a lack of transparency and failing on its duty to prevent human rights violations (Amnesty International, 2021; EuroNews, 2022).

As Clare explains, these agreements are problematic on a number of levels. On the one hand, they tie important policy areas to cooperation on migration "in ways that may undermine the EU's other policy goals and commitments". On the other hand, the incentives they involve are just not enough to mobilize African countries, since the remittances they get from their nationals living abroad are more significant than some of the offerings given by the EU (Clare, 2017:14). It can also be viewed as a way to tie migration to cooperation with development countries, thence their economic growth partly becomes conditioned to the way in which they deal with refugees internally. But it also fails to address the root causes of migration, linked to the political and economic situation of fragile states, and the lack of services related to education and labour, not to mention that the EU's goal to return third-country national

13 NATO (2016) 'NATO Defence Ministers Agree on NATO support to assist with the Refugee and Migrant Crisis', 11 February. Available at: https://www.nato.int/cps/en/natohq/news_127981.htm.

14 Akkerman, M. (2016) 'Border Wars: The arms dealers profiting from Europe's refugee tragedy', *Transnational Institute.*

overlooks the poor human rights records of certain countries they are cooperating with. As Oxfam International (2016) denounced, "by choosing to outsource third countries Europe's border control and the responsibility for managing refugees, Europe attempts to outsource its obligations to respect human rights". And what is more, demands have been made to these third countries to prevent irregular departures going to Europe, what Amnesty international has reported as being a way to put refugees, asylum seekers and migrants in general in their countries at risk for a prolonged and arbitrary detention, refoulement and ill-treatment (Amnesty International, 2014).

It is unclear to what extent these EU initiatives have been efficient or not, but the politics of fear have never been a good companion of human rights (Mourenza, 2016). And terrorist attacks cannot be used by states, nor by the European Union, to establish harsh measures that undermine the basic rights of both nationals and non-nationals (HRW, 2016). In sum, criticisms about the norms being applied by the EU on migration issues are already common. Its protection of the human rights of immigrants is not what would be expected seeing its internal common standards and framework on fundamental rights, and the fact that they negotiate with countries whose respect of human rights is also questionable is not exemplary of an advanced and protective organization.

These agreements, though framed as pragmatic tools of cooperation, are grounded in a logic of deterrence that positions refugees as liabilities to be contained elsewhere. The use of "safe third countries" and the outsourcing of asylum processing functionally displace EU responsibility while simultaneously casting refugees as external threats. This securitized outsourcing not only undermines international protection norms but also recasts refugeehood as a legal inconvenience to be managed beyond the EU's borders. What emerges is a system in which legal distance enables moral and political disavowal.

4 Conclusions

The EU's legal and operational responses to refugee flows demonstrate how protection is increasingly subordinated to risk management. This securitized framework not only reshapes how migration is governed but redefines who counts as a legitimate subject of rights. Refugees, despite formal legal status, are framed as actors whose presence must be deterred or outsourced. This tension between legal obligation and political framing lies at the heart of the global securitization of refugeehood, and constitutes a core thread uniting the case studies in this book.

As Strik argues (2017), if the EU continues focusing on the expulsion and fight against irregular migration when dealing with migration issues, other EU external policy objectives such as regional stability, cooperation, rule of law, peace, security, and economic growth might never come into the picture. A serious reflection should be made as to how to reach a coherent strategy that comprises equality and compliance with the human rights of all.

When the refugee was presented as a potential terrorist, society had to be protected from this transnational movement that could contaminate and attack our societies. During the refugee crisis, the migrant could take advantage of healthcare and other public services. And in the times of COVID-19, they were the ones to spread the virus across borders. These ideas, presented in political and media discourses, have extended the perception that refugees are security threats. Thence justifying the application of security measures, restricting their rights to secure national security.

These discourses alone are not the only element leading to the securitization of refugees. But these events are usually accompanied by financial difficulties such as economic crises or new terrorist attacks. It is in the context of a combination of factors that lead to insecurity that the notion of 'crisis' is construed. Some of the measures to contend immigration are aimed at refugees and are passed after declaring a state of emergency as a response, for instance, to a terrorist attack. In times of emergency, there can be restrictions on certain rights. Nevertheless, the principles of proportionality and necessity need to be balanced.

As Strik argues (2017), if the EU continues focusing on the expulsion and fight against irregular migration and incoming refugees when dealing with migration issues, other EU external policy objectives such as regional stability, cooperation, rule of law, peace, security, and economic growth might never come into the picture. A serious reflection should be made as to how to reach a coherent strategy that comprises equality and compliance with the human rights of all. Overall, what seems to be clear is that over time, and with more intensity after 9/11, the European Union has continuously securitized refugee groups, talking about the 'need' to protect EU borders from external threats.

As explained in a report by Statewatch and the Transnational Institute (Jones et al., 2022), "the EU is always keen to proclaim its origins in and ongoing commitment to upholding peace, human rights, democracy and the rule of law, and promoting diplomacy and soft power over militarism and war. Upon closer examination, however, the bloc's spending priorities make clear that its identity as a political project is shifting". Since 9/11, there has been a noticeable expansion of national and international security mechanisms which has by now been normalized. The intensification of border control and border externalization measures has been used in the name of the War on Terror, as a contention response to the refugee crisis, and more recently with the COVID-19 pandemic. Today, these measures have become everyday policies integrated in our societies and which many believe to be necessary for the normal functioning of the state. Instead of focusing only in ways to increase national security, we should also be finding ways to secure the rights of the most vulnerable groups in our societies.

In sum, the EU's legal and political instruments, from the Return Directive to migration partnerships, reveal a coherent shift in migration governance: from protection to control, from law to logistics, from rights to risk. This shift disproportionately impacts refugees, whose status is no longer shielded by humanitarian law but subjected to a security calculus that prioritizes exclusion and deterrence. In treating refugee flows as potential crises and external threats, the EU exemplifies the very dynamics of securitization this book aims to interrogate: a legal regime of protection gradually hollowed out by political imperatives of containment and fear.

As this chapter has shown, the EU's approach to refugee governance increasingly reflects a securitization logic that undermines its own legal commitments. Although refugees are formally protected under the 1951 Convention and the Charter of Fundamental Rights, they are routinely subjected to policies that prioritize deterrence, return, and externalization over access to protection. The portrayal of refugee movements as potential threats – particularly in the wake of terrorist attacks and political backlash – has contributed to a profound reframing of refugeehood itself. Within the EU framework, refugees are no longer treated primarily as rights-bearing individuals fleeing persecution, but as irregular entrants to be screened, contained, or removed. This shift exemplifies the broader puzzle at the heart of this book: how and why refugees, once at the core of the humanitarian regime, have come to be governed as risks to be managed.

References

Amnesty International (2014) 'The human cost of Fortress Europe. Human Rights violations against migrants and refugees at Europe's borders'. Available at: https://www.amnesty.org/download/Documents/8000/eur050012014en.pdf.

Amnesty International (2021) 'Greece: Pushbacks and violence against refugees and migrants are de facto border policy'. Available at: https://www.amnesty.org/download/Documents/8000/eur050012014en.pdf.

Amnesty International (2023) 'EU: Frontex's lack of transparency on Libyan cooperation to be heard in court'. Available at: https://www.amnesty.org/download/Documents/8000/eur050012014en.pdf.

Amnesty International (2024) 'EU: Migration and Asylum Pact reforms will put people at heightened risk of human rights violations'. Available at: https://www.amnesty.org/download/Documents/8000/eur050012014en.pdf.

Baerwaldt, N. (2018) 'The European Refugee Crisis: Crisis for Whom?', Border Criminologies, University of Oxford.

Betts, A. and Collier, P. (2018) *'How Europe Can Reform Its Migration Policy. The Importance of Being Sustainable', Foreign Affairs.* Available at: https://www.foreignaffairs.com/articles/europe/2018-10-05/how-europe-can-reform-its-migration-policy?cid=int-fls&pgtype=hpg.

Clare, C. (2017) 'The EU Migration Partnership Framework: time for a rethink?', *Deutsches Institut fur Entwicklungspolitik*, Discussion Paper No. 28/2017, ISBN 978-3-96021-053-5.

Cornelisse, G. (2020) 'Judicial dialogue about the Return Directive: Which role for courts in an era of executive governance?', *EU Immigration and Asylum Law and Policy*. Available at: https://eumigrationlawblog.eu/judicial-dialogue-about-the-return-directive-which-role-for-courts-in-an-era-of-executive-governance/.

Crépeau, F. (2015) 'Report of the Special Rapporteur on the human rights of migrants. Banking on mobility over a generation: follow-up to the regional study on the management of the external borders of the European Union and its impact on the human rights of migrants', 8 May 2015, A/HRC/29/36, UN Human Rights Council.

CRD (2024) 'The EU's new migration and asylum pact hollows out the right to asylum', *Civil Rights Defenders*, 11 April. Available at: https://crd.org/2024/04/11/the-eus-new-migration-and-asylum-pact-hollows-out-the-right-to-asylum/.

EuroMed (2023) 'EU Migration Pact to impose sweeping new human rights rollback', *EuroMed Rights*, 20 December. Available at: https://euromedrights.org/publication/eu-migration-pact-to-impose-sweeping-new-human-rights-rollback/.

EuroNews (2022) 'EU border agency Frontex covered up illegal migrant pushbacks, says report', 14 October. Available at: https://www.euronews.com/my-europe/2022/10/14/eu-border-agency-frontex-covered-up-illegal-migrant-pushbacks-says-report.

European Commission (2020) 'A fresh start on migration: Building confidence and striking a new balance between responsibility and solidarity', European Commission Press release, 23 September 2020. Available at: https://ec.europa.eu/commission/presscorner/detail/en/ip_20_1706.

European Commission (2024) *Pact on Migration and Asylum. A common EU system to manage migration*, European Commission. Available at: https://home-affairs.ec.europa.eu/policies/migration-and-asylum/pact-migration-and-asylum_en.

European Council (2019) 'A new strategic agenda 2019–2024', European Council. Available at: https://www.consilium.europa.eu/media/39914/a-new-strategic-agenda-2019-2024-en.pdf.

European Council (2024) 'Strategic agenda 2024–2029', European Council. Available at: https://www.consilium.europa.eu/en/european-council/strategic-agenda-2024-2029/#secure.

European Parliament (2008a) 'Parliament adopts directive on return of illegal migrants', European Parliament Press Release, Available at: https://www.europarl.europa.eu/sides/getDoc.do?pubRef=-//EP//TEXT+IM-PRESS+20080616IPR31785+0+DOC+XML+V0//EN.

European Parliament (2008b) 'Return Directive debate: political groups hold different positions ahead of vote', European Parliament Press Release, Available at: https://www.europarl.europa.eu/sides/getDoc.do?type=IM-PRESS&reference=20080616IPR31741&language=EN.

European Parliament (2019) 'The proposed Return Directive (recast) Substitute Impact Assessment', European Parliamentary Research Service. Available at: https://www.europarl.europa.eu/RegData/etudes/STUD/2019/631727/EPRS_STU(2019)631727_EN.pdf.

European Parliament (2020) *The Return Directive 2008/115/EC European Implementation Assessment*, European Parliamentary Research Service, June 2020. Available at: https://www.europarl.europa.eu/RegData/etudes/STUD/2020/642840/EPRS_STU(2020)642840_EN.pdf.

Frontex (2019) 'Non-Paper: Recast proposal of the Return Directive', European Border and Coast Guard Agency.

González, C. (2024) 'The EU Pact on Migration and Asylum: context, challenges and limitations', *Real Instituto El Cano*. Available at: https://www.realinstitutoelcano.org/en/analyses/the-eu-pact-on-migration-and-asylum-context-challenges-and-limitations/.

HRW (2022) 'EU: Frontex Complicit in Abuse in Libya', *Human Rights Watch*, 12 December. Available at: https://www.hrw.org/news/2022/12/12/eu-frontex-complicit-abuse-libya.

IDC (2015) *There are alternatives: A handbook for preventing unnecessary immigration detention (revised edition)*, International Detention Coalition. Available at: https://idcoalition.org/publication/there-are-alternatives-revised-edition/.

Joannin, P. (2019) 'From crisis exit to world challenges: The EU's Strategic Agenda 2019', Foundation Robert Schuman, European Issues n.521.

Jones, C., Kilpatrick, J. and Maccanico, Y. (2022) At What Cost? Funding the EU's security, defence, and border policies, 2021–2027. A guide for civil society on how EU budget works', *Statewatch and the Transnational Institute*.

Kilpatrick, J. (2019) 'The revised Returns Directive: a dangerous attempt to step up deportations by restricting rights', *Statewatch*. Available at: https://www.statewatch.org/media/documents/analyses/no-346-returns-directive.pdf.

Kirişci, K., Erdoğan, M. and Eminoğlu, N. (2020) 'The EU's "New Pact on Migration and Asylum" is missing a true foundation', *Brookings*, 6 November. Available at: https://www.brookings.edu/blog/order-from-chaos/2020/11/06/the-eus-new-pact-on-migration-and-asylum-is-missing-a-true-foundation/.

Lehne, S. (2016) 'Upgrading the EU's migration partnerships', *Carnegie Europe*. Available at: https://carnegieeurope.eu/2016/11/21/upgrading-eu-s-migration-partnerships-pub-66209.

Molinari C. (2019) 'The EU and its perilous journey through the migration crisis: informalisation of the EU return policy and rule of law concerns', *European Law Review*, Vol. 44, No. 6, 824.

OHCHR-UNHCR (2011) 'Global Roundtable on Alternatives to Detention of Asylum-Seekers, Refugees, Migrants and Stateless Persons: Summary Conclusions', 11–12 May 2011. Available at: https://www.ohchr.org/Documents/Issues/Migration/Events/SummaryConclusions.pdf.

Oxfam International (2016) 'Migration compact is attempt to outsource EU's obligation to respect human rights', 7 June. Available at: https://www.oxfam.org/es/node/9025.

Liukas, C. (2018) 'A crisis begins when we call it a crisis', University of Helsinki.

Manieri, M. G. and LeVoy, M. (2015) 'PICUM Position Paper on EU Return Directive', Platform for International Cooperation on Undocumented Migrants.

Manzanedo, C., Campos, A., Izuzquiza, D. and Trillo-Figueroa, J. (2014), 'CIE Informe 2013, Criminalizados, Internados, Expulsados'. Available at: https://www.entreculturas.org/files/documentos/estudios_e_informes/InformeCIE2013.pdf?download.

Martin, M. (2012) 'The Global Approach to Migration and Mobility: the state of play', *Statewatch*. Available at: https://www.statewatch.org/media/documents/analyses/no-215-gamm-state-of-play.pdf.

Moraru, M., Cornelisse, G., De Bruycker, P. (2020) *Law and Judicial Dialogue on the Return of Irregular Migrants from the European Union*, New York: Hart Publishing.

Sargentini, J. (2019) 'Draft Report on the proposal for a directive of the European Parliament and of the Council on common standards and procedures in Member States for returning illegally staying third-country nationals (recast)' 2018/0329 (COD), Committee on Civil Liberties, Justice and Home Affairs. Available at: https://www.europarl.europa.eu/doceo/document/LIBE-PR-632950_EN.pdf.

Statewatch (2019) 'EU: Common European Asylum System: deadlock in the Council as "frontline" Member States oppose mandatory "border procedures", *Statewatch News*, 30 April. Available at: https://www.statewatch.org/news/2019/april/eu-com

mon-european-asylum-system-deadlock-in-the-council-as-frontline-member-states-oppose-mandatory-border-procedures/.
Strik, T. (2017) 'The Global Approach to Migration and Mobility', *Groningen Journal of International Law*, Vol. 5(2).
Strik, T. (2020) 'Report on the implementation of the Return Directive (2019/2208 (INI)', Committee on Civil Liberties, Justice and Home Affairs, European Parliament. Available at: https://www.europarl.europa.eu/doceo/document/A-9-2020-0238_EN.html.
Sunderland, J. (2024) 'How Sweden Should Carry Out the EU Migration Pact', *Human Rights Watch*, 2 July. Available at: https://www.hrw.org/news/2024/07/02/how-sweden-should-carry-out-eu-migration-pact.
UNHCR (2019), 'Mediterranean situation', Operation Portal Refugee Situations, UNHCR. Available at: https://data2.unhcr.org/en/situations/mediterranean.
Zalan, E. (2020) 'Commissioner: No one will like new EU migration pact', EU Observer, 18 September 2020. Available at: https://euobserver.com/migration/149475.

CHAPTER 5

The Securitization of Refugees in the United States

The United States has a long history of immigration, being built itself by migrants from overseas. Nevertheless, it has also been a nation of strong anti-immigrant sentiments, which were reinforced after the September 11 events. Right after 9/11, new laws strengthening national security and in defence from the terrorist threat were passed, and in the following years legislators continued to focus on the same matters. However, the defence of national security has also involved a drawback on the rights of immigrant origin and non-citizens in the country.

Therefore, the chapter focuses specifically on how securitization dynamics in the United States have targeted refugees and asylum seekers. Despite their formal protection under US asylum law and the Refugee Convention, these groups have been recast as suspect populations, especially when originating from politically sensitive or majority-Muslim countries. This shift offers a stark example of how legal systems can be mobilized to erode protection through the lens of national security.

With the passing of the USA PATRIOT Act of 2001, a cluster of anti-immigrant laws arose, which has thence made the United States a nation at an advanced stage of the process of securitizing migration. In the following lines, the USA PATRIOT Act will be analysed to see which were its main additions and changes with respect to immigration, and later on I will complement them with some of the laws that were approved in the following years on the same line. Since many of them were passed in the aftermath of 9/11 but are still enforced today, they are still relevant to make this study. However, special emphasis is also made to legislation passed during the first Trump's administration, since those years were also a period where the same direction of uprising national security in connection with immigration law was enhanced, which had a real impact on non-citizens' rights, and particularly for refugees.

1 USA PATRIOT ACT 2001

One of the most important additions after the September 11 attacks of 2001 was the passing of the United and Strengthening America by Providing Appropriate Tools Required to Intercept and Obstruct Terrorism (USA PATRIOT Act) and new national security policies. In the aftermath of 9/11, the protection of

 | HTTPS://DOI.ORG/10.1163/9789004704527-007

the rights of refugees and other migrants trying to enter the US or those already in the territory was sacrificed in exchange for greater security measures to protect the country. Only seven weeks after the attacks the Act was enacted. In this sense, the focus has been on bringing together two figures: that of the immigrant, and that of the terrorist.

The USA PATRIOT Act was enacted on 26 October 2001 under the Bush administration, which defended the need for expanding the definition of terrorism because the Alien Terrorist Removal Court Act of 1996 did not suffice under current immigration threats to security (Friman, 2006). Furthermore, the range of aliens who could be deported from US territory on terrorism-related grounds was enlarged, while also reducing their procedural rights. Overall, the migrant – and also the refugee – is very much at the centre of this statute, being directly tackled and connected with terrorist offences.

1.1 The Concept of Terrorism

While one of the main goals of the Act was to identify and detain terrorist aliens, the Department of Homeland Security (DHS) prioritized the "apprehension and deportation" of criminal aliens as part of the war on terror (Friman, 2006).

One of the most controversial points of the USA PATRIOT Act is Section 411, establishing that any individual who "knows or reasonably should know" is giving material support to a terrorist organization will be committing an offence. As the definition of terrorist organization was expanded, so was the scope of Section 411, which would lead to include a wide range of organizations which were not until then thought to be related to terrorism. According to this Section, engaging in terrorist activity means:

> In an individual capacity or as a member of an organization, to: (1) commit or to incite to commit, under circumstances indicating an intention to cause death or serious bodily injury, a terrorist activity; (2) prepare or plan a terrorist activity; (3) gather information on potential targets for terrorist activity; (4) solicit funds or other things of value for a terrorist activity or a terrorist organization (with an exception for lack of knowledge); (5) solicit any individual to engage in prohibited conduct or for terrorist organization membership (with an exception for lack of knowledge); or (6) commit an act that the actor knows, or reasonably should know, affords material support, including a safe house, transportation, communications, funds, transfer of funds or other material financial benefit, false documentation or identification, weapons (including chemical, biological, or radiological weapons), explosives, or training for the commission

of a terrorist activity; to any individual who the actor knows or reasonably should know has committed or plans to commit a terrorist activity; or to a terrorist organization (with an exception for lack of knowledge).

Section 219 of the INA also designates a list of groups as foreign terrorist organizations. The USA PATRIOT Act retains this provision but in addition to this, it attaches immigration consequences to involvement with a terrorist organization. From the one hand, it establishes a second type of "designated organization", which can be determined by the Secretary of State when she finds out that an organization commits, incites, prepares, plans, gathers information for, solicits funds for or engagement in a prohibited conduct, or affords material support toward a terrorist activity. Describing terrorism as any crime involving the use of a "weapon or dangerous device (other than for mere personal monetary gain)" is such a broad definition can lead to the detention of many individuals committing a crime completely out of the realms of terrorism.

From the other hand, it also penalizes involvement is "undesignated organizations", broadening the concept of what a terrorist organization following Section 411. It is thence no longer limited to organizations that have been officially designated as terrorists and published in the Federal Register but according to Section 411, a terrorist organization is that designated as such under the INA or by the Secretary of State, and also "a group of two or more individuals, whether related or not, which engages in terrorist-related activities". While before the USA PATRIOT Act only non-citizens engaging in or supporting terrorist activities were deportable, with the approval of this Act the new definition of terrorism makes deportable all those having "any connection to a terrorist organization" (Patel, 2003). With the passing of Section 411, the mere association makes an immigrant guilty and deportable without even the need of proof between the immigrant's conduct and the terrorist activity, something that did not happen before (Vandenberg, 2004). If we connect this in light with the enlargement of the definition of a terrorist activity or terrorist organization, it becomes far too easy to detain and deport immigrants, and even asylum seekers.

As explained by Sinnar (2003:1422), Section 412 raises constitutional problems because the previous section expands the range of aliens who can be associated with terrorist offences which, in turn, means that the new criteria refer not only to individuals who plot to undertake a terrorist attack, "but also individuals who are more remotely affiliated with proscribed organizations". Thence this allows the Attorney General to certify immigrants as "suspected terrorists" without proof or even probable cause (ISPU, 2004).

Dority (2004) compares parts of the Act to legislation passed hundreds of years ago:

> Perhaps the most frightening thing about the Patriot Act – even putting aside these other impending instructions on civil liberties – is how similar the act is to legislation enacted in the eighteenth century. The Alien and Sedition Acts are notorious in history for their abuse of basic civil liberties. For example, in 1798, the Alien Friends Act made it lawful for the president of the United States "to order all such aliens, as he shall judge dangerous to the peace and safety of the United States, or shall have reasonable grounds to suspect are concerned in any treasonable or secret machinations against the government thereof, to depart out of the territory of the United States". For years Americans have pointed to legislation like this as a travesty never to be repeated. Yet now it is back!

It must be noted that not all prohibitions are dangerous only for immigrants, but for the general population. Section 802 states that "acts dangerous to human life that are a violation of criminal laws" which "appear to be intended to influence the policy of a government by intimidation of coercion" can actually lead to acts of civil disobedience being considered as attacks that violate the law and fall within the application of this Section. The definition is vague and broad, inviting the distant possibility of danger of becoming a pretext of an attempted terrorist attack. This is thus also threatening the right of free speech and assembly found in the First Amendment and international law.

1.2 The Nexus between Immigration and Terrorism

On 25 October 2001, the Attorney General John Ashcroft made a speech at the US Conference of Mayors and referred to the efforts being made to respond to the 9/11 terrorist attacks. Interestingly, he made special reference to immigrants in the country:

> If you overstay your visas even by one day, we will arrest you; if you violate a local law, we will hope that you will, and work to make sure that you are put in jail and be kept in custody as long as possible. We will use every available statute. We will seek every prosecutorial advantage. We will use all our weapons within the law and under the Constitution to protect life and enhance security for America.[1]

1 The full speech is available at: https://www.washingtonpost.com/wp-srv/nation/specials/attacked/transcripts/ashcrofttext_102501.html.

Although different parts are threatening for the rights of the general US population, many are directed exclusively to tackling migrants. Examples of this are Sections 201 and 203, which determinate that "unlawful presence" in US territory is a criminal rather than a civil offence, being subject to detention. As Friman (2006) says, "the length of sentence was not by accident; such a sentence would automatically result in an estimated 12 to 14 million migrants already illegally in the United States being designated as aggravated felons".

While detention would not be permitted in many cases under criminal law – like the requirement of a probable cause for arrest or the right to be brought before a judge within 48 hours of arrest – it is nevertheless now authorized if an individual violates immigration law. Thence arresting aliens under immigration charges enables the Department of Justice not only to deport them as it used to be the case, but also to keep them imprisoned while it continues to investigate and interrogate them about potential criminal activities they might have committed.

What is more, the Department of Justice has also created new immigration policies and procedures to limit the safeguards with which non-citizens used to count with. Thus, while most individuals were usually released after being accused of staying after their visas had expired or under other common immigration violations, now they can be kept in detention if there is a "special interest" if they are considered to be dangerous. Most of these arrested individuals because of "special interests" were foreign Muslim men (HRW, 2002).

After September 11, racial profiling became a recurrent tool to identify potential terrorists in the US, and most Americans will racially profile Arab males and non-citizens. As Vandenberg (2004:627–628) explains, the long history of racism in the United States can result in viewing as enemies those of members of minorities or immigrant origin, and "by permitting racial profiling to be an acceptable practice, non-citizens will be treated more like criminals and the rights of every U.S. citizen will subsequently decrease". And the fact that the perpetrations of the attacks were Arab male immigrants has led many to believe that it is necessary to pay closer attention to Arab-looking men (Cole, 2002). Proof of this perspective is the fact that after the 9/11 attacks, more than 1,200 non-citizens – mostly from Arab and South Asian origin – were apprehended (Taylor, 2002; Vandenberg, 2004), and later on in early 2002, the Department of Justice announced the apprehension and removal of 4,000 to 6,000 men of Arab countries such as Iraq, Iran, Libya, Sudan, Syria, Qatar, Somalia, Tunisia, Yemen, and Pakistan, among others (Vandenberg, 2004). Thence as Taylor (2002) affirms, "The arrest of hundreds of young men with Middle Eastern backgrounds has come to symbolize the fears within immigrant communities in the United States that current immigration enforcement policies are a product of federal discrimination" which raises serious questions on the protection of the rights of non-citizens of these origins, which may be sacrificed in exchange of ensuing the security concerns of the majority of the population.

1.3 Detention

Section 412 is probably one of the most contentious sections of the Act. It expands the Attorney General's powers of detention under the Immigration and Nationality Act (INA). She can certify that an alien is a terrorist when there are reasonable grounds to believe that she is affiliated with a designated terrorist organization or engaged in terrorist activities. And even when she cannot establish such connection, the person can also be detained if the Attorney General has reasons to believe that he endangers national security. Then this alien can be placed in removal proceedings, charged with a criminal offence, or released within seven days of being taken to custody. However, if the removal of aliens is unlikely in the near future or if it is threatening for national security "or the safety of the community or any person", they can be detained for up to six months. In addition to this, judicial review to habeas corpus is also limited and the right of appeal of any final order is also restricted.

Human Rights Watch (HRW, 2002) has contained that the Department of Justice has used immigration detention as a preventive detention to conduct criminal investigations and has deliberately maintained in custody these detainees for long periods of time even though lacking evidence that they would be a danger to society. After being detained, every person has the right to be represented by a legal counsel – and this is both ensured in international law but also in US constitutional law. And this becomes even more necessary in those cases relating to immigrants who are not familiar with the laws of a country that is not their own. Nonetheless, and as Human Rights Watch pointed in their investigations, many of the people who were detained after 9/11 could not exercise their right to counsel, and while immigration detainees do not have the right to free counsel for their immigration proceedings, they do have this right when they are being interrogated as part of a criminal investigation. This organization found that "special interest" detainees were, in fact, questioned in custody as part of a criminal procedure when, in fact, they were later on charged with immigration violations. Most of the times, these interrogations were made by FBI and Immigration and Naturalization Service (INS) agents.

During the interviews that this organization conducted to some of these detainees, they found out that some were told they would have the right to a lawyer and a phone call after FBI questioning. And after this phone call, they were then held incommunicado and in isolation for two weeks and denied access to any other phone call. In other cases, detainees were told they would get a lawyer only after the interrogation and were pressured to answer questions from FBI agents. Most of these persons were held in custody without being informed of their "Miranda rights".[2] Even more, they were not only denied these rights, but were also subject to abusive treatment (HRW, 2002).

In connection with what has been said, Sinnar gives an interesting insight on the changes introduced by Section 412 on detention for immigrants in the United States. She argues that the certification process triggers mandatory detention and while before the USA PATRIOT Act aliens suspected of involvement in terrorist activities could be arrested and then granted or denied bail depending on the discretionary decision of the INS, she would still retain a number of procedural rights to contest that determination. However, the USA PATRIOT Act introduces changes to these procedures (Sinnar, 2003):

> He had the right to request a hearing with an immigration judge to review the denial of bond, and could appeal a negative decision to the Board of Immigration Appeals. Beyond administrative review, an alien could also contest detention through appeal to a district court on a habeas petition. Under the new law [USA PATRIOT Act], detention is mandatory for aliens certified by the Attorney General, and any alien that the government has "reasonable grounds to believe" meets any of the broad grounds for inadmissibility or deportation in section 412, or is otherwise considered a national security threat, may be certified. Thus, certification could apply to an alien whose sole offense was a donation to an undesignated organization intended for charitable purposes, and who neither presents a danger to the public nor appears likely to abscond. Aliens may potentially be certified by the Attorney General for reasons other than threat to the public or bail risk. 30 Certified aliens are automatically ineligible for bail; there is no opportunity for an adversarial hearing to contest their detention. In sum, section 412 introduces an irrebuttable presumption that aliens subject to certification are unfit for release.

2 "Miranda Rights" are those found in the Fifth Amendment, which must be read by the police before custodial interrogation starts. These rights are that to remain silent, to know that anything the person says can and will be used against her in a court of law, the right to an attorney, and the right to get one appointed if not being able to afford one. They are made to protect against self-incriminating statements and to make sure one knows he has the right to have an attorney. They are called "Miranda rights" because of a historic 1966 US Supreme Court case called *Miranda v. Arizona*.

2 The Legal Aftermath of 9/11

The USA PATRIOT Act has not been the only piece of legislation developed in the line of securitizing migration and refugees, but it has been reinforced by other laws, edits, and orders, which have entered into force ever since. Sadly, these incorporations have been upheld by part of the population. As the United Nations Special Rapporteur on the human rights of migrants, already noted back in 2008, xenophobia and racism towards the immigrant population worsened after September 11, causing "a particularly discriminatory and devastating impact on many of the most vulnerable groups in the migrant population, including children, unaccompanied minors, Haitian and other Afro-Caribbean migrants, and migrants who are, or are perceived to be, Muslim or of South Asian or Middle Eastern descent" (Bustamante, 2008). Therefore, while these provisions target immigrants broadly, they have had a disproportionate impact on refugees and asylum seekers, particularly from Muslim-majority countries. The presumption of threat is extended to individuals seeking international protection, collapsing the legal and moral distinction between those fleeing persecution and those suspected of perpetrating it. This blurring of categories is central to refugee securitization, where risk perception overrides humanitarian obligation.

In this section, the norms that were passed shortly after 9/11 will be closely examined. This will be useful to see the reaction of the government to a terrorist attack and to have a broader view of the analysed USA PATRIOT Act and put it within the context of the national framework on security and migration developed at the time.

As explained in the Institute for Social Policy and Understanding's report (ISPU, 2004) which conducts a scrutiny of the USA PATRIOT Act, the dangers have thence been exacerbated by, for instance, the Bureau of Prisons surveillance order, approved by the Attorney General, which allows federal agents to breach the attorney–client privilege by listening to their conversations without obtaining judicial permission, whether before or after trial. And also related to the Act is the Attorney's General edict for increased surveillance of certain religious and political organizations, such as mosques and Islamic centres, allowed by the dismantling of the regulations prohibiting the Justice Department from conducting COINTELPRO operations, which were originally thought to protect US citizens from abuses by this Department. Thence by rescinding these operations "and thereby authorizing the FBI to monitor and conduct surveillance on certain religious and political groups without any evidence of wrongdoing, the edict opens the door to a new wave of COINTELPRO operations which are well known from past experience to be associated with effects that are unwanted in a free and democratic society: harassment and intimidation of people who disagree with the government on issues such as civil rights and the conduct of war". It must be noted that provisions that were to expire in this Act were reauthorized by succeeding legislation – USA Freedom Act of 2015 – in 2005, 2009, and 2015.

A key piece of legislation on national security is the Clear Law Enforcement for Criminal Alien Removal Act of 2003 (CLEAR Act), which was introduced on 9 July 2003. One of its most important changes was that it required state authorities and local law enforcement personnel to enforce Federal immigration laws. Section 101 allows them to investigate, apprehend, detain, and remove aliens from US territory. In addition to this, it also penalizes states and localities if these authorities fail to implement statutes which permit the enforcement of immigration laws. While there is not directly an obligation to do so, failing to enforce them does have consequences, which would be to discontinue providing federal funding, as seen in Sections 102 and 105. Furthermore, these state and local personnel count with remedies and protections, such as being immune from personal liability from suit for civil damages if they were acting in the scope of their duties (Section 110).

The CLEAR Act further contributes to allowing the detention of immigrants in the country. The text establishes in Section 103 that non-citizens being unlawfully present in the US are to be fined and imprisoned for a year and subject to asset forfeiture. Furthermore, it increases both civil and criminal penalties for illegal entry, while also reducing the time of amount granted to voluntarily leave the country.

Furthermore, Pretrial Detention and Lifetime Supervision of Terrorists Act of 2003 also introduces pretrial detention for anyone committing an act of terrorism even before investigations commence. While before, the government had to show that the person accused was a flight risk or a danger to the community, with this Act the judge can deny bail even without the government having to show that the accused is dangerous or likely to flee. Thence a person who is presumably not guilty and has not been found guilty of any crime can be held for months without even proof that she is dangerous or likely to flee. Another measure was the passing of the REAL ID Act of 2005 where the government wanted to reinforce national security by, for instance, denying driver's licences to illegal immigrants.

While the immediate response to the September 11 events was predominantly legislative, in the following years it was supplemented with presidential directives, regulations, and policy initiatives. These measures were once again connecting the strengthening of national security to dealing with refugees and other migrants. One example is the Absconder Apprehension Initiative, approved in 2002, directed to locate and apprehend approximately 314,000 non-citizens who were ordered deported but did not leave the country. The mission was conducted by immigrant and criminal law enforcement officials (Miller, 2005).

The Visa Security Program, the programme screening visa applications and also putting together these with terrorist watch lists and other intelligence information, has also played a critical role in relating refugees to security. In 2010, the programme screened 950,000 applicants, of which 26,000 were vetted and another 1,000 had recommendations for visa denials (Chishti and Bergeron, 2011). And since 2003, the U.S. Visitor and Immigration Status Indicator Technology Program (US-VISIT) has been collecting biometric information of all non-citizens entering the country. The Student and Exchange Visitor Information System (SEVIS) and the Electronic System for Travel Authorization (ESTA), launched in 2002 and 2009, respectively, are also other systems dedicated to collecting biometric data from foreigners to check them against criminal databases.

These data-driven systems reflect a shift from individualized assessments to algorithmic and bureaucratic filtering of refugee and migrant populations. Refugee status, once rooted in protection from persecution, is increasingly managed through predictive risk technologies. This bureaucratic securitization moves refugee governance into the realm of threat anticipation, aligning it with counterterrorism practices rather than human rights norms.

US intelligence has also been strengthened during these years. With the Intelligence Reform and Terrorism Prevention Act of 2004, the National Security Act of 1947 was reformed, and a new position of Director of National Intelligence as head of the intelligence community arose. Within the Office of the Director of National Intelligence, the National Counterterrorism Center was established as a knowledge bank for information about terrorist suspects and to centralize all counter-terrorism efforts (Kaczmarek et al., 2018).

The Department of Homeland Security was established in 2002 mainly as a consequence and response to the 9/11 terrorist attacks. Through the Homeland Security Act, the Immigration and Naturalization Service was dissolved and replaced by this new office. Very importantly, the Department addresses national security matters including all immigration-related functions, an addition that has remained ever since. This Department has seen a dramatic increase in staffing and budget since its creation. That same year, the National Security Entry-Exit Registration System (NSEERS) was expanded to require male nationals from Arab and Muslim-majority countries who had registered in the US before 9/11 to turn up to an immigration office and register with the INS. As explained previously, those who did not could be considered out of status and be sent back to their countries of origin.

In 2006, the Justice Department created the National Security Division to combat more effectively security threats to the nation, combining law enforcement and intelligence services. This was the first new Justice Department division in 49 years (Department of Justice, 2011).

In May 2006, the Immigration and Customs Enforcement was in charge of "Operation Return to Sender", an operation to look for dangerous immigrant fugitives and terrorists and which began. With the raids conducted by federal immigration agents, more than 23,000 people had been arrested nationwide and criticisms arose as to whether they were looking for criminal suspects or just targeting foreign-looking immigrants based on race (Mckinley, 2007). And later on, in 2008, the Foreign Intelligence Surveillance Act (FISA) of 2008 was approved, an Act which allowed intelligence agents to monitor terrorist communications much faster. The USA PATRIOT Act also expanded the FISA to allow the government to obtain personal records of ordinary Americans from libraries and Internet Service Providers although not having a connection with terrorism (ACLU, 2008).

As already noted by Bustamante in 2008, the US failed to comply with international legal obligations, with non-citizens being unable to enjoy some of their most basic human rights. Moreover, as the Rapporteur states in his country visit report, "A primary principle of United States immigration law is that United States citizens can never be denied entry into the country; neither can they ever be forcibly deported from the United States. By contrast, non-citizens, even those who have lived in the country legally for decades, are always vulnerable to mandatory detention and deportation" (Bustamante, 2008).

As one can easily see, a bunch of legal and organizational changes took place immediately after and the years following 9/11, added to the already punitive practices established in the country since 1996. And while this was just a glimpse of some of these changes in the national framework, we have seen laws and policies being approved in the same line ever since. This has become even more evident during the Trump administration, when a set of new executive orders on national security and affecting migration were passed just days after arriving to presidency.

3 Trump's Legislation on Security and Migration

After September 11, the United States has slowed immigration, conducted mass interviews of young Arab men, required registration of aliens from certain countries, made secret detentions, created the Department of Homeland Security, and even called for vigilance of ordinary citizens and aliens to fight the war on terror (Engle, 2004). The USA PATRIOT Act's Section 402 also allowed for the number of Border Patrol personnel, Customs personnel, and immigration inspectors along the Northern Border to be tripled, and also for adding a sum of $50 million to be directed to the Customs and INS to improve monitoring technology. Thence measures to fight the war on terror involve a wide range of tools, from protecting the border to enhancing surveillance. But in addition to this and up to this day, more laws connecting immigration to security matters have been passed. Part of these appeared during the Trump administration, where the link between immigration and national security matters was intensified.

On 25 January 2017, only five days after being sworn as President of the United States, Donald Trump issued two executive orders reinforcing the already existing process of securitization of migration in the country. With the Executive Order 13767 on Border Immigration Enforcement and with the Executive Order 13768 on Enhancing Public Safety in the Interior of the United States, the President approved building a massive wall between the US–Mexico border in addition to other proposals which undermined the basic rights of due process and the basic rights of those seeking asylum in the United States. The first of these instruments argues that the wall has to be built immediately and has to be monitored and supported by adequate personnel "so as to prevent illegal immigration, drug and human trafficking, and acts of terrorism" – Section 2(a). Other provisions of the Executive Order include the detention of individuals suspected of violating federal or state law (Section 2(b)) and the removal of individuals who are subject to removal under US immigration law (Section 2(d)).

The executive order titled Enhancing Public Safety in the Interior of the United States presents all types of immigrants with criminal conduct, alleging that "Many alien who illegally enter the United States and those who overstay or otherwise violate the terms of their visas present a significant threat to national security and public safety", as said in the introduction of the text. Section 5(a)(b) and (c) also state that aliens can be removed if committing "any criminal offence", being charged with such offence without having resolved it and omitting acts that can constitute a chargeable criminal offence are also considered crimes whose perpetrator, if an alien, has to be removed. This raises questions and concerns to the extent where these statements can be brought. Does an alien driving with an expired licence have to be removed from the US? Or for instance, since crossing the border illegally is a federal misdemeanour, anyone having done this in their past can fall within the definition of Section 5. These categories are so broad that any undocumented person can become a target according to this law.

These executive orders massively expand the use of detention, to allow the apprehension of individuals merely suspected of violating immigration law or criminal law. As condemned by the American Immigration Council, it also directs the Department of Homeland Security to detain all individuals in removal proceedings to the maximum extent of the law, regardless of whether they have had a court hearing or not, and whether the final order on deportation has been taken or not (AIC, 2017). If considering that legal counsel is not always easy to get by these individuals, who are not familiar with complex legal systems of countries not of their own, it makes it even more complicated for them to be able to defend themselves during these procedures.

Two days after passing these executive orders, Donald Trump also approved Executive Order number 13780 on Protecting the Nation from Foreign Terrorist Entry into the United States. One of the introductions of this executive order was to limit the ability of citizens from seven specific countries to travel to the US. These countries were Iraq, Syria, Sudan, Iran, Somalia, Libya, and Yemen. The main reason to do so was to protect the country from the terrorist threat, a threat which is made by organizations that seem to be operating in these seven countries. Terrorism, however, is a dynamic phenomenon, which can occur in many different places around the world, and which is constantly moving from one place to another. Any country may have secret organizations within its territory, and any country can be the object of these assaults. This executive order also limited the number of refugees to be admitted in the US to a maximum of 50,000 since any higher number would be "detrimental to the interests of the United States". The travel ban and cap on refugee admissions reinforced a symbolic reframing of the refugee as a potential enemy rather than a protected subject. These executive measures transformed refugee selection from a humanitarian duty into a filtering mechanism based on geopolitical and security calculations. In doing so, they institutionalized suspicion towards refugees within the broader national security framework.

On 8 October 2017, President Trump sent a letter to the House and Senate leaders[3] putting forth the principles for reforming the nation's immigration system. Three main subjects were addressed. The first refers to border security, and its main goals are to build a Southern border wall and "close legal loopholes that enable illegal immigration and swell the court backlog". Another of the measures to be applied regarding border security is to ensure

3 President Donald J. Trump's Letter to House and Senate Leaders and Immigration Principles and Policies, October 8, 2017. Available at: https://www.whitehouse.gov/briefings-statements/president-donald-j-trumps-letter-house-senate-leaders-immigration-principles-policies/?utm_source=link.

that unaccompanied children crossing the border can be returned. Before these measures were applied, children and their families were already being automatically and arbitrarily detained during immigration proceedings, even when the mother had passed the initial asylum screening (IACHR, 2015). But to add to this, President Trump argued that children arriving to the country illegally, instead of being removed, were sheltered in government facilities "at taxpayer expense" and then released to the custody of a family member "who often lack lawful status in the United States themselves". He calls for amending the law in order to "ensure the expeditious return" of these children. Furthermore, as Amnesty International denounced, the situation of these children is already critical in many detaining facilities. They found that those children seeking asylum held at the Homestead facility of Florida were in prolonged indefinite detention, staying far beyond the 20 days established in the law (AI, 2019). The administration also proposed to tighten standards in the asylum system and elevate the threshold standard of proof in credible fear interviews to lower the number of asylum applications and make it more difficult to obtain refugee status in the country. Another addition was to hire 370 immigration judges and 1,000 Immigration and Customs Enforcement attorneys to remove illegal border crossers swifter and faster. These are just some of the measures proposed for the first of the subjects to be addressed.

The second priority concerned the interior enforcement. The administration argued that many cities were in violation of 8 § U.S.C. 1373 of federal law, which states that state and local government entities and officials may not prohibit or restrict the sharing of information with the Department of Home Security regarding an individual's immigration status. These cities were called "sanctuary jurisdictions", and according to the letter, they "release dangerous criminals and empower violent cartels like MS-13 by refusing to turn over incarcerated criminal aliens to Federal authorities". In practice, what they are doing is to apply policies and regulations that make it harder for Immigration and Customs Enforcement to arrest non-citizens and make them deportable in response to the harshening measures applied by the Trump administration. They seek to protect low-priority immigrants from deportation, but they still turn over those immigrants having committed serious crime. The Trump administration wanted to block them from receiving certain federal grants. However, it must be noted that there is no official definition of "sanctuary".

Last but not least, the third area being addressed refers to the Merit-Based Immigration system. The immigration system prioritized the extended family-based chain over a skill-based system. What Trump was proposing was a merit-based immigration system that would prioritize high-skilled immigration to "protect U.S. workers and taxpayers".

These laws were passed during the first months of Trump's presidency, thence a long list of legislation, policies, reports, proposals and public speeches and comments on securitizing migration and securitizing refugees followed during his time in the White House. In 2019, authorities under the Trump administration forced over 59,000 asylum seekers to return to Mexico during the adjudication of their asylum claims. That same year, the government also announced its intention to decrease the annual number of refugee admissions of the following year to 18,000, the lowest number in the 40-year programme's history (AI, 2019).

Policies like Zero Tolerance, approved in April 2018, establishes that immigrants found crossing US borders could be referred by the Department of Homeland Security to the Department of Justice to be prosecuted. And the Migrant Protection Protocols (MPP) stated that all immigrants found trying to enter the country through the Southern border without legal documents are to be sent back to Mexico and forced to remain there while awaiting their removal proceedings. The Inter-American Commission on Human Rights condemned these policies arguing that they were having an impact on the effective enjoyment of human rights by all migrants including (i) the imposition of restrictions on the administrative and judicial mechanisms available to effectively access the right to request and be granted asylum; (ii) a dramatic increase in the use of migrant detention, immediately and, in some cases, for long periods, with the effect of separating families and discouraging the pursuit of ongoing asylum proceedings, and of migration to the United States more generally; (iii) the implementation of fast-track deportations through procedures without due process guarantees; and (iv) the forced return of individuals to the Mexican side of the border, as they progress through their immigration proceedings in the United States (IACHR, 2019).

It seems appropriate then to say that during his administration a more advanced framework to bring refugees and asylum seekers into the security realms was perfected. Migrants, refugees and asylum seekers, they were all often related to crime and considered a threat to the community, and migration-related matters became a key part of the national security agenda of the country. And with it, the rights of migrants in the country and those trying to seek refuge were diminished and put aside.

4 Recent Legislative Developments

Since Biden took office in January 2021, his administration has acted on a number of areas to reverse some of Trump's policies. In the field of immigration, Biden announced plans to boost refugee admissions and establish restrictions that were still in force following the COVID pandemic (Krogstad and Gonzalez-Barrera, 2022). With 535 immigrations after his first three years in presidency, the Biden administration has already outpaced the 472 immigration executive actions that Trump had enacted during his prior presidency (Chishti et al, 2024).

Despite announcing to end the use of Title 42 preventing individuals from seeking asylum by permitting rapid expulsions, Biden's administration has extended Title 42 to Cubans, Haitians, Nicaraguans, and Venezuelans (Chishti et al, 2024). Furthermore, externalization practices have also been developed, and policies related to accepting the return of nationals from Latin American countries have also been designed in an attempt to relief the number of migrant arrivals. In 2024, Biden issued an executive order directed to containing incoming migration through the Southern border with Mexico allowing officials to remove migrants entering the US illegally without processing asylum requests. This executive order was a response to the increasing number of migrants arriving through this border. In fact, since the start of the Biden's administration, numbers have exponentially increased compared to those during Trump's administration. In 2023, there were 2.4 million encounters by US patrols in the Southwest land border, compared to 500,000 in 2020 (ABC7, 2024).

Biden's approach during his campaign and during his initial days in presidency were to make an important distinction from his predecessor and move away from that restrictive immigration agenda that had taken place those previous years. As an example, in 2024 Biden also announced that he would give legal status through citizenship to almost half a million immigrants married to American citizens (Santana, 2024a). However, while the expectations that were created were partly met, as protection to thousands of migrants in the country had expanded, his administration has been unable to manage growing migration numbers at the border and has continued managing migrants and refugees through the focus on reinforcing border control. In June 2024, declarations from the White House upheld the actions taken by the administration, which focused on securing the border and addressing a broken immigration system. Some of these measures include the deployment of the largest number of agents and officers in the Southern border (White House, 2024a).

Following Executive Order 14013, the refugee resettlement program was restored, resulting in the resettlement of more than 100,000 refugees during fiscal year 2024, the highest annual figure in three decades (White House, 2024b). This was achieved by hiring more than 300 refugee officers, digitalising processes to improve efficiency, and launching the Safe Mobility initiative in partnership with UNHCR and the International Organization for Migration, which expanded lawful pathways to seek protection in the United States, Canada, and Spain. However, following Donald Trump's return to office in January 2025, US refugee and asylum policy shifted once again towards a more restrictive approach. The new administration reinstated a stronger emphasis on border enforcement, tightened access to asylum, and introduced new measures aimed at reducing refugee admissions and limiting humanitarian protection (White House, 2025; Chen and Dalal-Dheini, 2025). These developments illustrate the continued centrality of migration and refugee governance within the US national security agenda and confirm that the securitization of migration remains a defining feature of contemporary immigration policy.

5 Conclusions

Before 2001, the immigration system had already become more severe, some describing it as a "criminalization" of immigration law and others as a "convergence between the criminal justice and deportation systems" (Miller, 2005; Kanstroom, 2000). However, the connection between immigration and national security became much more evident after September 11, when the figure of the migrant was rapidly connected to that of a potential terrorist.

The USA PATRIOT Act was passed less than two months after the 9/11 attacks. There are a bunch of new measures introduced to reinforce US protection against terrorist threats and strengthen national security. Among these, for instance, there are greater surveillance mechanisms and information sharing between authorities and agencies related to security. One of the most significant provisions in this sense is Section 215, which allows the FBI to force anyone to turn over records on their clients and customers. It also increases powers to conduct secret searches to property without notice to the owner, searches of communications, allowance for looking at certain individual's activities records, and foreign intelligence information searches (Sections 213, 214, 215 and 218 respectively). However, the focus in this chapter has not been directed so much to analysing all of the controversial provisions of US legislation affecting the general population, but on particular parts of the law that contribute to affirming that there is, in fact, a securitization of *migration*. Securitization, nevertheless, happens in different spheres of the individual's life, be it a migrant or not. However, the figure of the migrant as a vulnerable person is further threatened and unprotected by securitizing provisions.

The instruments presented connect more closely immigrants and refugees to terrorism-related activities, with the USA PATRIOT Act at the forefront, facilitating the inadmissibility and deportation of migrants – including asylum seekers – while also enabling their indefinite detention. Thence this is not only a bill that reinforces border or surveillance technologies to protect from potential terrorist individuals or groups, but it also connects these to immigration and endures measures to detain and deport them.

After 9/11, the Attorney General, DOJ, FBI, and NSA designed the largest surveillance programme in the nation to track down terrorists and prevent from the terrorist threat and, most importantly, "most of the effort has been directed towards the Muslim community and has been spurred by ethnic considerations" (Wong, 2006). The continuous tendency to surpass national security has resulted in a deliberate, persistent, and dangerous detriment of individual rights, and especially those of immigrants. As summarized by the Center for Constitutional Rights (2002):

> The War on Terror has seriously compromised the First, Fourth, Fifth and Sixth Amendment rights of citizens and non-citizens alike. From the USA PATRIOT Act's over-broad definition of domestic terrorism, to the FBI's new powers of search and surveillance, to the indefinite detention of both citizens and non-citizens without formal charges, the principles of free speech, due process, and equal protection under the law have been seriously undermined.

Since September 11, immigration policy has been viewed through the lens of security. As Cole develops, while it may not have been *irrational* to focus on Arab-Muslim immigrants after the 9/11 attacks because of the origin of the attackers and in light of Al Qaeda's members' origins, it still does not justify denying them the basic guarantees of due process, political freedom, and equal protection (Cole, 2002: 978). It is also acceptable to waive partly some of our liberties to enhance the security of the nation, but after September 11 the citizens have not been the ones sacrificing their freedoms, but those of the non-citizens are the ones that have been at stake to protect from the citizens' insecurities.

Moreover, during the Trump administration the rights of non-citizens were also diminished and the link between immigration and national security was reinforced, placing migration as one of the main threats to the country and a necessary object to consider against the War on Terror. Migration was linked to crime and even terrorism and became one of the most important matters to be introduced to the national security agenda of the country. While the Biden administration has taken a different turn in his four years in presidency, border control has still been an important aspect of migration policies. It remains to be seen what the future holds for refugees and asylum seekers in the United States, but immigration clearly stands as one of the most controversial debates in the country, and securitization practices have not been left behind.

The case of the United States reveals a legal and discursive logic in which refugees, particularly from Muslim-majority countries, are treated less as rights-holders and more as potential national security threats. Post-9/11 legal instruments blurred the line between humanitarian protection and counter-terrorism enforcement, transforming asylum into a site of suspicion. This transformation, where individuals fleeing violence and persecution are reframed through the language of risk and prevention, lies at the heart of the securitization puzzle this book explores. It highlights how the protection regime can be retooled to serve sovereign security agendas, even in states that publicly champion refugee rights.

References

ABC7 (2024) 'Border encounters by the numbers: Here's what the data shows', 14 June. Available at: https://abc7.com/post/border-encounters-numbers-heres-what-data-shows/14945373/.

ACLU (2008) 'The Foreign Intelligence Surveillance Act – News and Resources', *American Civil Liberties Union*. Available at: https://www.aclu.org/other/foreign-intelligence-surveillance-act-news-and-resources.

AI (2019) 'United States of America 2019', *Amnesty International*. Available at: https://www.amnesty.org/en/countries/americas/united-states-of-america/report-united-states-of-america/.

AIC (2017) "Summary of Executive Order "Border Security and Immigration Enforcement Improvements", *American Immigration Council*, February 27. Available at: https://www.americanimmigrationcouncil.org/sites/default/files/research/summary_of_executive_order_border_security_and_immigration_enforcement_improvements.pdf.

Bustamante, J. (2008) 'Report of the Special Rapporteur on the human rights of migrants. Mission to the United States of America', *Human Rights Council*, A/HRC/7/12/Add.2.

Chen, G., and Dalal-Dheini, S. (2025). *Policy Brief: Trump Administration Day One Executive Orders*. Migration Policy Institute.

Chishti, M. and Bergeron, C. (2011) 'Post-9/11 Policies Dramatically Alter the U.S. Immigration Landscape' *Migration Policy Institute*. Available at: https://www.migrationpolicy.org/article/post-911-policies-dramatically-alter-us-immigration-landscape.

Chishti, K., Bush-Joseph, K. and Putzel-Kavanaugh, C. (2024) 'Biden at the Three-Year Mark: The Most Active Immigration Presidency Yet Is Mired in Border Crisis Narrative', *Migration Policy Institute*. Available at: https://www.migrationpolicy.org/article/biden-three-immigration-record.

Cole, D. (2002) 'Enemy aliens', *Stanford Law Review*, Vol. 54(5), pp. 953–1004.

Department of Justice (2011) 'Fact Sheet: the Department of Justice Ten Years After 9/11', Office of Public Affairs, Department of Justice of the United States. Available at: https://www.justice.gov/opa/pr/fact-sheet-department-justice-ten-years-after-911.

Dority, B. (2004) 'Your Every Move', *The Humanist*, Vol. 64(1), pp. 14–19.

Engle, K. (2004) 'Constructing good aliens and good citizens: Legitimizing the war on terror(ism)', *University of Colorado Law Review*, Vol. 75(1), pp. 59–114.

IACHR (2015) 'Human Rights situation of Refugee and Migrant Families and Unaccompanied Children in the United States of America', *Inter-American Commission on Human Rights*, OAS/Ser.L./V/II/155.

IACHR (2019) 'IACHR conducted visit to the United States' Southern Border', *Inter-American Commission on Human Rights*, No.228/19.

Kaczmarek, M., Lazarou, E., Guevara, M. and Fogel, B. (2018) 'US counter-terrorism since 9/11. Trends under the Trump administration', *European Parliament*. Available at: https://www.europarl.europa.eu/RegData/etudes/BRIE/2018/621898/EPRS_BRI(2018)621898_EN.pdf.

Kanstroom, D. (2000) 'Deportation, Social Control and Punishment: Some Thoughts About Why Hard Laws Make Bad Cases, *Harvard Law Review*, Vol. 113(8), pp. 1890–1935.

Krogstad, J. M. and Gonzalez-Barrear, A. (2022) 'Key facts about US immigration policies and Biden's proposed changes', *Pew Research Center*. Available at: https://www.pewresearch.org/short-reads/2022/01/11/key-facts-about-u-s-immigration-policies-and-bidens-proposed-changes/.

Friman, H. R. (2006) 'Migration and Security: Crime, Terror and the Politics of Order', *Ford Institute for Human Security*, Issue 2. Available at: https://www.files.ethz.ch/isn/28055/2006_2_Migration_Sec.pdf.

HRW (2002) 'Presumption of Guilt: Human Rights Abuses of Post-September 11 Detainees', in *Human Rights Watch World Report 2002*. New York, NY: Human Rights Watch. Available at: https://www.hrw.org/legacy/wr2k2/.

ISPU (2004) 'The USA PATRIOT Act Impact on the Arab and Muslim American Community', *The Institute for Social Policy and Understanding*. Available at: https://www.ispu.org/wp-content/uploads/2017/07/the-usa-patriot-act_farid-senzai.pdf.

McKinley, J. 2007 'San Francisco Bay Area Reacts Angrily to Series of Immigration Raids', *The New York Times*, April 28. Available at: https://www.nytimes.com/2007/04/28/washington/28immig.html?adxnnl=1&ref=us&adxnnlx=1177780418-U39IeJ5KGfAq2aUoerHNUw.

Miller, T. A. (2005) 'Blurring the boundaries between immigration and crime control after September 11th', *Boston College Third World Law Journal*, Vol. 25(1), pp. 81–123.

Patel, R. (2003) 'Immigration legislation pursuant to threats to us national security' *Denver Journal of International Law and Policy*, Vol. 32(1), pp. 83–104.

Santana, R. (2024a) 'Biden is offering some migrants a pathway to citizenship. Here's how the plan will work', *AP News*, 19 June. Available at: https://apnews.com/article/biden-immigration-order-spouse-border-54f6ad19bb5f645b9c6717e9c6256c9d.

Santana, R. (2024b) 'Biden has rebuilt the refugee system after Trump-era cuts. What comes next in an election year?', *AP News*, 19 June. Available at: https://apnews.com/article/refugees-resettlement-immigration-biden-trump-93cd3b6408fd45907645849da91e23bb.

Sinnar, S. (2003) 'Patriotic or Unconstitutional? The Mandatory Detention of Aliens Under the USA Patriot Act', *Stanford Law Review*, Vol. 55, pp. 1419–1456.

Taylor, M. A. (2002) 'Immigration enforcement post-September 11: Safeguarding the civil rights of Middle Eastern-American and immigrant communities', *Georgetown Immigration Law Journal*, Vol. 17(1), pp. 63–114.

Vandenberg, Q. H. (2004) 'How can the united states rectify its post-9/11 stance on noncitizens' rights', *Notre Dame Journal of Law, Ethics & Public Policy*, Vol.18(2), pp.605–646.

White House (2024a) 'Fact sheet: President Biden Announces New Actions to Secure the Border', 4 June. Available at: https://www.whitehouse.gov/briefing-room/statements-releases/2024/06/04/fact-sheet-president-biden-announces-new-actions-to-secure-the-border/.

White House (2024b) 'Fact sheet: Biden-Harris Administration on World Refugee Day Celebrates a Rebuilt US Refugee Admission Program', 20 June. Available at: https://www.whitehouse.gov/briefing-room/statements-releases/2024/06/20/fact-sheet-biden-harris-administration-on-world-refugee-day-celebrates-a-rebuilt-u-s-refugee-admissions-program/.

White House. (2025). *Protecting the American People Against Invasion* (Executive Order 14159). 20 January 2025.

Wong, K. (2006) 'The USA Patriot Act: A Policy of Alienation', *Michigan Journal of Race and Law*, Vol. 12, pp. 161–202.

CHAPTER 6

The Securitization of Refugees in South Africa

South Africa used to be known to have one of the most welcoming and safeguarding refugee systems not just of Africa but of the world. It has also ratified without reservations the 1951 Refugee Convention Relating to the Status of Refugees and the 1969 OAU Convention Governing the Specific Aspects of Refugee Problems in Africa. In the migration history of South Africa, the country has been known to welcome big refugee waves fleeing from armed conflicts and civil wars in the continent and who were seeking protection in this country.

However, since 2011 there has been a significant drop in the numbers of forced migrants compared to the first ten years of the millennium. The only country which has produced substantial internal and external displacement persons is the Democratic Republic of Congo (DRC) (UNHCR, 2019). But migration is still an important phenomenon in the African continent, and it will continue to be as long as political conflicts and environmental change (and its consequences, such as drought and food insecurity) continue hitting the continent. In the Southern Africa region in particular, migration is mostly driven for economic reasons, political instability, and environmental hazards. South Africa is the country with the higher estimated numbers of incoming migrants in the sub-region in mid-2020 with 2.9 million people (UN DESA, 2020). Most of these immigrants are from Zimbabwe (24%), Mozambique (12%), and Lesotho (7%) (UNDP, 2020), and three-quarters of the total number of immigrants in the country are from elsewhere of the African continent (Moyo, 2021).

And in the past decade, the southern region of Africa has started feeling certain reluctance to allow the free movement of migration for economic reasons. New restrictions have been approved, and border control has been reinforced by a variety of countries, which has led to more undocumented migration. Today, the continent is not only a refugee producer but also a refugee-hosting space, which has meant that the approach towards these immigrants has become much more restrictive than before (Khan and Rayer, 2020).

The point of this chapter is to analyse to what extent the phenomenon of securitizing migration has taken place in South Africa. This will be useful to provide a more global picture of the securitization of refugees, to show that this phenomenon does not only take place within the West – such as it has happened in the European Union and the United States, as we have seen in

 | HTTPS://DOI.ORG/10.1163/9789004704527-008

the two previous chapters – but also in other parts of the world. This chapter argues that although South Africa does not face transnational terrorism threats, it has nonetheless securitized refugees and asylum seekers through discourses of risk, crime, and economic burden, thus broadening the understanding of refugee securitization beyond the Global North and shows how protection norms can be undermined through domestic political pressures and administrative reform.

If the treatment over migration and over particularly vulnerable groups such as refugees and asylum seekers has changed so much in countries like South Africa, which used to be a protective one over these groups, we can think that we may really be seeing a change on the way we treat migration and that the securitization mechanisms towards these groups have really been spread across the globe. And what is more, if the laws of the countries have really become much more restrictive and are justifying these measures for national security reasons, we may also be facing a global change in the making of norms in relation to security and refugees.

1 South African Recent Legislation on Migration

The South African legislation on international migration is based on the 1999 White Paper on International Migration and implemented through the Immigration Act of 2002 and the Refugees Act of 1998. Both laws have been amended recently under the lead of the Department of Home Affairs, and new bills have been passed to address more recent migration movements and gaps in legislation.

This has meant that a series of changes in the way migration, and refugees, are treated in the country. More restrictions have been established, such as the reinforcement of borders, but other difficulties have also been imposed, such as bureaucratic burdens to obtaining asylum seeker permits to move freely within the country and exercise other basic rights. In this section, we will overview some of these recent changes in the legislation and policies of South Africa in relation to migration to analyse to what extent the securitization of refugees has also taken place in this African country.

1.1 The White Paper on International Migration

The White Paper on International Migration[1] sets out a framework on where immigration law in South Africa should move towards. White Papers are policy documents drawn by the Government which are used as proposals to set up a policy framework for future legislation. They may include a draft version of the future bill and are usually used for discussion before they are formally presented to Parliament. Released in 2017, this White Paper on migration introduces a series of changes regarding permanent residency, citizenship, the asylum system, and other immigration related issues. While the document recognizes that immigration in the country may be beneficial in some cases, it also links migration to security risks, trafficking, and corruption (Scalabrini, 2019). It is important to note that even though these concerns are framed in general migration terms, they implicitly encompass asylum seekers and refugees, who are increasingly absorbed into administrative and security control frameworks rather than treated as protected persons.

One of the changes that the White Paper introduces is to change how permanent residency and citizenship are granted. That is, temporary residency and refugee status would no longer lead to permanent residency, while permanent residency would also not lead to obtaining citizenship (Scalabrini, 2019). Permanent residency then could be renewed but would not count towards obtaining citizenship. The idea is to change the vision that immigrants have a right towards citizenship based on the years they have lived in South Africa, and in this way discourage further refugees and asylum seekers from coming to the country.

Instead, the South African government wants to establish a points-based system to encourage only high-skilled migration. The factors that would be considered for obtaining a visa would be based on qualifications, work experience, age, amount of money to invest in the country, type of business, and ability and willingness to transfer skills. There is then a clear focus on attracting the skills and investments of those who can contribute to the economy of the country. The document even states that "more skilled refugees could successfully apply to work and stay in South Africa under the Immigration Act if the required systems were established", showing a clear inclination only towards skilled migration.

While the Southern African Development Community (SADC) aimed to promote the free movement of people, goods, and capital, in reality most

1 *White Paper on International Migration for South Africa*, 28 July 2017, No. 41009, Department of Home Affairs of South Africa.

member states have not amended their policies in this direction. Various non-binding protocols were approved between member states to achieve these goals, but states have rarely shown real effort in working towards this line. The White Paper on International Migration of South Africa is another proof of this reality, although it offers some special conditions for citizens of SADC countries. For instance, there can be Special Dispensation Permits for the nationals of some countries, which are temporary permits that allow to work or study in South Africa for a limited period of time. On a similar trend, there is also the option to apply for a special work visa and a Small Medium Enterprise Visa for SADC nationals. All of these options are based and dependent on bilateral agreements.

More importantly, the White Paper also offered an explanation for why the country's migration system had to change. It states that South Africa has become an attractive destination for illegal immigrants "who pose a security threat to the economic stability and sovereignty of the country". It is argued that this happens because of different factors, one of which is that "human rights organizations and legal practitioners abuse the loopholes in the system to secure the release of the illegal immigrants, at the expense of the government". It seems that the government is clearly mistreating human rights organizations, legal practitioners, and even the judicial process, when the attitude towards them should be of service disposition.

The Department of Home Affairs now follows a risk-based approach which seeks to keep security threats out of the country because "immigration that is not managed through a risk-based approach is poorly managed immigration". The White Paper's executive summary states that the current migration system of the country "serves to perpetuate irregular migration, which in turn leads to unacceptable levels of corruption, human rights abuse and national security risks. The new White Paper argues that the current policy does not enable South Africa to adequately embrace global opportunities while safeguarding our sovereignty and ensuring public safety and national security". This link between illegal immigration and national security threats is not a new phenomenon, as we have already seen it in other countries, but it is a clear new way of dealing with immigration in the country which, unfortunately, puts in danger the rights of certain unwanted migrant groups, such as refugees, in South Africa. This vision reframes refugees not as individuals entitled to international protection, but as part of a broader challenge to state sovereignty and internal stability, a shift that reflects the logic of securitization.

1.2 Border Management Authority Act 2 of 2020

The Border Management Authority Act was passed in 2020 and is meant to make the control of border more efficient. The project of the law was deliberated for many years, but a new border regime was finally approved (Erasmus, 2020). While South Africa's borders used to be managed by different government departments, the Act establishes a single authority, a new Border Management Authority under the Department of Home Affairs, to oversee all aspects related to border control including land, air and seaports of entry. The bill has been very controversial and criticized for creating "an increasingly securitized and militarized presence along the country's borders" (Bornman, 2020).

The border crisis that the government has been referring to and which resulted in this bill is based on problems in relation to illegal migration, contraband, and smuggling, which altogether with corruption have made national boundaries porous. The border is 4,400 kilometres long and has 72 ports of entry, through which 39 million people pass annually (Erasmus, 2020). Thence one of the reasons to give all the responsibility in these matters to a single body is to reduce corruption and prevent illicit trafficking (Maunganidze and Mbioyozo, 2020), but it is argued that it will also offer better policing and enhanced security at the borders.

One of the most controversial parts of the bill is Chapter 6. Article 18 of this gives extensive powers to border officials to search, seize, and arrest any person "if the officer on reasonable grounds believes that a warrant will be issued if applied for". The powers given to these officers are quite wide and may be easily used against a wide range of persons for what could be unjustified reasons. The Article is written as follows:

> (1) An officer may, with or without a warrant, within the border law enforcement area or at a port of entry –
> (a) enter any premises;
> (b) search any person, goods, premises or vehicle;
> (c) inspect any goods, documents, premises or vehicle;
> (d) seize anything found in that search or inspection that may be lawfully seized;
> (e) question any person about any matter related to the passage of persons, goods or vehicles through a port of entry or across the border law enforcement area and confirm their responses in a written declaration; and
> (f) arrest or detain any person reasonably suspected of contravening any provision of this Act.

(2) An officer may, without a warrant, exercise any power in terms of subsection (1) if –
  (a) a person who is competent to do so consents to the entry, search, inspection or seizure; or
  (b) the officer on reasonable grounds believes that –
    (i) a warrant will be issued if applied for; and
    (ii) the delay in obtaining the warrant is likely to defeat the object of such warrant.

Signs that such a bill would be passed have long been shown by some of the politicians in the government. Aaron Motsoaledi, former Minister of Health and who later on became the Minister of Home Affairs, used to blame immigrants – including refugees – for the bad state of the health system of the country, and in his new position claims for more border protection. He, and other members of the African National Congress (ANC) – the ruling party – ran the 2019 elections with border controls as one of its main demands and have often shown their anti-immigrant position. As Bornman (2020) explains: "It would be easy to dismiss the bill as some form of Trumpian legislation, or something that mirrors the rhetoric and actions against migrants emerging from countries such as Hungary, Poland and the United Kingdom. But this bill has been in development since long before Donald Trump ran for president of the United States." The bill has been criticized for using justifications such as the prevention of smuggling and human trafficking and to stop the terrorist threat as a mechanism for securitizing migration and undermining regional governance initiatives (Landau and Kihato, 2017).

Moreover, the bill was passed on 21 July 2020, in the midst of the COVID-19 outbreak, and this is something that is reflected in the Preamble of the Act. While the document acknowledges that the bill is passed to prevent illegal cross-border movement, smuggling, and trafficking of human beings and goods, and to make border law enforcement functions more effective, it also recognizes that it is needed to "protect the Republic from harmful and infectious diseases, pests and substances", which may be another way of reinforcing border protection and refrain outsiders from entering the country and bringing more COVID-19 cases. As Moyo and Zanker (2022) point out, legislation taken during the pandemic was just a continuation of existing refugee and migration governance responses in the country which dismantled the distinction between refugees and migrants.

This has been a piece of legislation which has put into practice many of the securitization priorities of the White Paper. Some commentators have noted that the Border Management Act shares many similarities with some of the securitization measures on immigration developed by the European Union which could result in a new paradigm where "millions will be detained in facilities across Africa or condemned to die along land and water borders" (Landau and Kihato, 2017).

By prioritizing territorial control over individual rights, the Border Management Authority Act demonstrates how refugee governance in South Africa is increasingly shaped by securitized logics, even in the absence of a formal terrorism threat.

1.3 Refugees Amendment Act 11 of 2017

In the post-Apartheid period, South Africa ratified some international human rights treaties including the 1951 Geneva Convention relating to the Status of Refugees, the 1967 New York Protocol relating to the Status of Refugees, as well as other regional instruments such as the 1969 Convention Governing the Specific Aspects of Refugee Problems in Africa (which is a OAU Convention). The latter even broadened the definition of refugee from the previous instruments, to include "every person who, owing to external aggression, occupation, foreign domination or events seriously disturbing public order in either part or the whole of his country of origin or nationality, is compelled to leave his place of habitual residence in order to seek refuge in another place outside his country of origin or nationality".[2]

The Refugees Amendment Act 11 of 2017 (hereafter RAA 2017) is, as its name says, an amendment to the Refugees Act 130 of 1998 (hereafter RA 1998). The RA 1998 was a progressive law which incorporated international refugee law into the legal framework of South Africa and put the country at the forefront of refugee protection within the region. The refugee system became, ever since, an advanced, modern, and tolerant one, outstanding within the continent.

Nevertheless, with the approval of the RAA 2017 and its entering into force on January 1, 2020, the refugee system and refugee protection of the country has substantially and detrimentally been altered (Ziegler, 2020). On the one hand, it complicates access to the asylum regime, while, on the other, it denies asylum seekers certain rights which they used to enjoy. This change has not come from one day to another, but it has been built by the implementation of different restrictive policies which have slowly but steadily constricted refu-

2 See Article 1(2) of the 1969 Convention. Regarding the interpretation and application of this Article, see Harerimana v Chairperson of the Refugee Appeal Board [2013] ZAWCHC 209, (2014) (5) SA 550 (WCC) which held that the OAU definition of refugee should be considered to define the concept of refugee in Africa.

gees' rights. These legal incorporations meant more restrictions to asylum status through "pre-screening procedures; refusal to renew permits originally issued at another Refugee Reception Office (RRO) elsewhere in South Africa; close of RROs and foot-dragging in implementation of court orders that instructed their re-opening; as well as corruption in their operation, and refusal to issue permits to delayed applicants", while in terms of their substantive rights they have "restricted access to employment, education, basic medical care, and marriage (at least) until and unless asylum-seekers are formally recognised as refugees" (Ziegler, 2020:69). They can even lose their refugee status for voting or participating in any political activity of their country of origin. While presented as a legal refinement of the asylum process, these changes impose a presumption of abuse and bad faith on asylum seekers, effectively treating the act of seeking refuge as a potential security risk. This presumption aligns with a broader shift in state posture: one that approaches protection claims with suspicion and exclusion. This framing positions mobility itself – regardless of cause or legal entitlement – as a potential breach of sovereignty. As such, the Act reinforces the logic that refugees, like irregular migrants, represent a threat that must be contained at the border. As declared by Jon Temin, director of Africa programmes at Freedom House, "the South African government should immediately revise the Refugees Amendment Act to safeguard the rights of refugees and asylum seekers and ensure that the Act conforms to South Africa's constitution and international law" (Freedom House, 2020).

One of the practical problems that refugees face in South Africa is related to admissibility after crossing the border, as they face refusal to entry the country, which is an infringement of the principle of non-refoulement. Once a refugee enters the country, she automatically enjoys the protections given by the RA 1998 and should therefore also have an opportunity to apply.[3] What is more, if one is able to enter the country, she must gain an asylum seeker permit dispensed by a Refugee Status Determination Officer. According to Section 21 of the RA 1998, applications for such permits must be in person. However, an appointment system which adjudicates dates as far away as six months to a year has been set up. And while these asylum seekers wait for their appointment, their status is considered to be that of an illegal migrant. Other similar problems are also not rare, such as those in relation to being refused the renovation of a permit because it was originally issued at another Refugee Reception Office, refusal to issue a permit that has been submitted with delay – although that should not be a justification to deny someone refu-

---

3 *Abdi & Another v Minister of Home Affairs & Others* [2011] ZASCA 2, 2011 (3) SA 37 (SCA).

gee status as it would deny the rights established in the 1951 Convention, refusal to renew permits to detainees, among others (Ziegler, 2020).

Furthermore, Section 4(1)(h) denies recognition to those who have entered the country illegally and Section 4(1)(i) those who have failed to report to the Refugee Reception Office within five days of entry into the country. However, let's explain the complications to reporting within five days. The Regulations accompanying the Refugees Amendment Act alter the position of newcomer asylum seekers. Regulation 7 states that those arriving to the country and wishing to apply for asylum must declare their intention to do so when entering South Africa. Only then will they be issued an Asylum Transit Visa in the terms of Section 23 of the Immigration Act, which is valid for five days only. Once they have declared their intention to apply for asylum and have obtained an Asylum Transit Visa, they can go to a Refugee Reception Office in less than five days to formally apply for asylum. As said, according to Section 4(1)(i) of the RAA 2017, if they fail to report to a Refugee Reception Office within five days of entering the country, they will be excluded from refugee status. The problem is that obtaining such a visa is not an easy task, and asylum seekers may unintentionally forget to apply for this visa or do not know how to do so. Five days is a short period for filling lengthy asylum applications without any or very limited assistance. But what is more, there is a practice called "nationality days" at these Offices which establish specific days for specific nationalities to assist them in their applications. For instance, the Somali nationality day is on Thursdays, meaning that Somalis may only enter Refugee Reception Offices on Thursdays. If a five-day Asylum Transit Visa is issued on a Thursday for a Somali national, the moment of her arrival, this visa will unavoidably have expired by the following Thursday, when the newcomer wants to enter a Refugee Reception Office to apply for asylum. And if violating this period, she is then at risk of being excluded from having her refugee status recognized as she is in violation of the immigration laws of the country. If, to this practical barrier to applying for asylum, we add the decision of the Director-General of Home Affairs of 2011, Mkuseli Apleni, of closing three of the six Reception Offices in the Country[4] (that of Johannesburg, Port Elizabeth, and Cape Town) more complications are added to the chances of applying for asylum, which

4 The Port Elizabeth Refugee Reception Office reopened in 2018 after Lawyers for Human Rights brought an application on behalf of the Somali Association of South Africa's Eastern Cape branch challenging the decision to close this Port Elizabeth's office, and the Court ruled that closing these offices increased barriers for asylum seekers to accessing asylum and was irrational and unlawful. This was held in *Minister of Home Affairs and Others v. Somali Association of South Africa, Eastern Cape* (*SASA EC*) *and Another* (831/2013) [2015] ZASCA 35.

increases the hurdles to being recognized with this legal status (Ncube and Tracey, 2020).

But even when one has gained recognition, she may still have issues maintaining such status. That is because RAA 2017 has introduced a series of circumstances which will lead to the cessation of the status of refugee, thus having expanded the reasons under which refugee status could be withdrawn. Among these cases, engagement with consular authorities of the country of origin may be a basis for withdrawal of refugee status and, given that certain legal documentation such as birth certificates, which are often asked by the authorities of South Africa, can only be issued by the country of origin, in many cases one may find herself either uncapable of getting these documentation or under the threat to have her refugee status unrecognized or removed (Ziegler, 2020). Failing to report to a Refugee Reception Office within one month or more after the expiry of their asylum permit will also lead to cessation of refugee status according to Section 22(12). Once one of the conditions to lose refugee status are met, she "may not re-apply for asylum and must be dealt with as an illegal foreigner in terms of section 32 of the Immigration Act" as established by Section 22(13).

More concerning is Section 28(1) which states that refugees and asylum seekers can be removed from South Africa "on grounds of national security, national interest or public order". Definition of these three grounds are not given anywhere in the document. Such vague wording may contribute to providing wide interpretations which may lead to detention and removal. Some have even called these measures as moving South Africa "closer to Donald Trump's America" (Shivji, 2020) and is, again, another proof of the intention to securitize migration in the country. Such legislative changes and introduction of restrictions have been characterized by a shift towards a security-oriented model by the Department of Home Affairs (Duncan, 2020), which in turn gives "excessive emphasis on security in government policy" in justification of responding to the terrorist threat (Hobden, 2020).

Even though different parts of the migration legislation are questionable and may lead to arrest and repatriation in cases where it should not, if the legislative branch may have wronged, it is the turn of the judiciary to make sure that all of the provisions are interpreted according to international human rights norms, which are predominant over national law. In *Ruta v. Minister of Home Affairs*,[5] Mr. Ruta had entered South Africa illegally in 2014 and remained under such status until he was arrested in 2016 for a traffic violation. The

5 *Ruta v Minister of Home Affairs* [*2018*] *ZACC 52*, South Africa: Constitutional Court, 20 December 2018.

Department of Home Affairs wanted to deport him to Rwanda, his country of origin, but he requested to apply for asylum as he claimed he would face death if returned to that country, an application which was opposed by the Department arguing that he had already been in the country for over a year, and it was not too late to apply. The Constitutional Court ruled that the principle of non-refoulement, a customary international norm which has been widely recognized in human rights law, had to be considered in this case. Similarly, even though he had no refugee status by the time, the 1951 UN Convention protects those who have not yet been granted such status. Therefore, the Court found that even though delay might be a factor for determining an asylum claim, Mr. Ruta's application could still be made and could not be disqualified for making such application only because of his delay in doing so (Ncube and Tracey, 2020). While this is a 2018 decision, it will be interesting to see how South African Courts will continue interpreting the Refugee Amendment Act of 2017 and whether they will consider if any provisions are in violation of international law.

The Refugees Amendment Act thus exemplifies how securitization does not always rely on overt emergency discourse but can also operate through legal instruments that quietly erode access to rights.

1.4 Recent Legislative Proposals

The Department of Home Affairs published in November 2023 the "White Paper on Citizenship, Immigration and Refugee Protection: Towards A Complete Overhaul of the Migration System in South Africa" (hereafter new White Paper).[6] The new White Paper had been four years under negotiations and the final version was finally published in April 2024. After a public consultation process, the Minister of Home Affairs published a revised draft which, by the time of writing, is again under public consultation. Once this stage is finalized by early 2026, the White Paper is expected to be presented as a bill before the National Assembly.

When the new White Paper was released, the Minister of Home Affairs, Aaron Motsoaledi, made a public statement in which it declared that it was a mistake not to have made any reservations to the 1951 Refugee Convention and its Protocol and that, as a result, national Courts had applied the law in ways that were not favourable to South Africa. As a result, one of the policy framework recommendations of the new White Paper is to withdraw from these

6 The new proposal is available here: https://www.gov.za/sites/default/files/gcis_document/202311/49690gon4061.pdf.

international instruments to then re-accede with reservations (Motsoaledi, 2023). However, it is important to recall that South Africa would still be bound internationally by the 1969 OAU Convention, as this also contains key principles similar to those of the 1951 Refugee Convention. In addition, it would still have to comply with the customary principle of non-refoulement.

And yet, the reality that refugees face in South Africa is of an arduous path before gaining, for instance, permanent residency. The Refugees Act allows for certification to apply for permanent residence only ten years after gaining refugee status. The Scalibrini Centre, an organization designed to facilitate the arrival and integration of migrants based in Cape Town, has stated that, from their experience, it actually usually takes from 20 to 25 years for refugees to gain citizenship (Scalibrini Centre, 2024).

Both the 2017 White Paper and the new White Paper endorse negative language towards immigration, contributing to rising tensions between nationals and foreigners in the country. With the latest statements by Motsoaledi, it is even shown that there is no differentiation between migrant groups, considering equally important to contend economic migration and refugees or asylum seekers. Unwanted migration has thus become a wide group encompassing all types of immigrants. As UNHCR (2024) has declared, proposals in the new White Paper "risk isolating the refugee community and exposing them to hostility, without offering effective and sustainable responses to the challenges of migration that face the country".

2 Xenophobia in South Africa

Discrimination has a long history in South Africa, shaped by colonialism and apartheid, during which racialized exclusion was formally institutionalized against the country's black population. Today, despite the formal dismantling of apartheid, deep social inequalities persist, and xenophobia has emerged as a distinct and enduring problem within the post-apartheid order (Misago, 2017).

While Apartheid constitutes a crucial historical backdrop for understanding contemporary patterns of exclusion in South Africa, it should not be conflated with present-day xenophobia. Apartheid was a legally entrenched system of racial domination, whereas xenophobia in post-apartheid South Africa emerges in a formally rights-based constitutional order and targets primarily non-nationals rather than racialized citizens. Nonetheless, apartheid-era governance left enduring institutional, spatial, and socio-economic legacies, particularly regarding mobility control, policing practices, and the construction of "outsiders", that continue to shape how migration and foreignness are framed today. In this sense, Apartheid functions not as an equivalent to contemporary xenophobia, but as a historical precedent that helps explain the persistence of exclusionary logics within a radically transformed political context.

It was not until 1994 with the fall of the Apartheid government that the new executive decided to move away from the policy of exclusion to one based on the protection of fundamental rights. With the ratification of the OAU Refugee Convention in 1995 and of the UN Refugee Convention and its Protocol in 1996, South Africa was entering a new era in which a new refugee approach would begin. One year later, in 1997, the Green Paper on migration was approved, which evolved into two White Papers,[7] one for Refugee Law and one for Immigration Law (Khan and Rayer, 2020).

Even with these legislative changes incorporating a new and more friendly framework towards immigration, and specially refugees, xenophobic sentiments persisted among certain groups, now primarily directed at non-nationals rather than racialized citizens". As Abdul Hassan, chairperson of the Somali Association of South Africaplaces, explains: "They [South Africans] didn't get what was promised to them after the 1994 elections. So they think that the little that they have [is] being shared by [people] from African countries who have come to South Africa. They [South Africans] don't want that" (Adjai and Lazardis, 2013).

The reality that the migrant community faces in the country is one of exclusion, produced through contemporary administrative and policing practices rather than formal racial segregation. Ataboungwoung and Nkoko (2025) illustrate how Francophone African immigrants in South Africa find it difficult to find employment because of exclusive laws and language barriers.

In areas most affected by xenophobic violence, exclusion is increasingly articulated through spatialized notions of rights and belonging that draw on historically sedimented forms of territorial ordering. These understandings are mobilized to expel "unwanted" African migrants and reclaim control over local spaces (Landau & Misago, 2009; Thompson, 2016).

As a result, struggles over belonging are increasingly expressed through spatial practices, where violence becomes a means of asserting territorial authority and social membership. Using the case of Somali migrants' in South Africa, Pineteh shows how exclusionary performances of belonging can generate reactive forms of resistance among migrants with established ties to South Africa.

7 Green Papers are documents used as proposals and set out for discussion, while White Papers are statements of policy which establish the proposals for legislative changes. Green Papers precede White Papers. And White Papers precede formal Bills.

The article links Somali migrants' perceptions of xenophobia with South Africans' claims to spatial entitlement, framing these dynamics around control, belonging, and social inclusion. It shows how Somali business clustering both heightens vulnerability to xenophobic attacks and enables collective identity, territorial presence, and rapid mobilization in response to violence.

As Nduru (2005) pointed, police officers resorted to routinely confiscate and destroy refugees' documents to justify arresting them as illegal migrants. And all this happened before the more restrictive changes in the law that have succeeded in recent years and which have been analysed in this chapter, such as the White Paper of 2017. Furthermore, as mentioned previously, the Refugees Amendment Act 11 of 2017 also introduced a series of changes that make the process of applying for asylum excessively bureaucratic and poses many difficulties to obtaining the status, such as the limitation of five days to report to a Refugee Reception Office or the closure of some of these offices around the country. And this is just one of the many examples which can be found in these most recent legislative changes. While in theory the South Africa refugee system used to be one of the most generous, its implementation is in truth much more restrictive and is based on domestic legitimacy gains through exclusion and "a state-led bureaucratized merging of refugees and migrants, in the shadow of institutionalized xenophobia leading to increasing securitization" (Moyo et al., 2021).

One of the reasons which reinforce this xenophobic feeling towards refugees and which promotes the securitization of migration in South Africa is that the government has taken an active role in targeting foreigners by blaming them for negatively contributing to the worsening of the economic system of the country, which continues to foster this negative image of the refugee and asylum seeker coming to South Africa among the population. There have been certain political moves directed towards the migrant population to accuse them of damaging the economy of the country. One example is that of Operation Hardstick by which the Limpopo police was instructed to shut down those businesses owned by refugees and asylum seekers (Carciotto, 2020). Later on, the Supreme Court of Appeal[8] ruled in 2014 that the actions taken by the police were unlawful. In other occasions, foreigners have also been accused of dominating the informal trade sector and on being the source of the country's socio-economic problems, beliefs which even led to xenophobic demonstrations in Gauteng and KwaZulu-Natal during 2015 (Kharsany, 2015). Unfortunately, actions in the same negative lines have also been approved by

8 *Somali Association of South Africa v Limpopo Department of Economic Development, Environment and Tourism* (48/2014) ZASCA 143 (26 September 2014).

provincial governments such as those of Limpopo, which wanted to remove Zimbabwean migrants from the province and have even led to their deportation (Carciotto, 2020) and several other xenophobic violent actions against non-nationals have taken place during the last decade (HRW, 2020).

Some of the conditions that foreigners face in South Africa are a result of governmental actions to detain undocumented persons. Documentation raids have often taken place and have led to arrests to both documented and undocumented migrants, who have later on remained under arrest for several days or even weeks while their legal status was being verified and without access to their lawyer. Some have even reported being beaten by law enforcement officials. But some of the mistreatment also comes from nationals who verbally and physically harass them because they blame them for high unemployment and crime rates, among other issues (HRW, 2020).

Furthermore, the current migration system in South Africa does not consider gendered aspects of migration and thus fails to compensate the vulnerabilities that these groups suffer. While women represent almost half of the migration population in the continent, migrant women in the country have quadrupled in the last 15 years (Mbiyozo, 2018). And while South Africa's National Development Plan 2030 implements as some of its goals those in relation to both migration and women and some legislation has been passed to achieve gender equality in some sectors, in the case of migration this has not been the case (Farley, 2019).

Violence has been exacerbated in recent years following xenophobic attacks. Operation Fiela is a joint operation by the South African Police Service and other departments of the South African government. The operation was designed to conduct raids to arrest irregular migrants in the country. An example of these actions is when the police detained 235 immigrants in the Central Methodist Church of Johannesburg, where they took shelter. Following the arrests, President Zuma stated that "the government will not tolerate illegal immigrants" (NWI, 2023). Civil society has also mobilized, which has resulted in a new anti-migrant movement. After "Put South Africa First", now Operation Dudula (which means "push back", in Zulu language) is a new branch of the organization which started in Soweto in July 2021 after President Zuma was sentenced to jail for contempt of court. The movement, originated by Nhlanhla 'Lux' Dlamini, has been followed by the launch of other anti-immigrant groups, and they are driven by the belief that immigration is restricting access to nationals to health services, job opportunities, social grants, and are a source of criminality.

Unlike apartheid, which relied on explicit racial hierarchies enshrined in law, contemporary xenophobia operates through administrative exclusion, discretionary enforcement, and political narratives of economic threat, rendering it both formally lawful and socially normalized. Xenophobia in South Africa does not just manifest as societal prejudice: it is increasingly institutionalized through laws, policing practices, and political rhetoric. Refugees, in particular, are frequently portrayed as contributors to economic strain and public disorder, reinforcing their image as undesirable outsiders. This association contributes to their securitization, as the state justifies exceptional restrictions and enforcement not only against undocumented migrants but also against those legally entitled to protection. The result is a discursive merger of "refugee" and "threat", where fear of the foreigner legitimates the erosion of refugee rights.

Major instances on xenophobic violence started in 2008. Almost 20 years later, xenophobia is still a persistent problem in the country. In 2022 and 2023 Xenowatch reported 170 incidents (HRW, 2024). In the words of Crush (2022), "One consequence of two decades of xenophobia governance by displacement in South Africa is, in fact, intensified xenophobia on the ground as there is no countervailing discourse about the benefits of migration." The anti-immigrant rhetoric used by politicians in the country is fuelling xenophobia and resulting in more violence against immigrants. Measures to fight xenophobia and to ensure the integration of immigrants in the country are urgently needed, and specially to protect those more vulnerable groups such as that of refugees.

Several scholars have noted that South African authorities have been reluctant to publicly acknowledge xenophobia or their own role in producing the temporal and legal marginalization of non-citizens. While anti-immigrant rhetoric has become increasingly visible in electoral politics, the government has tended to deny responsibility for fostering hostile attitudes or enabling violence against migrants. Instead, official discourse often reframes such violence either as *Afrophobia* (attributed to apartheid-era conditioning) (Ochonu, 2021) or as ordinary criminality (Tagwirei, 2019). Both narratives deflect state accountability, deny citizen agency, and recast anti-immigrant violence as an inherited or inevitable consequence of historical inequality rather than as a contemporary political failure. By portraying migrants as illegal competitors for jobs, services, and economic opportunities – and even as instruments of entrenched economic power – these framings legitimize exclusionary practices while reinforcing a security-oriented approach to migration governance.

Taken together, these dynamics illustrate how xenophobia in South Africa is not merely a societal pathology but a politically mediated and institutionally sustained phenomenon. Through the normalization of anti-immigrant rhetoric, the denial of state responsibility, and the framing of migration as a security and economic threat, exclusionary practices are rendered legitimate and durable. For refugees and asylum seekers, this environment translates into heightened vulnerability, diminished protection, and the erosion of rights within a formally rights-based constitutional order. Xenophobia thus becomes both a driver and a consequence of the securitization of migration, reinforcing a cycle of exclusion that the current legal and policy framework has yet to disrupt.

3 Conclusions

In this chapter we have seen how recent legislative changes in South Africa have affected immigration and, in particular, the rights of asylum seekers and refugees. In recent years, the government has shown through the White Paper on International Migration of 2017 its plan to further control immigration and prioritize skilled migrants only. New laws like the Border Management Authority Act 2 of 2020 and reforms like that of the Refugees Amendment Act 11 of 2017 have difficulted the processing of visas for those seeking refuge, but also the integration of the overall migrant population in the country. Critics have repeatedly said that the asylum system in the country is characterized by years-long backlogs and lengthy appeals, and rejection rates reached as high as 96% in 2019 (Moyo, 2021).

The history of this Southern African country is partly, but importantly, linked to xenophobia. First, against the black population during colonial times, and which lasted until the very end of the Apartheid. But later on, and to this day, immigrants have also been victims of several attacks in the hands of South Africans. These attacks have been more common specially in times of regression and economic crisis. But what is more, the COVID-19 pandemic has made life even more difficult for these groups which, already vulnerable, are struggling to keep their jobs and get access to health. The government has used these strenuous times to progress in their plans to securitize refugees by setting stricter border controls and making it more burdensome to apply for asylum and to get visas to stay legally in the country. It has even established a points-based system so that only those with sufficient skills or economic stability can stay in the country.

The Department of Home Affairs now uses a risk-based approach that connects immigration with national security. The 2017 White Paper is clear in this sense: "The current paradigm exposes South Africa to many kinds of risk in a volatile world and by default strengthens colonial patterns of labour, production and trade. It also serves to perpetuate irregular migration, which in turn leads to unacceptable levels of corruption, human rights abuse and national security risks." This risk-based approach will be used to manage "the secure and efficient cross-border movement of people", which are associated with "serious risks such as terrorism and drug smuggling". This strategy will be used to prioritize the deportation of "high-risk migration" over "low-risk migration". What is considered to be a high-risk migrant is yet to be completely identified, as risks to national security can be broadly interpreted.

This was a country that used to be friendly towards asylum seekers and refugees, but while on paper they used to have many rights, in practice it was harder to enjoy them. Today, with these legislative changes, even more. This complex situation serves again as another example of how securitization measures are taking place globally, and not only in Western countries. The ways in which countries deal with immigration groups, including refugees, are more commonly linked to national security strategies which regress in the rights that migrant communities had gained in many countries. The terrorist threat has been one of the most popular arguments which have been used to connect immigrants, and even refugees, to terrorist attacks and potential security threats for the country. But the COVID-19 has also been used as another justification to continue approving measures that refrain and control immigration, furthering in these processes of securitizing migration and securitizing refugees particularly.

What emerges across the chapters is a shared discursive pattern: the refugee, once a symbol of vulnerability and protection, is reframed as a figure of potential risk. In South Africa, this shift is fuelled not by transnational terror concerns but by populist narratives linking foreignness to crime, unemployment, and disorder. The result is a securitization logic that spreads through legal, administrative, and symbolic means, a logic that displaces humanitarian commitments in favour of exclusionary state practices. This is not a regional aberration, but a sign of global convergence in the governance of displacement.

As Kandjii () explains, exclusion in South Africa operates through a self-reinforcing cycle in which public fears of outsiders shape electoral preferences, political rhetoric, and policy choices. Politicians amplify anti-immigrant narratives to mobilize support, which in turn legitimizes societal hostility and violence against migrants, often in the absence of accountability. Media dynamics further entrench this cycle by reinforcing dominant exclusionary frames.

South Africa's case highlights how securitization can take root through domestic logics that differ from the terrorism frameworks dominant in Western states. Refugees and asylum seekers are increasingly portrayed as burdens on public resources and threats to social order. Legislative reforms have curtailed rights once available to them and reinforced a narrative that conflates forced displacement with illegality and insecurity. This case demonstrates that the securitization of refugees is not a Western anomaly, but a global trend in which legal protections are reinterpreted through the lens of sovereignty, control, and exclusion. A core concern of this book's comparative inquiry. The cases of the European Union, the United States, and South Africa are just some of the few examples which can be found in this direction, but many other countries have taken similar steps or plans of action to deal with international migration. It will be then gripping to see to what extent we can continue forgetting about the rights of the most vulnerable in the name of security.

References

Adjai, C., and Lazaridis, G. (2013) 'Migration, xenophobia and new racism in post-apartheid South Africa', *International Journal of Social Science Studies*, Vol.1(1), pp. 192–205.

AlJazeera (2020) 'South Africa to build 40km fence along Zimbabwe border', *AlJazeera*. Available at: https://www.aljazeera.com/news/2020/3/20/south-africa-to-build-40km-fence-along-zimbabwe-border.

Ataboungwoung, G. and Nkoko, M. (2025) 'A Qualitative Case Study of Experience of Xenophobia Among Francophone African Informal Immigrant Entrepreneurs in Pretoria', *International Journal of Applied Research in Business and Management*, Vol. 6(5).

Bornman, J. (2020) 'SA's border bill another anti-migrant development', *New Frame*, 26 July. Available at: https://www.newframe.com/sas-border-bill-another-anti-immigrant-development/.

BusinessTech (2020) 'South African taxpayers spent R40 million on a fence that doesn't work -what went wrong', 19 August. Available at: https://businesstech.co.za/news/government/426830/south-african-taxpayers-spent-r40-million-on-a-fence-that-doesnt-work-what-went-wrong/.

Carciotto, S. (2020) 'In the cross-hairs: foreigners in SA's informal sector', *Institute for Security Studies*, 7 December. Available at: https://issafrica.org/iss-today/in-the-cross-hairs-foreigners-in-sas-informal-sector.

Chirume, J. (2021) 'About 180,000 Zimbabweans in SA face uncertain future', *Citizenship Rights in Africa Initiative*, May 27. Available at: https://citizenshiprightsafrica.org/about-180000-zimbabweans-in-sa-face-uncertain-future/.

Coertzen, P. (2011) 'The Huguenots of South Africa in History and Religious identity', *Stellenbosch Theological Journal*, Vol. 122, pp. 45–57.

Crush, J. (2022) 'Xenophobia Denialism and the Global Compact for Migration in South Africa', *Governing Migration for Development from the Global Souths*, Vol. 14.

Du Plessis, C. (2020) 'Zimbabweans stuck in SA because of pandemic slapped with five-year ban', *Daily Maverick*, 21 May. Available at: https://www.dailymaverick.co.za/article/2020-05-21-zimbabweans-stuck-in-sa-because-of-pandemic-slapped-with-five-year-ban/.

Duncan, J. (2020) 'South Africa's emerging Department of Homeland Security', *Daily Maverick*, 20 January. Available at: https://www.dailymaverick.co.za/article/2020-01-20-south-africas-emerging-department-of-homeland-security/.

Erasmus, G. (2020) 'New Border Management for South Africa amidst unresolved systemic Issues', *Tralac*, 12 February. Available at: https://www.tralac.org/blog/article/14393-new-border-management-for-south-africa-amidst-unresolved-systemic-issues.html.

Farley, A. (2019) 'South African Migration Policy: A Gendered Analysis', Policy Insights, *South African Institute of International Affairs*, No. 70.

Feldbaum, H., Patel, P., Sondorp, E. and Lee, K. (2006) 'Global health and national security: the need for critical engagement', *Medicine Conflict and Survival*, Vol. 22(3), pp. 192–198.

FHR (2018) 'SEJA Baselina Survey', Foundation for Human Rights. Available at: https://static.pmg.org.za/SEJA_Report.pdf.

Freedom House (2020), 'South Africa: Authorities Must Improve Treatment of Refugees and Asylum Seekers', *Freedom House*. Available at: https://freedomhouse.org/article/south-africa-authorities-must-improve-treatment-refugees-and-asylum-seekers.

Hicks, T. F. (1999) 'The constitution, aliens control act, and xenophobia: The struggle to protect Africa's pariah the undocumented immigrant', *Indiana Journal of Global Legal Studies*, Vol. 7(1), pp. 393–418.

Hobden, C. (2020) 'South Africa takes fresh steps to restrict rights of refugees', *The Conversation*, 5 February. Available at: https://theconversation.com/south-africa-takes-fresh-steps-to-restrict-rights-of-refugees-130606.

HRW (2020) "They Have Robbed Me of My Life": Xenophobic Violence Against Non-Nationals in South Africa', *Human Rights Watch*. Available at: https://www.hrw.org/report/2020/09/17/they-have-robbed-me-my-life/xenophobic-violence-against-non-nationals-south.

HRW (2024) 'South Africa: Toxic Rhetoric Endangers Migrants', *Human Rights Watch*. Available at: https://www.hrw.org/news/2024/05/06/south-africa-toxic-rhetoric-endangers-migrants.

IOM (2020) 'Migration Factsheet No. 6 – The impact of COVID-19 on migrants', International Organization for Migration. Available at: https://www.iom.int/sites/default/files/our_work/ICP/MPR/migration_factsheet_6_covid-19_and_migrants.pdf.

Kandjii, J. (2025) 'Hunger, Anger and Strangers: Assembling Refugee Exclusion and Food Insecurity among Refugees and Asylum Seekers in South Africa' in Crush, J., Chikanda, A. and Ramachandran, S. (eds.) in *New Directions in South South Migration*. Springer: Switzerland.

Khan, F. and Rayner, N. (2020) 'Country Fiche: South Africa', ASILE Project. Available at: https://www.asileproject.eu/wp-content/uploads/2021/03/Country-Fiche_South-Africa_Final_Pub.pdf.

Kharsany, S. (2015) 'Uneasy calm in Johannesburg after anti-immigrant riots', *AlJazeera*, 19 April. Available at: https://www.aljazeera.com/news/2015/4/19/uneasy-calm-in-johannesburg-after-anti-immigrant-riots.

Landau, L. B. and Kihato, C. (2017) 'Securitising Africa's Borders is Bad for Migrants, Democracy and Development', *The New Humanitarian*, 5 July. Available at: https://www.thenewhumanitarian.org/fr/node/259499.

Landau, L. B., and J. P. Misago (2009) 'Who to Blame and What's to Gain? Reflections on Space, State, and Violence in Kenya and South Africa', *Africa Spectrum*, Vol. 44-(1), pp. 99–110.

Maunganidze, O. A. and Mbiyozo, A. (2020) 'South Africa's Border Management Authority dream could be a nightmare', *Institute for Security Studies*, 11 August. Available at: https://issafrica.org/iss-today/south-africas-border-management-authority-dream-could-be-a-nightmare.

Mbiyozo, A. N. (2018) 'Gender and Migration in South Africa: Talking to Women Migrants', Southern Africa Report, *Institute for Security Studies*. Available at: https://issafrica.org/research/southern-africa-report/gender-and-migration-in-south-africa-talking-to-women-migrants.

Mbiyozo, A. N. (2018) 'Aligning South Africa's migration policies with its African vision', *Institute for Security Studies*.

Misago, J. P. (2017) 'Politics by other means? The political economy of xenophobic violence in South Africa', *The Black Scholar*, Vol. 47(2), pp. 40–53.

Misago, J. P. and Landau, L. B. (2023) 'Running Them Out of Time:' Xenophobia, Violence, and Co-Authoring Spatiotemporal Exclusion in South Africa', Geopolitics, Vol. 28(4).

Moyo, K., Sebba, K. R. and Zanker, F. (2021) 'Who is watching? Refugee protection during a pandemic -responses from Uganda and South Africa', *Comparative Migration Studies*, Vol. 9(37).

Motsoaledi, Aaron (2023) 'Press statement on the release of the white paper on Citizenship, Immigration and Refugee Protection: Towards a complete overhaul of the migration system in South Africa', *Department of Home Affairs of the Republic of South Africa*, 12 November. Available at: https://www.dha.gov.za/index.php/statements-speeches/1724-press-statement-on-the-release-of-the-white-paper-on-citizenship-immigration-and-refugee-protection-towards-a-complete-overhaul-of-the-migration-system-in-south-africa.

Mukumbang, F. C. (2020) 'Are asylum seekers, refugees and foreign migrants considered in the COVID-19 vaccine discourse?', *British Medical Journal Global Health*, Vol. 5.

Ncube, W. and Tracey, C. (2020) 'Monitoring policy, litigious and legislative shifts in immigration detention in South Africa', *Lawyers for Human Rights*. Available at: https://www.lhr.org.za/wp-content/uploads/2020/06/Detention-Report-Final-Final-Digital-1.pdf.

Ndenze, B. (2020) 'Mapisa-Nqakula: Beitbridge border fence is useless', *Eyewitness News*, October. Available at: https://ewn.co.za/2020/10/06/mapisa-nqakula-beitbridge-border-fence-is-useless.

Nduru, M. (2005) 'SA doesn't roll out welcome mat for all immigrants', *Mail and Guardian*, 22 August.

Ochonu, M. E. (2021) 'Black South African intellectuals went from pan-Africanism to insular afrophobia', London School of Economics Blog. Available at: https://blogs.lse.ac.uk/africaatlse/2021/03/03/black-south-african-intellectuals-went-from-pan-africanism-to-insular-afrophobia/.

OECD (2020) 'What is the impact of the COVID-19 pandemic on immigrants and their children?', Organisation for Economic Co-operation and Development. Available at: https://read.oecd-ilibrary.org/view/?ref=137_137245-8saheqv0k3&title=What-is-the-impact-of-the-COVID-19-pandemic-on-immigrants-and-their-children%3F&_ga=2.235258882.222265795.1629270819-1426864779.1629270818.

Moyo, K. (2021) 'South Africa Reckons with Its Status as a Top Immigration Destination, Apartheid History, and Economic Challenges', *Migration Policy Institute*. Available at: https://www.migrationpolicy.org/article/south-africa-immigration-destination-history.

Moyo, K. and Zanker, F. (2022) 'No Hope for the 'Foreigners': The Conflation of Refugees and Migrants in South Africa', *Journal of Immigrant and Refugee Studies*, Vol. 20(2), pp. 253–265.

NWI (2023) 'Operation Fiela: Raids Illegal Immigrants', *New World Immigration*.

Pineteh, E. (2017) 'Spatial Contestation, Victimisation and Resistance during Xenophobic Violence: The Experiences of Somali Migrants in Post-Apartheid South Africa', *International Migration*, Vol. 56(2), pp. 133–145.

Scalabrini (2019) 'What Is The White Paper On International Migration?', *Scalabrini Centre of Cape Town*. Available at: https://www.scalabrini.org.za/news/what-is-the-white-paper-on-international-migration/.

Scalabrini (2024) 'Submission on the White Paper on Citizenship, Immigration and Refugee Protection: Towards a Complete Overhaul of the Migration System in South Africa', *Scalabrini Centre of Cape Town*. Available at: https://www.scalabrini.org.za/wp-content/uploads/2024/02/White_Paper_Submission_2024.pdf.

Shivji, N. (2020) 'Change to the Refugees Act moves South Africa much closer to Donald Trump's America', *Daily Maverick*, 4 February. Available at: https://www.dailymaverick.co.za/article/2020-02-04-change-to-the-refugees-act-moves-south-africa-much-closer-to-donald-trumps-america/.

STATS SA (2021) 'Statistical Release P0302. Mid-year population estimates, 2020'. Department of Statistics of South Africa. Available at: http://www.statssa.gov.za/publications/P0302/P03022020.pdf.

Tagwirei, C. (2019) 'A New Word is Needed for Xenophobia, but It's Not Criminality, *Business Day*, 14 September. Available at: https://www.businessday.co.za/bd/opinion/2019-09-14-a-new-word-is-needed-for-xenophobia-but-its-not-criminality/.

Thompson, D. K. (2016) 'Risky Business and Geographies of Refugee Capitalism in the Somali Migrant Economy of Gauteng, South Africa', *Journal of Ethnic and Migration Studies*, Vol. 42(1), pp. 120–135.

UNAIDS (2020) 'UNAIDS Data 2020'. Available at: https://www.unaids.org/sites/default/files/media_asset/2020_aids-data-book_en.pdf.

UNDP (2020), 'International Migrant Stock 2020: Destination and Origin', United Nations Population Division.

UNHCR (2019) 'Global Trends: Forced Displacement in 2019'. Available at: https://www.unhcr.org/afr/statistics/unhcrstats/5ee200e37/unhcr-global-trends-2019.html.

UNHCR (2024) 'UNHCR's Observations on the 'White Paper on Citizenship, Immigration and Refugee Protection: Towards a Complete Overhaul of the Migration System in South Africa', *United Nations High Commissioner for Refugees*. Available at: https://www.refworld.org/policy/polrec/unhcr/2024/en/147563?destination=search.

Vearey, J., de Gruchy, T. and Maple, N. (2021) 'Global health (security), immigration governance and Covid-19 in South(ern) Africa: An evolving research agenda', *Journal of Migration and Health*, Vol. 3.

Ziegler, R. (2020) 'Access to Effective Refugee Protection in South Africa: Legislative Commitment, Policy Realities, Judicial Rectifications?', *Constitutional Court Review*, Vol. 10, pp. 65–106.

Conclusions

This manuscript has demonstrated that the securitization of migration, and of refugees in particular, has become a widespread and entrenched practice across multiple national and regional contexts. The attacks of September 11, 2001, marked a turning point, significantly shaping the discourse and legal frameworks used to justify increasingly restrictive measures, especially under the banner of counter-terrorism. Since then, a wave of legislation and policy reforms has expanded state powers to control borders and limit the rights of those seeking protection. While the origins of this latest wave of securitization lie in the "War on Terror", it has since evolved to address broader concerns around irregular migration and demographic control. This was most clearly evident in the response to the migratory crisis in 2015–2016, which further solidified the treatment of refugee movements as matters of national and regional security.

Therefore, even though many states have used the terrorist justification to apply these measures, the fight against the terrorist threat is not the only ground on which the approval of these laws and policies is based. It was just the beginning. As seen in the case of South Africa, non-Western states are also securitizing migration, and they are not always doing so in the name of the war on terror. In this case, as explained in Chapter 6, measures have been said to be necessary to protect from illegal immigration, as it is considered a security threat to economic stability, sovereignty, and blamed for higher criminality rates. The securitization of migration is then not only constructed on the fight against the terrorist threat, but it is also securitized following a wide range of argumentations other than terrorism. However, the case of every country is different, showing that this is not a homogeneous phenomenon, as it has been applied with different degrees depending on the country, as seen in the cases of the European Union, the United States, and South Africa in Chapters 4 to 6.

Practices securitizing migration also show that there is a preference for national security over human security. National self-interests and the protection of national territory come first, even before the security of vulnerable groups such as that of refuges. What the securitization of refugee groups shows in this respect is that changes in the political paradigm strongly affect the rights of unprotected or more exposed groups. States are prioritizing national security strategies over human security, and this has a great impact on the rights of the most vulnerable groups of our societies. As a result, refugees have become even more vulnerable.

 | HTTPS://DOI.ORG/10.1163/9789004704527-009

1 Key Findings

The analysis carried out across the three case studies has led to several important findings. First, the securitization of refugees is neither incidental nor marginal but has become a normalized and institutionalized component of migration governance. Despite the formal protections granted by the 1951 Refugee Convention and international human rights law, refugees have increasingly been subject to policies and legal frameworks that prioritize security over protection. Second, the discursive portrayal of refugees as threats is not limited to associations with terrorism. In all three cases, refugees are also linked to broader societal anxieties, from economic strain and unemployment to threats to cultural identity and national sovereignty. Third, the trend towards securitization marks a deeper shift from human security to state-centric security paradigms. Rather than emphasizing the rights and vulnerabilities of forcibly displaced persons, the focus increasingly lies on controlling movement, mitigating perceived risks, and protecting national borders. Lastly, while the language and mechanisms of securitization have diffused globally, their application is context-dependent, revealing both shared logics and distinctive regional priorities.

The analysis of the European Union, the United States, and South Africa has shown that while the logic of securitization is common across these cases, the specific justifications and modalities differ according to historical, political, and regional contexts. In the European Union, securitization has largely been driven by the need to control large refugee flows, particularly after the 2015–2016 migratory crisis, and has focused on externalizing border controls and strengthening return mechanisms. In the United States, the securitization of migration has been deeply intertwined with counter-terrorism efforts, particularly following 9/11, and has been characterized by expansive security legislation, detention practices, and travel bans. In South Africa, although the direct threat of terrorism has been less pronounced, migration has been increasingly framed as a security risk to economic stability and national sovereignty, leading to restrictive immigration reforms and heightened border controls.

Looking at each case more deeply, in the European Union we see that the post-2015 asylum crisis was a decisive moment, intensifying an already existing trend towards externalizing borders and increasing return mechanisms. The EU's approach, shaped by collective but uneven national interests, has emphasized containment over integration, often outsourcing migration control to third countries under the logic of protecting the Schengen space. Refugees are framed as an unmanageable flow that burdens welfare systems and jeopardizes internal cohesion, leading to the erosion of protection standards across member states.

In the United States, the securitization of refugees is deeply embedded in post-9/11 national security architecture. Legal and institutional responses such as the USA PATRIOT Act, the creation of the Department of Homeland Security, and successive executive orders have entrenched a link between forced migration and terrorism. Refugees, particularly from Muslim-majority countries, have been cast as latent threats, and entry has been conditioned by extreme vetting, suspension programmes, and categorical exclusions. Here, securitization has functioned both as policy and performance, reinforcing broader narratives of internal threat and sovereign protection.

South Africa presents a distinct yet complementary case. Although not facing transnational terrorism, the country has witnessed a progressive conflation of refugees with irregular migration, crime, and economic instability. Policies and political discourse have framed asylum seekers as competitors for scarce resources and threats to public order. This has led to increasingly restrictive legislative proposals, the erosion of durable solutions like permanent residency, and a reliance on enforcement and deterrence. Unlike the EU and US cases, securitization in South Africa emerges more from domestic socio-economic pressures than from transnational security logics, but the effects on refugee rights and access to protection are no less severe.

While each case has its own political and legal history, a comparative reading reveals important parallels in how securitization narratives are constructed and deployed. Despite their vastly different histories, institutional frameworks, and exposure to terrorist threats, the EU, the US, and South Africa have all developed securitized approaches to refugee governance. In the US, the post-9/11 era institutionalized a direct link between asylum and terrorism; in the EU, security concerns are framed more broadly, tied to border control and integration challenges; in South Africa, securitization emerges from internal political pressures and economic precarity. In each context, the refugee becomes a proxy for deeper fears: fear of violence, of demographic change, of systemic crisis. The convergence lies not in identical policies but in the logic that underpins them: that managing refugee flows is a matter of national security, not international responsibility.

2 Presenting Refugees as a Threat

Dramatic increasing refugee flows can be overwhelming and difficult to manage for some states, which is one of the things that have happened in the past years (Loescher, 1993). There may be different reasons why the citizenry may be worried about the arrival of foreigners to their countries. Mandel (1997) explains that there is, for instance, a difference between developing and developed countries. While the first worry about economic disruptions, the latter are usually more concerned about political ones. Thus, the way in which migrants – and refugees – are seen by the host society is also dependant on the specific states we are looking at. As it has been previously said, the situation that each state may be facing at a given time – whether there is a time of crisis or need, for instance – but also the history of the country with migration – is also a determinant factor affecting the perception of immigrants within the host state. Altogether, linking migration to burdens and risks leads to a generalized perception that refugees lead the country to scarcity and degradation, and the feeling that refugee flows are a threat is spread across territories. And at times, these arguments are also used as a tool by political parties to blame refugee for domestic problems, whether these are related to economic regressions or public budget cuts, crime, overpopulation, and a long etcetera. If on top of that, we add ethnic or cultural nationalism as a tool to manipulate the citizens to reinforce their identity in connection to the political leaders and in detriment of the refugee population, these tendencies to connect migration to national security threats increase the difficulties of integrating them into the country. Bello (2017) summarizes this process in the following words:

> When migrants are treated as criminals, detained in immigration centres or deported, this will indeed increase prejudiced attitudes towards them (…) Therefore, the securitization of migration is a spiral that has started with particular frames of interpreting our world. These, mixed with actual facts, policies, practices, narratives and techniques, have engendered a spiralling progression that each of these factors has contributed to speeding. Therefore, it is crucial to stop the intensity of its driving forces in order to avoid that this securitization flows, from the societal, into different domains.

Securitization is inherently linked to the logic of exception. The greater the perceived threat, the easier it becomes for states to justify the use of extraordinary measures that depart from normal political procedures. Ideally, such measures should be reserved for truly exceptional circumstances – when ordinary tools like diplomacy, development cooperation, or law enforcement are insufficient. By definition, exceptional measures must be temporary and proportionate to the threat they seek to address and should be lifted once that threat subsides. In theory, once an issue is no longer an urgent security concern, it should be "desecuritized" (Buzan, Wæver, and de Wilde, 1998) and returned to the realm of ordinary politics. However, in practice, the exceptional measures introduced in the wake of 9/11 have persisted, expanded, and been repurposed – justified by a shifting set of social, political, and economic arguments. This normalization of exceptionality raises serious concerns. It is therefore crucial to assess whether such measures remain proportionate, necessary, and justified. This book has aimed to contribute to that task by showing that securitizing migration – and particularly portraying refugees as threats – often lacks a reasonable or evidence-based foundation and instead reflects broader political strategies of exclusion and control.

As previously explained, the establishment of this relationship between migration and security has pursued self-interested political purposes in order to legitimize privileged positions (Karyotis, 2007; Messina, 2014) and approve measures that would otherwise be hard to implement. Accepting an issue such as immigration as a common security threat can become an opportunity for politicians to reinforce collective identification and generate greater loyalties (Boswell, 2007); thus, it is important to detect when this happens and report it.

Conflicts around the world always involve migration movements, either with internal displacements or with people fleeing their home countries searching for safety elsewhere. As a response to these migratory flows, immigration legislation and policies have harshened globally, making it more difficult for them to feel secure in host countries. These refugees are in very vulnerable positions, and having their rights restrained once leaving their homes, makes it even harder for them to protect themselves and their families. Today, migration is approached through the lens of national security. Terrorist attacks, economic recession and times of crisis have paved the way for politicians to justify harder security measures, not only restricting the rights of its own citizens at times, but also restricting specifically those of non-nationals.

This reflects a shift in state priorities, where national security increasingly takes precedence over human security, a trend that is especially significant given the transformations currently reshaping the international order, with direct and far-reaching implications for individuals. Rather than placing the individual at the centre of concern, the state continues to occupy that central position. A truly universalist approach, one that prioritizes the protection of all human beings and reflects a collective international responsibility, has yet to materialize. While there were moments when international cooperation appeared to be moving in that direction, these efforts have largely fallen short of achieving their stated aspirations. Instead of going beyond a state-centric world politics in which each state is responsible only of the security of its sovereignty, territory, and population, we have remained right there. And while migration is also part of the international debate, it has mostly been dealt with at the state level. We have seen mass refugee flows around the world, and yet many states have been resilient to accept asylum seekers into their countries for considering them a potential terrorist threat, or an economic burden, or both. And an international response has not been appropriately given.

Finally, it is important to mention the part that racism and discrimination play in this securitization process. Those using anti-immigrant discourses in the West blame a particular image of the migrant. The male national from Arab and Muslim-majority countries is the most often immigrant looked at with distrust, and the one most often linked to a national security threat. But refugees from developing countries in general, especially if coming from third non-Western countries, are all equally blamed by some for economic recession, regression in healthcare assistance, or insecurity. However, what the Russian–Ukrainian 2022 conflict has shown is that European countries have not been so unwilling to welcome refugees to their homes. They have not really seen them as security threats -even though this had become the fastest refugee crisis in the world since 1950, as confirmed by Flippo Grandi, UN High Commissioner for Refugees (Aragó, 2022). While refugees from Syria, Libya, and other countries have many times had to arrive illegally to Europe in order to be able to apply for asylum, border barriers have been lifted for Ukrainians (Townsend, 2022; Hedayat, 2022). It is as if this conflict had revealed Europe's "selective empathy on refugees" (Saifi, 2022). This raises concerns, as it once again shows that the connection between national security and migration is a result of a social construction. And this link is established only for immigrants from certain countries, following the interests of the political elite. Thus, there is a strong racist component, one that is reinforced only by political and media discourses which later on materialize into further restricting legislation against particular communities.

A comparative perspective highlights both common patterns and distinctive trajectories. All three cases exhibit the prioritization of national security over human security, the expansion of executive powers, and the marginalization of migrant and refugee rights. However, the intensity and framing of securitization vary: while the EU and US responses are deeply shaped by terrorism-related discourses, South Africa's securitization is more closely linked to economic and social stability concerns. The study also finds that securitization practices disproportionately affect vulnerable groups, particularly refugees and asylum seekers, who are increasingly portrayed as security threats rather than individuals in need of international protection. This reframing challenges the fundamental premises of international refugee law and undermines the principle of non-refoulement and other core humanitarian protections.

3 Raising Awareness

These trends point to a broader transformation in the treatment of displaced populations, which raises critical questions about the underlying drivers and justifications of securitization.

This book began by asking how and why refugees – who are entitled to international protection – have come to be framed as security threats in such different political and regional contexts. The analysis of the European Union, the United States, and South Africa has shown that while the drivers and discourses of securitization differ, the outcome is strikingly consistent: a retreat from protection in favour of exclusion, control, and deterrence. The securitization of refugees operates as both a policy framework and a symbolic process, reflecting broader anxieties about sovereignty, identity, and global disorder. It is not simply a reaction to terrorism or irregular migration but a deeper shift in the priorities of international governance.

Once we have seen the negative consequences of securitizing measures on refugees and the symbolism of these practices within the current changing international order, it is also interesting to try to think on the prospects that are awaiting.

The case studies examined in this book demonstrate that the securitization of migration – and of refugees in particular – is not confined to Western states or rooted solely in counter-terrorism agendas. Rather, it is a global phenomenon that manifests across diverse legal, political, and social contexts. While the United States developed a robust securitization framework in the wake of 9/11, reinforcing this logic over time through legislation and executive action, countries like South Africa have more recently begun to adopt similar approaches. Though the stages and justifications vary, from terrorism to economic instability or social unrest, a common thread emerges: the growing association between immigration and national security across legal systems and political regimes.

The problem lays precisely in the fact that measures do not seem to cease or decrease. But on the contrary, political discourses on the need to protect from external threats associated with immigration are very vivid today. Extraordinary measures restricting peoples' rights should only be in force so long as the threat is still menacing the state. That is precisely the reason why they are 'extraordinary'. However, terrorism seems to have given states the sense that this is a potential danger that is constantly threatening them, and they seem to be unwilling to withdraw the mechanisms they have established. Therefore, as long as states prioritize national security over human security, it seems unlikely that the phenomenon of securitization on migration – but also in other areas – will cease.

This book seeks to modestly contribute to emphasizing the importance of securitization processes and the consequences of related measures. It wants to warn that securitizing migration has an impact on the rights of refugees, but that this is also a sign that the liberal values as we had construed them can be in danger if we do not act to further protect them. Thence instead of focusing solely on protecting the security of the nation, it is also important to reinforce that of the individual, and even more for those individuals who are in particularly vulnerable positions. Trying to establish more diverse and tolerant societies should be the goal of states to enhance social cohesion. Helping those coming from abroad to integrate into host societies should be the solution, not to further isolate them.

Securitization is not a new phenomenon, and migration has been subject to it in various forms throughout history. However, recent years have seen a new wave of securitization measures, shaped by shifting global power dynamics and evolving conceptions of threat. This new phase is particularly concerning because it risks undermining some of the most basic rights and protections embedded in international law. Recognizing when a law genuinely serves public safety, and when it is unjustifiably invoked in the name of security, is essential. This book aims to expose those distinctions. It is critical that we remain vigilant about such measures to ensure that core values are preserved and that human security, not just state security, remains at the forefront of international policymaking.

In this sense, the book's findings offer a direct response to the initial questions posed. These findings confirm the central argument advanced in the introduction: that the global rise in the securitization of refugees is not simply a matter of policy drift, but a structural transformation in the international order. The shift from a logic of protection to one of control reflects not only geopolitical anxieties but also deeper reconfigurations of law, legitimacy, and power. By tracing this transformation across multiple legal and political regimes, this book contributes to a growing critical literature that seeks to reassert the centrality of human rights, legal accountability, and ethical responsibility in the governance of forced migration.

Yet while this structural shift has been driven by institutional and political forces, its effects are also deeply felt at the societal level. In recent years, anti-immigrant sentiment – particularly towards refugees – has gained traction in many countries, often amplified by economic pressures and politicized narratives that blame migrants and refugees for deeper systemic shortcomings. Although not all citizens embrace these narratives, a significant portion of the public has been persuaded that refugee arrivals pose a threat to national welfare and social cohesion. In this context, it becomes all the more urgent to produce impartial, evidence-based analysis that critically examines the validity of such claims. Academic research has a crucial role to play in demystifying securitizing discourses and defending the legal and ethical principles at the heart of refugee protection.

Ultimately, the securitization of refugees is not only a legal or political concern, it is a moral and humanitarian one. At stake is the future of a global order that either upholds the principles of protection, dignity, and solidarity or retreats into a logic of fear, exclusion, and exceptionalism. This book has shown that the choices made by states today will shape not only the rights of refugees, but the broader fabric of international norms and values. As the pressure to govern through security continues to grow, the imperative to defend human security, and to reclaim refugeehood as a site of rights rather than risk, is more urgent than ever.

References

Aragó, L., (2022) 'La Guerra de Ucrania causa el éxodo de refugiados más rápido de la historia', *La Vanguardia*, March 17. Available at: https://www.lavanguardia.com/internacional/20220317/8130331/guerra-ucrania-causa-exodo-refugiados-mas-rapido-historia.html.

Barber, L., Foy, H. and Barker, A. (2019) 'Vladimir Putin says liberalism has 'become obsolete', *Financial Times*, June 28. Available at: https://www.ft.com/content/670039ec-98f3-11e9-9573-ee5cbb98ed36.

Beckley, M. (2022) 'Enemies of My Enemy: How Fear of China Is Forging a New World Order', *Foreign Affairs*, March/April.

Bello, V. (2017) *International Migration and International Security: Why Prejudice Is a Global Security Threat.* London: Routledge.

Betts, A. (2014) 'From Persecution to Deprivation', in Betts, A. and Orchard, P., *Implementation and World Politics: How International Norms Change Practice.* Oxford: Oxford Scholarship Online.

Betts, A. and Orchard, P. (2014a) 'The Normative Institutionalization-Implementation Gap', in Betts, A. and Orchard, P., *Implementation and World Politics: How International Norms Change Practice.* Oxford: Oxford Scholarship Online.

Betts, A. and Orchard, P. (2014b) 'Norms and the Politics of Implementation', in Betts, A. and Orchard, P., *Implementation and World Politics: How International Norms Change Practice.* Oxford: Oxford Scholarship Online.

Boese, V. A., Alizada, N., Lundstedt, M., Morrison, K., Natsika, N., Sato, Y., Tai, H. and Lindberg, S. I. (2022) 'Autocratization Changing Nature? Democracy Report 2022', *Varieties of Democracy Institute*. Available at: https://v-dem.net/media/publications/dr_2022.pdf.

Boffey, D. (2022) 'EU leaders announce intention to collectively rearm in face of Putin threat', The Guardian, March 11. Available at: https://www.theguardian.com/world/2022/mar/11/eu-leaders-announce-intention-collectively-rearm-putin-threat-russia-ukraine.

Boswell, C. (2007). Migration control in Europe after 9/11: Explaining the absence of securitisation'. *Journal of Common Market Studies, 45*(3), 589–610.

Brzozowski, A. (2022) 'With war at its doorstep, EU agrees to move on defence', *Euractiv*, March 11. Available at: https://www.euractiv.com/section/defence-and-security/news/with-war-at-its-doorstep-eu-agrees-to-move-on-defence/.

Buzan, B., Waever, O., & Wilde, J. (1998). *Security: A New Framework for Analysis*. Lynne Reinner Publishers.

Cave, D. (2022) 'The War in Ukraine Holds a Warning for the World Order', *The New York Times*, March 6. Available at: https://www.nytimes.com/2022/03/04/world/ukraine-russia-war-authoritarianism.html.

Christou, G., Croft, S., Ceccorulli, M. and Lucarelli, S. (2010) 'European Union security governance: putting the "security" back in', *European Security*, Vol. 19(3), pp. 341–359.

Ferrero, R. (2017) 'Los principales retos de la gobernanza de las migraciones. El binomio migración y seguridad a debate' in Escuela Superior de las Fuerzas Armadas, *Las migraciones internacionales, percepción y realidad. Un análisis desde la perspectiva de la seguridad*. Madrid: Ministry of Defence of Spain.

Gaskarth, J. (2013) 'Security and global governance', in Harman, S. and Williams D., *Governing the world?*. London: Routledge.

Hedayat, N. (2022) 'The response to Ukraine is laudable. But as a British Afghan, I'm a little jealous', *The Guardian*, March 19. Available at: https://www.theguardian.com/commentisfree/2022/mar/19/response-ukraine-laudable-british-afghan-jealous-kabul-crisis.

Ikenberry, G. J. (2022) 'The real liberal bet' in 'A Rival of America's Making? The Debate Over Washington's China Strategy', *Foreign Affairs*, March/April.

Karyotis, G. (2007). European migration policy in the aftermath of September 11: The security–migration nexus. *Innovation: The European Journal of Social Science Research, 20*(1), 1–17.

Karyotis, G. (2011) 'The fallacy of securitizing migration: elite rationality and unintended consequences', in Karyotis, G., Lazaridis, G. (eds) *Security, Insecurity and Migration in Europe*, Farnham, pp. 13–30.

Kirchner, E. (2007) 'Regional and global security: changing threats and institutional responses', in Kirchner, E. and Sperling, J., *Global Security Governance*. London: Routledge.

Klare, M. T. (2022) La resurrección de una superpotencia', *Le Monde Diplomatique*, March. Available at: https://mondiplo.com/la-resurreccion-de-una-superpotencia.

Lanchester, J. (2018) 'After the fall', *London Review of Books*, pp. 3–8.

Leali, G. and Moens, B. (2022) 'Ukraine war gives Macron's drive for EU autonomy new impetus', *Politico*, March 9. Available at: https://www.politico.eu/article/war-in-ukraine-versailles-france-emmanuel-macrons-strategic-autonomy/.

Loescher, G. (1993) *Beyond Charity: International Cooperation and the Global Refugee Crisis*. New York: Oxford University Press.

Mandel, R. (1997) 'Perceived Security Threat and the Global Refugee Crisis', *Armed Forces and Society*, Vol. 24(1), pp.77–103.

Mearsheimer, J. (2019) 'Bound to Fail: The Rise and Fall of the Liberal International Order', *International Security*, Vol. 43(4), pp. 7–50.

Messina, A. (2014). Securitizing immigration in the age of terror. *World Politics*, 66(3), 530–559.

Nathan, A. J. 'The China threat in perspective' in "A Rival of America's Making? The Debate Over Washington's China Strategy", *Foreign Affairs*, March/April 2022.

Papademetriou, D. and Collett, E. (2011) 'A new Architecture for Border Management', *Migration Policy Institute*.

Saifi, Z. (2022) 'How the Ukraine war revealed Europe's selective empathy on refugees, *CNN*, March 18. Available at: https://www.cnn.com/2022/03/16/middleeast/mideast-summary-03-16-2022-intl/index.html.

Townsend, M. (2022) 'Stranded Nigerians accuse UK of ignoring pleas of black refugees fleeing Ukraine, *The Guardian*, March 19. Available at: https://www.theguardian.com/world/2022/mar/19/stranded-nigerians-accuse-uk-of-ignoring-pleas-of-black-refugees-fleeing-ukraine.

Index

 | HTTPS://DOI.ORG/10.1163/9789004704527-010

www.ingramcontent.com/pod-product-compliance
Lightning Source LLC
LaVergne TN
LVHW020046251026
850939LV00003B/29